Longman

Listening
mentor joy

4
LEVEL

P Pearson

Longman
Listening Mentor Joy 4

지은이 교재개발연구소
편집 및 기획 English Nine
발행처 Pearson Education South Asia Pte Ltd.
판매처 inkedu(inkbooks)
전화 02-455-9620(주문 및 고객지원)
팩스 02-455-9619
등록 제13-579호

ISBN 979-11-88228-61-4
잘못된 책은 구입처에서 바꿔 드립니다.

INTRODUCTION

Listening Mentor Joy 시리즈는 총 5권 5레벨로 구성되어 있으며,
각 권마다 15회의 모의고사가 수록되어 있습니다.

단계	대상	활용 방안
	**초등 3학년**	<ul><li>정확한 알파벳 소리를 익힌다.</li><li>영어 단어의 정확한 발음과 의미를 익힌다.</li><li>한 문장으로 된 간단한 지시, 명령을 이해한다.</li><li>간단한 대화의 내용을 이해한다.</li><li>간단한 질문을 이해하고 대답할 수 있는 능력을 키운다.</li></ul>
	**초등 3-4학년**	<ul><li>영어 단어의 정확한 발음과 의미를 익힌다.</li><li>한 문장으로 된 간단한 지시, 명령을 이해한다.</li><li>일상생활에 관련된 쉽고 간단한 대화를 듣고 이해한다.</li><li>수와 시각에 관한 간단한 대화를 듣고 이해한다.</li><li>간단한 대화를 듣고, 대화가 일어난 장소와 시간 등을 안다.</li></ul>
	**초등 4-5학년**	<ul><li>한두 문장으로 된 명령이나 지시를 듣고 이해한다.</li><li>간단한 대화를 듣고, 대화가 일어난 장소와 시간 등을 안다.</li><li>일상생활과 관련된 쉽고 간단한 말을 듣고, 중심 낱말을 찾는다.</li><li>시간과 수량에 관한 대화를 이해하고 대답할 수 있다.</li><li>두 사람 간의 대화를 통해 내용을 이해할 수 있다.</li><li>의문사를 이용한 질문을 이해하고 대답할 수 있다.</li></ul>
	**초등 5-6학년**	<ul><li>일상생활에 관한 쉽고 간단한 내용을 듣고, 의도나 목적을 이해한다.</li><li>간단한 대화를 듣고 주제를 이해한다.</li><li>간단한 말을 듣고 세부 사항을 이해한다.</li><li>앞으로 일어날 일에 관한 간단한 말을 듣고 이해한다.</li><li>의문사를 이용한 질문을 이해하고 답할 수 있다.</li><li>대상을 비교하는 쉬운 말을 듣고 이해한다.</li><li>간단한 전화 대화를 이해한다.</li></ul>
	예비중학생	<ul><li>자기소개를 하거나 위치를 묻고 말하는 내용을 이해한다.</li><li>과거시제를 이용한 대화를 이해한다.</li><li>대화를 듣고 세부 정보를 파악하거나 화자 간 관계를 추론할 수 있다.</li><li>대화를 통해 화자의 의도나 목적을 추론할 수 있다.</li><li>대화를 듣고 화자의 심정이나 태도 추론이 가능하고 관용적인 표현을 이해한다.</li><li>간단한 전화 대화를 이해할 수 있으며, 좀 더 복잡한 시간과 수를 영어로 이해한다.</li></ul>

CONSTRUCTION

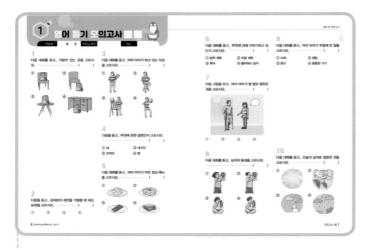

영어 듣기 모의고사

실제 모의고사에 나오는 다양한 문제들을 풀면서
영어 듣기 평가 시험에 대비합니다.

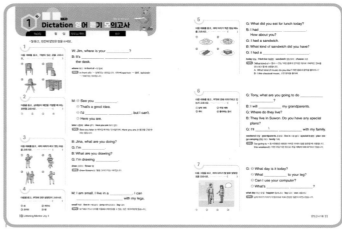

Dictation 영어 듣기 모의고사

모의고사에 나오는 단어와 문장, 표현들을 Dictation을
통해서 확인하고, 듣기 집중력과 청취력을 향상시킵니다.

Word Check

모의고사에 등장하는
핵심 단어들을 듣고
확인합니다.

Sentence Check

모의고사에 등장하는
핵심 문장을 듣고
확인합니다.

Vocabulary

모의고사 15회에
등장하는 모든 단어들을
회별로 다시 한 번 더
확인합니다.

정답 및 해석

모의고사와 Dictation의
답을 확인할 수 있으며,
모의고사에 등장하는
단어와 문장, 대화의
해석을 확인합니다.

CONTENTS

영어 듣기 모의고사

보통 속도   빠른 속도

학습일	월 일	부모님 확인	점수

1

다음 대화를 듣고, 가방이 있는 곳을 고르시오. ·················· (   )

①

②

③

④

2

다음을 듣고, 상대방의 제안을 거절할 때 하는 표현을 고르시오. ·················· (   )

①   ②   ③   ④

3

다음 대화를 듣고, 여자 아이가 하고 있는 모습을 고르시오. ·················· (   )

①

②

③

④

4

다음을 듣고, 무엇에 관한 설명인지 고르시오. ·· (   )

① 새   ② 개구리

③ 코끼리   ④ 뱀

5

다음 대화를 듣고, 여자 아이가 먹은 점심 메뉴를 고르시오. ·················· (   )

①

②

③

④

6

다음 대화를 듣고, 무엇에 관해 이야기하고 있는지 고르시오. ···················· (   )

① 방학 계획

② 주말 계획

③ 취미

④ 좋아하는 음식

9

다음 대화를 듣고, 여자 아이가 주말에 한 일을 고르시오. ···················· (   )

① 숙제

② 캠핑

③ 등산

④ 동물원 가기

7

다음 그림을 보고, 여자 아이가 할 말로 알맞은 것을 고르시오. ···················· (   )

①   ②   ③   ④

8

다음 대화를 듣고, 남자의 동생을 고르시오.
···················· (   )

10

다음 대화를 듣고, 오늘의 날씨로 알맞은 것을 고르시오. ···················· (   )

11

다음 대화를 듣고, 남자 아이 아버지의 직업을 고르시오. ················· (   )

① 의사   ② 요리사
③ 소방관   ④ 선생님

14

다음 대화를 듣고, 두 사람이 만나기로 한 시각을 고르시오. ············· (   )

① 6시   ② 6시 20분
③ 6시 30분   ④ 7시

12

다음 대화를 듣고, 남자가 사려는 물건과 개수가 바르게 짝지어진 것을 고르시오.
·· (   )

① 토마토 – 5개
② 토마토 – 6개
③ 감자 – 5개
④ 감자 – 6개

13

다음 대화를 듣고, 내용과 일치하는 그림을 고르시오. ···················· (   )

①    ②

③    ④

15

다음 대화를 듣고, 대화가 이루어지고 있는 장소를 고르시오. ················ (   )

① 도서관   ② 지하철역
③ 가방가게   ④ 분실물 보관소

16

다음 대화를 듣고, 두 사람의 대화가 <u>어색한</u> 것을 고르시오. ·· (　　　)

① 　　② 　　③ 　　④

17

다음 그림을 보고, 여자가 할 말로 알맞은 것을 고르시오. ·· (　　　)

① 　　② 　　③ 　　④

18

다음 대화를 듣고, 이어질 말로 알맞은 것을 고르시오. ·· (　　　)

B _____

① 　　② 　　③ 　　④

19

다음 대화를 듣고, 이어질 말로 알맞은 것을 고르시오. ·· (　　　)

M _____

① No, I don't have any pets.
② There are three cats over there.
③ Yes, I want a dog.
④ Yes, I love all animals.

20

다음 대화를 듣고, 이어질 말로 알맞은 것을 고르시오. ·· (　　　)

W _____

① Yes, I have some water.
② I don't drink coffee.
③ No, we don't have milk.
④ Orange juice, please.

보통 속도 | 빠른 속도

정답 및 해석 p. 2

Dictation 영어 듣기 모의고사

| 학습일 | 월 | 일 | 부모님 확인 | 점수 |

● 잘 듣고, 빈칸에 알맞은 말을 쓰세요.

1

다음 대화를 듣고, 가방이 있는 곳을 고르시오. ·················· (   )

① ② ③ ④

W: Jim, where is your _____?

B: It's _____ _____ _____ the desk.

where 어디 | in front of ~의 앞에

TIPS in front of는 '~ 앞에'라는 의미입니다. 이밖에 next to는 '~ 옆에', behind는 '~ 뒤에'라는 의미입니다.

2

다음을 듣고, 상대방의 제안을 거절할 때 하는 표현을 고르시오. ·················· (   )

① ② ③ ④

M: ❶ See you _____.

❷ That's a good idea.

❸ I'd _____ _____, but I can't.

❹ Here you are.

later 나중에 | idea 생각 | here you are 여기 있다

TIPS See you later.는 헤어질 때 하는 인사말이며, Here you are.는 물건을 건넬 때 하는 말입니다.

3

다음 대화를 듣고, 여자 아이가 하고 있는 모습을 고르시오. ·················· (   )

① ② ③ ④

B: Jina, what are you doing?

G: I'm _____.

B: What are you drawing?

G: I'm drawing _____.

draw 그리다 | flower 꽃

TIPS draw flowers는 '꽃을 그리다'라는 의미입니다.

4

다음을 듣고, 무엇에 관한 설명인지 고르시오. ·················· (   )

① 새 ② 개구리
③ 코끼리 ④ 뱀

M: I am small. I live in a _____. I can _____ _____ with my legs.

small 작은 | live in ~에 살다 | pond 연못 | jump 뛰어오르다 | leg 다리

TIPS 보기에서 작고 다리를 이용해서 뛰어오를 수 있는 것은 개구리밖에 없습니다.

5

다음 대화를 듣고, 여자 아이가 먹은 점심 메뉴를 고르시오. .... ( )

① ② ③ ④

G: What did you eat for lunch today?

B: I had _____ _____. How about you?

G: I had a sandwich.

B: What kind of sandwich did you have?

G: I had a _____ _____.

today 오늘 | fried rice 볶음밥 | sandwich 샌드위치 | cheese 치즈

TIPS [What kind of + 명사 ~?]는 '어떤 종류의 것'이란 의미로 구체적인 정보를 얻으려고 할 때 사용합니다.
A : What kind of music do you like? 어떤 종류의 음악을 좋아하니?
B : I like classical music. 고전 음악을 좋아해.

6

다음 대화를 듣고, 무엇에 관해 이야기하고 있는지 고르시오. .... ( )

① 방학 계획　　② 주말 계획
③ 취미　　④ 좋아하는 음식

G: Tony, what are you going to do _____ _____?

B: I will _____ my grandparents.

G: Where do they live?

B: They live in Suwon. Do you have any special plans?

G: I'll _____ _____ with my family.

weekend 주말 | grandparents 조부모 | live in ~에 살다 | special 특별한 | plan 계획 | go camping 캠핑 가다 | family 가족

TIPS [be going to + 동사원형]은 예정된 가까운 미래의 일을 표현할 때 사용합니다.
this weekend는 '이번 주말'이란 뜻으로 주말 계획에 대해 얘기하고 있습니다.

7

다음 그림을 보고, 여자 아이가 할 말로 알맞은 것을 고르시오. .... ( )

① ② ③ ④

G: ❶ What day is it today?

❷ What _____ to your leg?

❸ Can I use your computer?

❹ What's _____ _____?

what day 무슨 요일 | happen 일어나다 | leg 다리 | use 사용하다

TIPS 남자 아이가 다리가 다쳤으므로 이와 관련된 질문이 자연스럽습니다.

8

다음 대화를 듣고, 남자의 동생을 고르시오.
.... (   )

① ② ③ ④

W: Is your brother in this room?

M: Yes, he's _____ _____.

W: Do you mean the boy with long hair?

M: No, he has _____ _____.

He is playing _____ _____

_____.

over there 저쪽에 | **mean** 의미하다 | **long hair** 긴 머리 | **short hair** 짧은 머리 | **ball** 공

TIPS 전치사 with는 '~을 가진', '~이 달린' 등의 의미를 가지고 있습니다. 또한 '~을 써서', '~을 이용하여'라는 의미도 있습니다.
a girl with red hair 머리가 빨간[빨간 머리의] 소녀
play with a doll 인형을 가지고 놀다

9

다음 대화를 듣고, 여자 아이가 주말에 한 일을 고르시오. .... (   )

① 숙제　　　　② 캠핑
③ 등산　　　　④ 동물원 가기

G: What did you do yesterday, Jim?

B: I went to the zoo.

G: Did you have fun?

B: Yes, very much. How was _____

_____? Did you go camping?

G: No, I stayed home and did _____

_____.

yesterday 어제 | **zoo** 동물원 | **fun** 재미 | **weekend** 주말 | **stay** 머무르다 |
homework 숙제

TIPS · stay [at] home은 '집에 머물다'라는 의미입니다.
· 의문사 how는 '어떻게'의 의미로 '즐거움이나 성공 여부를 물을 때' 사용할 수 있습니다.
A: How was your trip? 여행 어땠어?　　　B: It was good. 좋았어.

10

다음 대화를 듣고, 오늘의 날씨로 알맞은 것을 고르시오. .... (   )

① ② ③ ④

M: How's the _____ today? Is it sunny?

W: No, it isn't. It's _____.

M: Is it cold?

W: No, it isn't, but it's _____.

weather 날씨 | **today** 오늘 | **sunny** 맑은 | **cloudy** 흐린 | **windy** 바람이 부는

TIPS How's the weather today? 대신 What's the weather like today?라고 할 수 있습니다.

11

다음 대화를 듣고, 남자 아이 아버지의 직업을 고르시오. ·········· (　)

① 의사 　　　　② 요리사
③ 소방관 　　　④ 선생님

G: What does your father do?

B: Do you mean my _____ _____?

G: Yes.

B: He's a _____. His job is to put out fires.

mean 의미하다 | job 직업 | firefighter 소방관 | put out 끄다 | fire 불, 화재

TIPS　What does your father do?(너의 아버지는 무슨 일을 하시니?)는 직업을 물을 때 사용하는 표현으로, What does your father do for a living?(너의 아버지는 생계를 위해서 무슨 일을 하시니?)으로 물을 수도 있습니다.

12

다음 대화를 듣고, 남자가 사려는 물건과 개수가 바르게 짝지어진 것을 고르시오.
·········· (　)

① 토마토 – 5개
② 토마토 – 6개
③ 감자 – 5개
④ 감자 – 6개

W: May I help you?

M: Yes, I'm looking for _____ _____.

W: They're over there. How many potatoes do you need?

M: I _____ _____.

look for ~을 찾다 | potato 감자 | over there 저쪽에 | need 필요하다

13

다음 대화를 듣고, 내용과 일치하는 그림을 고르시오. ·········· (　)

① ② ③ ④

M: What are you doing, Cindy?

G: I'm looking for my _____ _____. Did you see it?

M: Yes, I saw it _____ _____ _____ over there a few minutes ago.

G: Oh, thanks.

M: No problem.

look for ~을 찾다 | over there 저쪽에 | a few minutes ago 몇 분 전에 | no problem 천만에

TIPS　cap은 앞부분에 챙이 달린 모자를 의미이며 hat은 둥근 테가 있는 모자입니다.　cap:　　hat:

14

다음 대화를 듣고, 두 사람이 만나기로 한 시각을 고르시오. ·················· (　　　)

① 6시　　　　② 6시 20분
③ 6시 30분　　④ 7시

B: Do you remember our plan for tomorrow?
G: Sure. The basketball game starts at 7 o'clock.
　_____ _____ shall we meet?
B: _____ _____ 6 o'clock?
G: That's too early. _____ _____ at 6:30 in front of the gym.
B: Okay. See you then.

remember 기억하다 | plan 계획 | start 시작하다 | how about ~은 어때 | too 너무 | early 이른 | in front of ~ 앞에 | gym 체육관

TIPS 상대방에게 뭔가를 제안할 때 [How about ~ ?]을 이용합니다.

15

다음 대화를 듣고, 대화가 이루어지고 있는 장소를 고르시오. ·················· (　　　)

① 도서관　　　② 지하철역
③ 가방가게　　④ 분실물 보관소

M: How can I help you?
W: I _____ _____ _____ on the bus yesterday.
M: Do you remember the bus number?
W: I _____ bus number 30.
M: What does your bag _____ _____?
W: It is red and rectangular.

left 남기다(leave)의 과거형 | yesterday 어제 | number 번호 | took 타다(take)의 과거형 | look like ~처럼 생기다 | rectangular 직사각형의

TIPS 가방을 버스에 두고 내려 찾는 내용으로 대화가 이루어지는 장소를 유추할 수 있습니다.
took는 take의 과거형으로 '교통수단을 타다, 이용하다'라는 의미입니다.
take the train 기차를 타다

16

다음 대화를 듣고, 두 사람의 대화가 어색한 것을 고르시오. ·················· (　　　)

①　　②　　③　　④

❶ B: What did you do last Sunday?
　G: I went shopping.
❷ B: _____ _____ your vacation?
　G: I went there _____ _____.
❸ B: What do you think of my picture?
　G: Wow, you're very good at painting.
❹ B: What do you want to be in the future?
　G: I want to be a _____.

last Sunday 지난 일요일 | go shopping 쇼핑하다 | vacation 방학, 휴가 | by train 기차로 | think 생각하다 | be good at ~을 잘하다 | in the future 장래에 | pianist 피아니스트

TIPS How was your vacation?이라는 질문에는 It was fun.(재미있었어.) / It was amazing.(좋았어.) / Not so bad.(나쁘지 않았어.) 등으로 답할 수 있습니다.

17

다음 그림을 보고, 여자가 할 말로 알맞은 것을
고르시오. ·············· (   )

① ② ③ ④

18

다음 대화를 듣고, 이어질 말로 알맞은 것을 고
르시오. ·············· (   )

B _____

① ② ③ ④

19

다음 대화를 듣고, 이어질 말로 알맞은 것을 고
르시오. ·············· (   )

M _____

① No, I don't have any pets.
② There are three cats over there.
③ Yes, I want a dog.
④ Yes, I love all animals.

20

다음 대화를 듣고, 이어질 말로 알맞은 것을 고
르시오. ·············· (   )

W _____

① Yes, I have some water.
② I don't drink coffee.
③ No, we don't have milk.
④ Orange juice, please.

W: ❶ Where is your computer?
   ❷ Can I play computer games?
   ❸ Could you _____ _____ the
      computer game?
   ❹ Whose computer is this?

where 어디에 | computer game 컴퓨터 게임 | stop 멈추다 | whose 누구의

TIPS [stop + 동명사]는 '~하는 것을 멈추다'라는 의미입니다.
My dad stopped smoking. 내 아빠는 담배를 끊으셨다.

B: You _____ _____ today.
   Do you have any good news?
G: Yes, I won _____ _____ in the
   English language competition.
B: ❶ That's too bad.
   ❷ Wow! _____!
   ❸ See you later.
   ❹ It's warm and windy.

news 소식 | win 승리하다, 따다 | first prize 1등 | language 언어 | competition 대회 |
congratulations 축하해 | later 나중에 | warm 따뜻한

TIPS 여자 아이가 영어 말하기 대회에서 1등을 했으므로 '축하한다'는 표현이 어울립니다.
That's too bad.는 '그것 참 안됐다, (그렇다니) 유감이다'라는 의미입니다.
A: I failed the test. 나 시험에 떨어졌어. B: That's too bad. 그것 참 안됐다.

M: Do you like dogs, Amy?
W: Yes, I love dogs. _____ _____ you?
M: I like dogs very much.
W: Do you like cats, too?
M: _____

love 사랑하다 | what about ~은 어때? | very much 매우 | too 역시, 또한

M: May I help you?
W: I'd like a sandwich, please.
M: _____ _____ _____?
W: _____

help 돕다 | sandwich 샌드위치 | anything 무엇 | drink 마시다

TIPS Anything to drink?는 Would you like anything to drink?를 줄여서 표현한
것입니다. 이때 필요 없으면 No, thank you.라고 합니다.

● 다음 들려주는 단어의 의미를 쓰세요.

	단어	의미
01	later	나중에
02	sandwich	
03	weekend	
04	special	
05	plan	
06	happen	
07	mean	
08	stay	
09	firefighter	
10	remember	
11	gym	
12	number	
13	rectangular	
14	think	
15	competition	

● 앞에 모의고사에 나오는 문장들을 잘 듣고, 빈칸을 완성하세요.

01 That's a ___good___ ___idea___.

02 I can _____ _____ with my legs.

03 I will visit my _____.

04 He is _____ _____ a ball.

05 I _____ _____ and did my homework.

06 His job is to _____ _____ _____.

07 I'm _____ _____ some potatoes.

08 I saw it on the desk over there a few _____ _____.

09 The basketball game _____ _____ 7 o'clock.

10 Let's meet at 6:30 _____ _____ _____ the gym.

11 I _____ _____ _____ on the bus yesterday.

12 You're very _____ _____ painting.

13 I won _____ _____ in the English language competition.

14 That's _____ _____.

15 _____ to drink?

보통 속도   빠른 속도

학습일	월 일	부모님 확인	점수

1

다음 대화를 듣고, Jim이 하고 있는 것을 고르시오. ····························· (   )

①  ②

③  ④

2

다음 대화를 듣고, 두 아이가 좋아하는 운동을 고르시오. ····························· (   )

① 테니스   ② 축구

③ 야구   ④ 농구

3

다음 그림을 보고, 남자가 할 말로 알맞은 것을 고르시오. ····························· (   )

①   ②   ③   ④

4

다음을 듣고, 무엇에 관한 내용인지 고르시오.
····························· (   )

①    ②

③   ④

5

다음 대화를 듣고, 여자 아이가 부탁한 것을 고르시오. ················· (   )

① 함께 책 읽기

② 수학 숙제 도와주기

③ 도서관에 함께 가기

④ 물건 빌려주기

6

다음 대화를 듣고, 무엇에 관해 이야기하고 있는지 고르시오. ····················· (   )

① 방학 계획　　② 주말 계획

③ 취미　　④ 좋아하는 음식

7

다음 대화를 듣고, 현재의 날씨를 고르시오. ······································ (   )

① 　②

③ 　④

8

다음 대화를 듣고, 남자가 가리키는 표지판으로 알맞은 것을 고르시오. ········ (   )

① 　②

③ 　④

9

다음 대화를 듣고, 오늘이 무슨 요일인지 고르시오. ······································ (   )

① 월요일　　② 화요일

③ 수요일　　④ 목요일

10

다음 대화를 듣고, 남자 아이가 캠핑을 가지 못한 이유를 고르시오. ············ (   )

① 바빠서　　② 아파서

③ 돈이 없어서　　④ 늦잠을 자서

11

다음 대화를 듣고, 남자 아이 어머니의 직업을 고르시오. ·····················(   )

① 과학자   ② 의사
③ 간호사   ④ 선생님

12

다음을 듣고, 내용과 일치하지 <u>않는</u> 것을 고르시오. ······························(   )

① John은 캐나다에서 왔다.
② John은 지난해 서울로 이사했다.
③ John의 아버지는 자동차 회사에서 일하신다.
④ John이 좋아하는 음식은 피자다.

13

다음 대화를 듣고, 대화가 이루어지고 있는 장소를 고르시오. ·····················(   )

① 거실   ② 정원
③ 침실   ④ 부엌

14

다음 대화를 듣고, 두 사람의 대화가 <u>어색한</u> 것을 고르시오. ·····················(   )

①   ②   ③   ④

15

다음 대화를 듣고, 남자 아이 형이 몇 살이 되는지 고르시오. ·····················(   )

① 12살   ② 14살
③ 15살   ④ 16살

16

다음 대화를 듣고, 민지 여동생을 고르시오.
.................................( )

① ②

③ ④

17

다음 대화를 듣고, 현재 시각을 고르시오.
.................................( )

① 5시   ② 5시 10분

③ 5시 20분   ④ 5시 30분

18

다음 대화를 듣고, 이어질 말로 알맞은 것을 고르시오. ....( )

B _____

①   ②   ③   ④

19

다음 대화를 듣고, 이어질 말로 알맞은 것을 고르시오. ....( )

W _____

① I want to talk to you.
② You too! See you later.
③ Long time no see.
④ I don't feel good today.

20

다음 대화를 듣고, 이어질 말로 적절하지 <u>않은</u> 것을 고르시오. ....( )

M _____

① No, I don't have money.
② It looks good, but I want a yellow shirt.
③ How much is it?
④ It's too small for me. Do you have one in a larger size?

● 잘 듣고, 빈칸에 알맞은 말을 쓰세요.

1

다음 대화를 듣고, Jim이 하고 있는 것을 고르시오. ……………………… (   )

① ② ③ ④

W: Where is Jim?

M: He's in the _____.

W: Is he cooking?

M: No, he's _____ _____

_____.

kitchen 부엌 | cook 요리하다 | wash the dishes 설거지하다

TIPS wash the dishes는 '설거지하다'라는 의미입니다.

2

다음 대화를 듣고, 두 아이가 좋아하는 운동을 고르시오. …………………… (   )

① 테니스   ② 축구
③ 야구   ④ 농구

B: Jina, what's your _____ _____?

G: I like table tennis. How about you?

B: I like soccer. Do you like soccer?

G: No, I don't, but I like _____.

B: I like baseball, _____.

favorite 좋아하는 | sport 운동 | table tennis 탁구

TIPS 운동이름(soccer, baseball, table tennis, volleyball 등) 앞에는 관사를 붙이지 않습니다.

3

다음 그림을 보고, 남자가 할 말로 알맞은 것을 고르시오. …………………… (   )

① ② ③ ④

M: ❶ Are you _____ to _____?

❷ Have some more pizza.

❸ Do you need any help?

❹ Happy birthday, Alice. This is _____

_____.

ready 준비된 | pizza 피자 | need 필요하다 | birthday 생일

TIPS This is for you.는 '이것은 너를 위한 거야.'라는 의미로 여기서 this는 선물을 의미합니다.

4

다음을 듣고, 무엇에 관한 내용인지 고르시오.
.... ( )

① ② ③ ④

M: I am a bird, but I _____ _____.
I'm good at swimming, and I like to _____
_____.

bird 새 | fly 날다 | be good at ~을 잘하다 | swim 수영하다 | fish 물고기
TIPS 새지만 날 수 없고 수영을 잘하는 동물은 펭귄입니다.

5

다음 대화를 듣고, 여자 아이가 부탁한 것을 고르시오. .... ( )

① 함께 책 읽기
② 수학 숙제 도와주기
③ 도서관에 함께 가기
④ 물건 빌려주기

G: Mike, what are you going to do after school?

B: I don't have any _____ _____.

G: Then, can you help me do my _____
_____?

B: Sure. Let's meet at the library at 4.

G: Okay.

after school 방과 후에 | special 특별한 | plan 계획 | library 도서관
TIPS help me do my math homework(내 수학 숙제를 도와줘)를 이해하면 정답을 쉽게 알 수 있습니다.

6

다음 대화를 듣고, 무엇에 관해 이야기하고 있는지 고르시오. .... ( )

① 방학 계획   ② 주말 계획
③ 취미   ④ 좋아하는 음식

W: What do you do in your _____ _____?

M: I play computer games. How about you?

W: I usually play the piano or _____
_____.

M: That's good. I like reading, too.

free time 여가 시간 | usually 보통 | play the piano 피아노를 치다
TIPS What do you do in your free time? 대신 Do you have any hobbies?로 바꿔 표현할 수 있습니다.

7

다음 대화를 듣고, 현재의 날씨를 고르시오.
.... ( )

① ② ③ ④

W: Are you going out?

M: Yes, I'm going to the library now.

W: I think you should _____ _____
_____.

M: Is it raining now?

W: No, it's not, but it looks like it will _____
_____.

go out 외출하다 | library 도서관 | now 지금 | umbrella 우산 | look like ~일 것 같다 |
soon 곧
TIPS 지금은 비가 오고 있지 않으나 비가 곧 올 거라는 내용이므로 현재 날씨가 흐리다는 것을 알 수 있습니다.

8

다음 대화를 듣고, 남자가 가리키는 표지판으로 알맞은 것을 고르시오. ……… (   )

① ② ③ ④

M: Julie, what are you doing?

W: I'm talking _____ _____

_____ .

M: Look at that sign. You _____

_____ your cellphone here.

W: Oh! I see. I didn't know that.

talk 말하다 | phone 전화기 | sign 표지판 | cellphone 휴대폰 | here 여기

TIPS Do not park. 주차 하지 마세요.
Do not eat here. 여기서 먹지 마세요.
Do not use your cellphone. 휴대폰을 사용하지 마세요.
Do not swim here. 여기서 수영하지 마세요.

9

다음 대화를 듣고, 오늘이 무슨 요일인지 고르시오. ……………… (   )

① 월요일   ② 화요일
③ 수요일   ④ 목요일

M: Stella, where are you going?

W: I'm going to the shopping mall.

M: _____ _____ is it today?
Is it Tuesday or Wednesday?

W: It's _____ .

M: The shopping mall is _____ on Tuesdays.

shopping mall 쇼핑몰 | close 닫다 | on Tuesdays 화요일마다

10

다음 대화를 듣고, 남자 아이가 캠핑을 가지 못한 이유를 고르시오. ………… (   )

① 바빠서   ② 아파서
③ 돈이 없어서   ④ 늦잠을 자서

G: Did you _____ _____ yesterday?

B: No, I didn't.

G: Why? Were you busy?

B: No, I _____ _____ , so I stayed home _____ _____ .

G: Oh, that's too bad.

go camping 캠핑 가다 | yesterday 어제 | busy 바쁜 | sick 아픈 | all day 하루 종일

TIPS go camping(캠핑 가다)처럼 go를 이용한 다양한 표현이 있습니다.
go fishing 낚시 가다   go shopping 쇼핑 가다

11

다음 대화를 듣고, 남자 아이 어머니의 직업을 고르시오. ····················· (   )

① 과학자   ② 의사
③ 간호사   ④ 선생님

B: What do you want to be _____
_____ _____?

G: I'd like to be a scientist. How about you, Mike?

B: I want to be _____ _____
_____ my mother.

G: Your mom is a nurse?

B: Yes. She works at the _____ next to our
school.

in the future 장래에 | **scientist** 과학자 | **nurse** 간호사 | **hospital** 병원 | **next to** ~ 옆에

TIPS I want to be a nurse like my mother.에서 like는 동사가 아니고 '~처럼'이란
의미의 전치사입니다.

12

다음을 듣고, 내용과 일치하지 <u>않는</u> 것을 고르시오. ····················· (   )

① John은 캐나다에서 왔다.
② John은 지난해 서울로 이사했다.
③ John의 아버지는 자동차 회사에서 일하신다.
④ John이 좋아하는 음식은 피자다.

B: Hello, everyone. I'm John Brown. _____
_____ Canada. I moved to Seoul last
year. _____ _____ works at a
computer company here in Korea. I like playing
baseball. My _____ _____ is
pizza. I'm happy to meet you.

everyone 모두 | **be from** ~ 출신이다 | **move** 이사하다 | **last year** 작년 |
computer company 컴퓨터 회사 | **here** 여기

TIPS 아버지는 컴퓨터 회사에서 근무합니다.

13

다음 대화를 듣고, 대화가 이루어지고 있는 장소를 고르시오. ····················· (   )

① 거실   ② 정원
③ 침실   ④ 부엌

B: What's for lunch today?

W: _____ _____ fried rice.
Do you like it?

B: Yes, that's one of _____ _____
foods.

W: Good. Lunch will be ready soon. Wash your
hands _____ _____.

B: Okay.

fried rice 볶음밥 | **favorite** 좋아하는 | **ready** 준비된 | **soon** 곧 | **before** ~ 전에

TIPS 대화상 어머니가 부엌에서 볶음밥을 만들고 있는 것을 유추할 수 있습니다.

14

다음 대화를 듣고, 두 사람의 대화가 <u>어색한</u> 것을 고르시오. ·········· (　　)

① 　　　② 　　　③ 　　　④

❶ M: What's wrong?

W: I have a _____.

❷ M: Cathy, what are you doing?

W: I'm cleaning my room.

❸ M: _____ shall we meet tomorrow?

W: Let's meet at 7 o'clock.

❹ M: How was your _____ _____?

W: It was wonderful.

wrong 잘못된 | have a headache 두통이 있다 | tomorrow 내일 | vacation 휴가 | wonderful 멋진

TIPS　Where로 물으면 Let's meet at the bus stop.(버스 정류장에서 만나자.)처럼 장소와 관련된 답을 해야 합니다.

15

다음 대화를 듣고, 남자 아이 형이 몇 살이 되는지 고르시오. ·········· (　　)

① 12살 　　　② 14살
③ 15살 　　　④ 16살

G: Jim, where are you going?

B: I'm going to the _____ _____.

G: Why?

B: I'm going to buy a birthday present for my

_____ _____.

Tomorrow is his birthday.

G: He is turning sixteen years old, isn't he?

B: No, he's turning _____ _____ old.

shopping mall 쇼핑몰 | birthday present 생일 선물 | older brother 형, 오빠

16

다음 대화를 듣고, 민지 여동생을 고르시오.
·········· (　　)

① 　　　②

③ 　　　④

M: Where is your sister, Minji?

W: She's over there.

She's wearing _____ _____.

M: Do you mean the girl _____ _____?

W: No, she's not wearing glasses. She has a _____ in her _____.

M: Oh, I found her.

over there 저쪽에 | wear 입다 | skirt 치마 | mean 의미하다 | wear glasses 안경을 쓰다 | hand 손 | found 찾다(find)의 과거형

TIPS　여동생은 치마를 입었고, 안경을 쓰지 않았습니다. 안경처럼 쌍으로 이루어진 것들을 복수형으로 씁니다.

pants 바지　　scissors 가위　　shoes 신발

17

다음 대화를 듣고, 현재 시각을 고르시오. ·········· ( )

① 5시 　　　　② 5시 10분
③ 5시 20분 　　④ 5시 30분

18

다음 대화를 듣고, 이어질 말로 알맞은 것을 고르시오. ·········· ( )

B _____

① 　　② 　　③ 　　④

19

다음 대화를 듣고, 이어질 말로 알맞은 것을 고르시오. ·········· ( )

W _____

① I want to talk to you.
② You too! See you later.
③ Long time no see.
④ I don't feel good today.

20

다음 대화를 듣고, 이어질 말로 적절하지 않은 것을 고르시오. ·········· ( )

M _____

① No, I don't have money.
② It looks good, but I want a yellow shirt.
③ How much is it?
④ It's too small for me. Do you have one in a larger size?

G: Billy, _____ _____ does the swimming class start?

B: It starts at 5:30.

G: What time is it now?

B: It's _____ _____ _____.

G: Really? Let's hurry.

class 수업 | start 시작하다 | now 지금 | hurry 서두르다
TIPS ten past five는 '5시 10분'이란 의미로 past 대신 after를 사용할 수 있습니다. to를 이용하여 ten to five라고 하면 '5시 10분 전'이란 의미입니다.

G: Do you have any _____ after school?

B: No, I don't.

G: Then, _____ _____ swimming.

B: ❶ That's a _____ _____.

　　❷ You had a great time.

　　❸ Yes, I need some water.

　　❹ Thank you so much.

plan 계획 | after school 방과 후에 | go swimming 수영하러 가다 | so much 무척
TIPS Why not?(왜 아니겠어?)은 상대방의 제의에 동의를 나타낼 때 사용합니다.

W: What are you going to do this _____?

M: I'm going to visit my grandparents. How about you?

W: I am going to the beach with my cousins.

M: _____ _____ good weekend, Cindy. _____ _____ on Monday.

W: _____

weekend 주말 | grandparents 조부모 | beach 해변
TIPS See you.는 '잘 있어, 잘 가, 또 봐.' 등의 의미로 헤어질 때 하는 인사말입니다. See you.대신 See you around. / See you again. 등으로 말할 수 있습니다.

W: May I help you?

M: Yes, I'm _____ _____ a T-shirt.

W: _____ _____ this red one?

M: _____

help 돕다 | T-shirt 티셔츠 | how about ~은 어때?
TIPS red one에서 one은 티셔츠를 의미합니다.

● 다음 들려주는 단어의 의미를 쓰세요.

단어	의미
01 beach	해변
02 kitchen	
03 usually	
04 free time	
05 special	
06 present	
07 cellphone	
08 sign	
09 nurse	
10 company	
11 soon	
12 wrong	
13 wonderful	
14 hurry	
15 grandparents	

● 앞에 모의고사에 나오는 문장들을 잘 듣고, 빈칸을 완성하세요.

01 _____Have_____ _____some_____ more pizza.

02 I'm _____ _____ swimming and I like to eat fish.

03 I don't have any _____ _____.

04 I _____ _____ the piano or read books.

05 _____ _____ you should take an umbrella.

06 It looks like it will _____ _____.

07 You can't use your _____ _____.

08 The shopping mall is closed _____ _____.

09 I was sick, so I stayed home _____ _____.

10 I want to be a nurse _____ _____ _____.

11 My dad works at a _____ _____ here in Korea.

12 Lunch will _____ _____ soon.

13 I'm going to buy a birthday present for my _____ _____.

14 She has a book _____ _____ _____.

15 Have a _____ _____.

보통 속도   빠른 속도

| 학습일 | 월 일 | 부모님 확인 | 점수 |

1

다음 그림을 보고, 그림과 일치하는 대화를 고르시오. ···································· (   )

① ② ③ ④

2

다음 대화를 듣고, 남자 아이가 어제 잠자러 간 시각을 고르시오. ···················· (   )

① 11시 10분   ② 11시 20분
③ 11시 30분   ④ 11시 40분

3

다음 대화를 듣고, 무엇에 관해 이야기하고 있는지 고르시오. ···················· (   )

① 음악 수업   ② 연주하는 악기
③ 취미   ④ 좋아하는 운동

4

다음 대화를 듣고, 여자 아이의 어머니를 고르시오. ···································· (   )

①    ②

③    ④

5

다음 그림을 보고, 남자 아이가 할 말로 알맞은 것을 고르시오. ···················· (   )

① ② ③ ④

6

다음 대화를 듣고, 파티가 열리는 요일을 고르시오. ⸺⸺⸺⸺⸺⸺⸺ (　　)

July
7

Sun	Mon	Tue	Wed	Thu	Fri	Sat
					1	2
3	4	5	6	7	8	9
10	11	12	13	14	15	16
17	18	19	20	21	22	23
24/31	25	26	27	28	29	30

① 월요일　　　　② 화요일
③ 목요일　　　　④ 일요일

7

다음 대화를 듣고, 남자 아이가 가을을 좋아하는 이유를 고르시오. ⸺⸺⸺⸺ (　　)

① 단풍을 좋아해서
② 사과를 좋아해서
③ 시원한 날씨를 좋아해서
④ 가을에 생일이 있어서

8

다음 대화를 듣고, 남자 아이가 사려는 것을 고르시오. ⸺⸺⸺⸺⸺⸺⸺ (　　)

① 　　②

③ 　　④

9

다음 대화를 듣고, 내용과 일치하지 <u>않는</u> 것을 고르시오. ⸺⸺⸺⸺⸺⸺ (　　)

① 민수는 주말에 조부모님을 방문했다.
② 민수의 조부모님은 인천에 사신다.
③ 여자 아이는 주말을 즐겁게 보냈다.
④ 여자 아이는 주말 동안 집에 있었다.

10

다음 대화를 듣고, 남자가 이용한 교통수단을 고르시오. ⸺⸺⸺⸺⸺⸺ (　　)

① 버스　　　　② 지하철
③ 택시　　　　④ 자전거

11

다음 대화를 듣고, Alice가 하고 있는 것을 고르시오. ·····················( )

12

다음 대화를 듣고, 현재 시각을 고르시오.
····························· ( )

① 10시 50분

② 10시 55분

③ 11시 10분

④ 11시 20분

13

다음 대화를 듣고, 여자가 원하는 풍선의 개수를 고르시오. ·····················( )

① 12개   ② 13개

③ 14개   ④ 15개

14

다음 대화를 듣고, 두 사람의 대화가 <u>어색한</u> 것을 고르시오. ·····················( )

①   ②   ③   ④

15

다음 대화를 듣고, 대화가 이루어지는 장소를 고르시오. ·····················( )

① 백화점   ② 병원

③ 서점   ④ 학교

16

다음을 듣고, 그림과 일치하는 설명을 고르시오. ································ (   )

① ② ③ ④

17

다음 대화를 듣고, 상대방의 제안을 거절하는 대화를 고르시오. ··················· (   )

① ② ③ ④

18

다음 대화를 듣고, 이어질 말로 알맞은 것을 고르시오. ································ (   )

M _____

① That's a good idea.
② No, thanks. I'm full.
③ How about this one?
④ I'll have iced tea.

19

다음 대화를 듣고, 이어질 말로 알맞은 것을 고르시오. ································ (   )

M _____

① I play soccer three times a week.
② It's 20 dollars.
③ What a nice hobby!
④ I'd like to, but I can't.

20

다음 대화를 듣고, 이어질 말로 적절하지 않은 것을 고르시오. ··················· (   )

M _____

① It was fun. I went camping.
② I will stay at a hotel.
③ It was great! I went to Hawaii with my cousin.
④ It was amazing.

● 잘 듣고, 빈칸에 알맞은 말을 쓰세요.

1

다음 그림을 보고, 그림과 일치하는 대화를 고르시오. ····················· (　　　)

① ② ③ ④

❶ W: Is he cooking?

M: No, he's _____ the car.

❷ W: What does your mother do?

M: She's a _____.

❸ W: Would you like something to drink?

M: Orange juice, please.

❹ W: Would you like to _____

_____ _____?

M: Sure, thanks.

cook 요리하다 | wash a car 세차하다 | chef 주방장 | try 먹어보다

TIPS 여성이 남자에게 케이크를 권하는 대화가 가장 적절합니다. 동사 try 다음에 음식이 오면 '~을 먹어보다'라는 의미입니다.

2

다음 대화를 듣고, 남자 아이가 어제 잠자러 간 시각을 고르시오. ················· (　　　)

① 11시 10분　② 11시 20분
③ 11시 30분　④ 11시 40분

B: I'm so sleepy.

G: What did you do last night?

B: I did my homework _____ _____ at night.

G: What time did you go to bed?

B: I _____ _____ _____ at 11:40 and got up at 5:30 today.

sleepy 졸린 | homework 숙제 | until late 늦게까지 | at night 밤에 | go to bed 자러 가다 | get up 일어나다

3

다음 대화를 듣고, 무엇에 관해 이야기하고 있는지 고르시오. ················· (　　　)

① 음악 수업　② 연주하는 악기
③ 취미　④ 좋아하는 운동

B: Michelle, can you play the flute?

G: Yes, I can.

B: What other musical instruments can you play?

G: I can _____ the _____ and the _____. How about you?

B: I can play the _____.

flute 플루트 | other 다른 | musical instrument 악기 | violin 바이올린 | guitar 기타

TIPS 동사 play와 함께 악기 이름이 오면 악기 이름 앞에 정관사(the)를 써야 합니다.

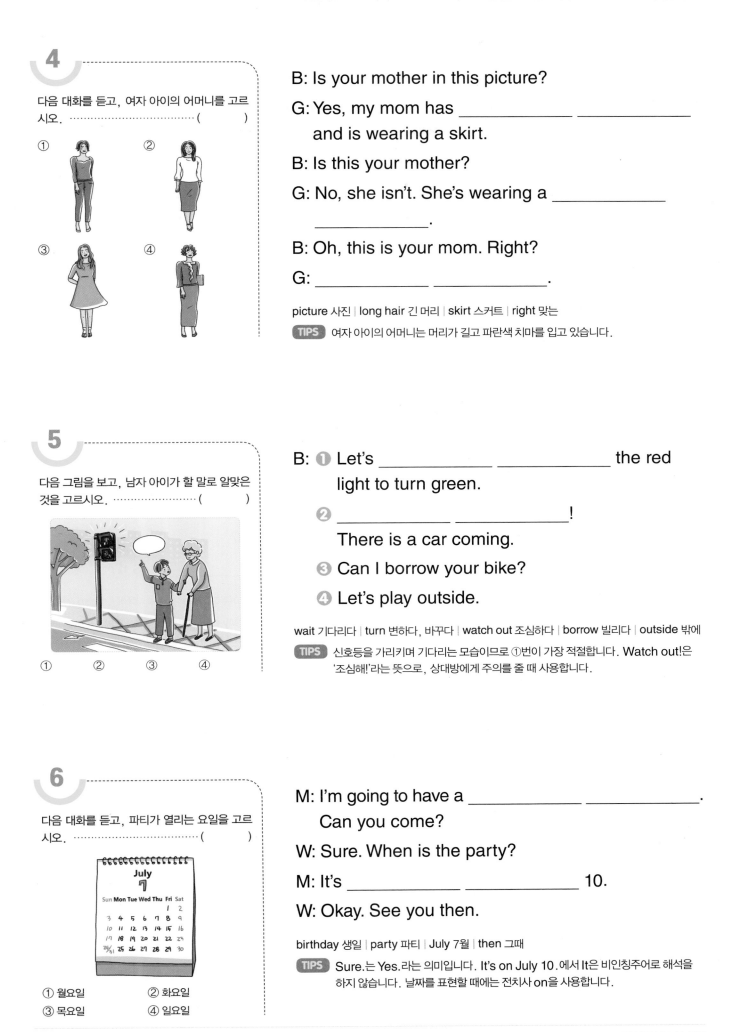

4

다음 대화를 듣고, 여자 아이의 어머니를 고르시오. ·········· (   )

① ② ③ ④

B: Is your mother in this picture?

G: Yes, my mom has _____ _____ and is wearing a skirt.

B: Is this your mother?

G: No, she isn't. She's wearing a _____ _____.

B: Oh, this is your mom. Right?

G: _____ _____.

picture 사진 | long hair 긴 머리 | skirt 스커트 | right 맞는

TIPS 여자 아이의 어머니는 머리가 길고 파란색 치마를 입고 있습니다.

5

다음 그림을 보고, 남자 아이가 할 말로 알맞은 것을 고르시오. ·········· (   )

① ② ③ ④

B: ❶ Let's _____ _____ the red light to turn green.

❷ _____ _____! There is a car coming.

❸ Can I borrow your bike?

❹ Let's play outside.

wait 기다리다 | turn 변하다, 바꾸다 | watch out 조심하다 | borrow 빌리다 | outside 밖에

TIPS 신호등을 가리키며 기다리는 모습이므로 ①번이 가장 적절합니다. Watch out!은 '조심해!'라는 뜻으로, 상대방에게 주의를 줄 때 사용합니다.

6

다음 대화를 듣고, 파티가 열리는 요일을 고르시오. ·········· (   )

July 7

Sun Mon Tue Wed Thu Fri Sat
        1 2
3 4 5 6 7 8 9
10 11 12 13 14 15 16
17 18 19 20 21 22 23
24/31 25 26 27 28 29 30

① 월요일   ② 화요일
③ 목요일   ④ 일요일

M: I'm going to have a _____ _____. Can you come?

W: Sure. When is the party?

M: It's _____ _____ 10.

W: Okay. See you then.

birthday 생일 | party 파티 | July 7월 | then 그때

TIPS Sure.는 Yes.라는 의미입니다. It's on July 10.에서 It은 비인칭주어로 해석을 하지 않습니다. 날짜를 표현할 때에는 전치사 on을 사용합니다.

7

다음 대화를 듣고, 남자 아이가 가을을 좋아하는 이유를 고르시오. ·········· (   )

① 단풍을 좋아해서
② 사과를 좋아해서
③ 시원한 날씨를 좋아해서
④ 가을에 생일이 있어서

B: Alice, do you like spring?

G: Yes, I do. How about you, Tony?

B: I like spring, too. But my _____ _____ is autumn.

G: _____ do you like autumn most?

B: I like _____ _____.

spring 봄 | too 역시, 또한 | favorite 좋아하는 | season 계절 | autumn 가을 | cool 시원한

TIPS 가을은 autumn 대신 fall이라고 표현해도 됩니다.

8

다음 대화를 듣고, 남자 아이가 사려는 것을 고르시오. ·········· (   )

① ② ③ ④

W: May I help you?

B: Yes, I'm looking for a _____ for my sister.

W: How about this Barbie doll?

B: She has many Barbie dolls. Can you show me the _____ _____ over there?

W: Do you mean this one?

B: Yes, _____ _____ is it?

look for ~을 찾다 | present 선물 | show 보여주다 | over there 저쪽에 | mean 의미하다

TIPS one은 teddy bear를 의미합니다. My computer is old. I want a new one. (내 컴퓨터가 낡았다. 나는 새 것을 원한다.)에서 one은 computer를 의미합니다.

9

다음 대화를 듣고, 내용과 일치하지 않는 것을 고르시오. ·········· (   )

① 민수는 주말에 조부모님을 방문했다.
② 민수의 조부모님은 인천에 사신다.
③ 여자 아이는 주말을 즐겁게 보냈다.
④ 여자 아이는 주말 동안 집에 있었다.

G: How was your weekend, Minsu?

B: It was great. I visited my _____.

G: Where do they live?

B: They _____ _____ Incheon. How about you? Did you have a good weekend?

G: No, _____ _____. I stayed home the whole weekend because I was _____.

weekend 주말 | visit 방문하다 | grandparents 조부모 | whole 전체의 | sick 아픈

TIPS It was great. 대신 It was good. / It was amazing. 등으로 답할 수 있습니다.
Where는 장소에 관한 정보를 얻기 위해 질문할 때 사용하는 의문사입니다.

10

다음 대화를 듣고, 남자가 이용한 교통수단을 고르시오. ·················· ( )

① 버스   ② 지하철
③ 택시   ④ 자전거

W: What did you do last Sunday?

M: I went to the museum.

W: Where is the museum?

M: It is in the _____ _____ Seoul.

W: Did you take a bus?

M: No. I _____ the _____.

last Sunday 지난 일요일 | museum 박물관 | center 중심지 | subway 지하철

TIPS 동사 took은 take의 과거형이며, '탈것을 이용하다', '탈것에 타다' 등의 의미를 가지고 있습니다.

11

다음 대화를 듣고, Alice가 하고 있는 것을 고르시오. ·················· ( )

① ② ③ ④

B: Mom, where is Alice?

W: She's in the front yard.

B: _____ is she _____ there?

W: She's _____ _____

_____.

B: Really? I'll go and help her.

front 앞의 | yard 마당 | wash one's car 세차하다 | help 돕다

12

다음 대화를 듣고, 현재 시각을 고르시오.
·················· ( )

① 10시 50분
② 10시 55분
③ 11시 10분
④ 11시 20분

W: What time does our train leave?

M: It leaves here at 11:20.

W: _____ _____ is it now?

M: Oh, it's _____ _____

_____. I mean it's 10:50.

W: I see.

leave 출발하다 | here 여기 | now 지금 | mean 의미하다

TIPS It's ten to eleven. 대신 It's ten before eleven.으로 표현할 수 있습니다. 또한 When(= What time) does our train leave?로 표현할 수 있습니다.

13

다음 대화를 듣고, 여자가 원하는 풍선의 개수를 고르시오. ·················· ( )

① 12개   ② 13개
③ 14개   ④ 15개

M: May I help you?

W: I need _____ _____ for a birthday party.

M: How many balloons do you want?

W: I want _____ blue balloons and _____ red balloons.

need 필요하다 | balloon 풍선 | birthday party 생일 파티

TIPS 정확한 수를 알기 위해서는 [How many + 복수명사 ~?]로 물어야 합니다.

14

다음 대화를 듣고, 두 사람의 대화가 어색한 것을 고르시오. ·············· (   )

①   ②   ③   ④

❶ B: This present is for you.

   G: Thank you very much.

❷ B: _____ _____ is this?

   G: It's mine.

❸ B: Where are you _____?

   G: I'm _____ _____

   _____.

❹ B: Who is that girl?

   G: She's my friend, Sally.

present 선물 | very much 무척 | mine 내 것 | classroom 교실

TIPS Where are you from?은 '어디에서 왔니?'라는 의미로 I'm from Korea. 등으로 답할 수 있습니다. I'm in the classroom.의 대답을 얻기 위해서는 Where are you?라고 물어야 합니다.

15

다음 대화를 듣고, 대화가 이루어지는 장소를 고르시오. ························· (   )

① 백화점   ② 병원
③ 서점   ④ 학교

M: What's wrong?

W: I have a fever and a _____ _____.

M: Let me check. I think you _____

_____ _____.

W: Do I have to _____ _____?

M: No, you don't have to. Instead, drink lots of water and get some rest.

wrong 잘못된 | fever 열 | runny nose 콧물 | check 확인하다 | medicine 약 | instead 대신에 | rest 휴식

TIPS a fever, a runny nose, check, medicine 등의 의미를 알고 있으면 대화가 일어나는 장소를 알 수 있습니다. [don't have to + 동사원형]은 '~할 필요가 없다' 라는 의미입니다.

16

다음을 듣고, 그림과 일치하는 설명을 고르시오. ························· (   )

①   ②   ③   ④

W: ❶ There is _____ _____ on the tree.

  ❷ Leaves are _____ _____ the tree.

  ❸ There are many flowers in the garden.

  ❹ Some people are _____ in the river.

leaves 나뭇잎(leaf)의 복수형 | fall from ~에서 떨어지다 | flower 꽃 | garden 정원 | people 사람들 | river 강

TIPS leaves는 leaf의 복수형입니다. −f나 −fe를 지우고 −ves를 붙여 복수형을 만드는 명사에는 이외에도 wolf(늑대 − wolves), wife(부인 − wives), knife(칼 − knives) 등이 있습니다.

17

다음 대화를 듣고, 상대방의 제안을 거절하는
대화를 고르시오. ·············· (　　)

① 　　② 　　③ 　　④

① B: What are you doing?

G: I'm listening to music.

② B: What's wrong with him?

G: He has the flu.

③ B: _____ _____ to the library.

G: I'm sorry, but _____ _____.

④ B: How do you go to school?

G: I go to school _____ _____.

listen to music 음악을 듣다 | flu 독감 | library 도서관 | by bus 버스로

TIPS I'm sorry, but I can't. 대신 I'd like to, but I can't.를 사용할 수 있습니다.

18

다음 대화를 듣고, 이어질 말로 알맞은 것을 고
르시오. ·············· (　　)

M _____

① That's a good idea.
② No, thanks. I'm full.
③ How about this one?
④ I'll have iced tea.

W: Would you like _____ _____ to drink?

M: Sure. What do you have?

W: We have three kinds of fruit juice and

_____ _____.

M: _____

something 무언가 | kind 종류 | fruit juice 과일 주스 | iced tea 아이스티 | idea 생각

19

다음 대화를 듣고, 이어질 말로 알맞은 것을 고
르시오. ·············· (　　)

M _____

① I play soccer three times a week.
② It's 20 dollars.
③ What a nice hobby!
④ I'd like to, but I can't.

W: Do you have _____ _____?

M: I enjoy playing soccer.

W: Sounds interesting!

_____ _____ do you play soccer?

M: _____

hobby 취미 | enjoy 즐기다 | interesting 재미있는 | often 자주 | time 번

TIPS How often은 '얼마나 자주'라는 의미로 다음과 같이 대답할 있습니다.
Once a week. 일주일에 한 번 / Twice a month. 한 달에 두 번

20

다음 대화를 듣고, 이어질 말로 적절하지 <u>않은</u>
것을 고르시오. ·············· (　　)

M _____

① It was fun. I went camping.
② I will stay at a hotel.
③ It was great! I went to Hawaii with my
cousin.
④ It was amazing.

M: Jenny. Long time no see.

_____ _____ you been?

W: Pretty good. _____ was your vacation?

M: _____

pretty 꽤, 무척 | vacation 휴가 | hotel 호텔 | cousin 사촌 | amazing 멋진

TIPS How have you been?으로 물으면 Great.(좋아.) / Not bad.(잘 지내.) /
Never been better.(이보다 더 좋을 순 없어.) 등으로 답할 수 있습니다.

● 다음 들려주는 단어의 의미를 쓰세요.

단어	의미
01 turn	변하다, 바꾸다
02 borrow	
03 outside	
04 pretty	
05 season	
06 autumn	
07 whole	
08 center	
09 fever	
10 check	
11 instead	
12 rest	
13 fall	
14 great	
15 something	

● 앞에 모의고사에 나오는 문장들을 잘 듣고, 빈칸을 완성하세요.

01 I ___did___ ___my___ ___homework___ until late at night.

02 She's wearing a _____ _____.

03 Let's _____ _____ the red light to turn green.

04 I'm _____ _____ _____ a birthday party.

05 Can you _____ _____ the teddy bear over there?

06 I stayed home the whole weekend because I _____ _____.

07 It is _____ _____ _____ of Seoul.

08 She's _____ _____ _____.

09 It _____ _____ _____ 11:20.

10 I have a fever and a _____ _____.

11 Leaves are _____ _____ _____ _____.

12 I need _____ _____ for a birthday party.

13 Would you like _____ _____ to drink?

14 Do you have _____ _____?

15 Long time _____ _____.

보통 속도 빠른 속도

| 학습일 | 월 일 | 부모님 확인 | 점수 |

1

다음 그림을 보고, 남자 아이가 할 말로 알맞은 것을 고르시오. ·················· (　　　)

①　　　　②　　　　③　　　　④

2

다음을 듣고, 상대방에게 음식을 권할 때 쓰는 표현을 고르시오. ················ (　　　)

①　　　②　　　③　　　④

3

다음 대화를 듣고, 도서관의 위치로 알맞은 것을 고르시오. ··············· (　　　)

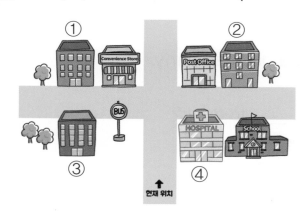

①　　　　②　　　　③　　　　④

4

다음 대화를 듣고, 무엇에 관해 이야기하고 있는지 고르시오. ·················· (　　　)

① 학교 숙제　　　　② 장래 희망

③ 방학 계획　　　　④ 좋아하는 음악

5

다음 대화를 듣고, 여자 아이가 저녁식사 후 하는 것을 고르시오. ··············· (　　　)

① 　②

③ 　④

6

다음 대화를 듣고, 내용과 일치하지 <u>않는</u> 것을 고르시오. ·················· (　　　)

① 민수는 12시 30분에 점심식사를 한다.
② 민수는 점심식사 후 축구를 한다.
③ 수업은 3시에 끝난다.
④ 방과 후 민수는 태권도 수업을 듣는다.

7

다음 대화를 듣고, 오이 한 개의 가격을 고르시오. ····························· (　　　)

① 100원　　　　② 200원
③ 400원　　　　④ 1,000원

8

다음 대화를 듣고, 여자가 부탁을 거절한 이유를 고르시오. ····················· (　　　)

① 잡지가 너무 재미없어서
② 잡지를 반납해야 해서
③ 집에 가야해서
④ 다른 친구에게 잡지를 빌려줘야 해서

9

다음 대화를 듣고, 어떤 상황에서 이루어지는 대화인지 고르시오. ················ (　　　)

① 사과하는 상황
② 헤어지는 상황
③ 오랜만에 만난 상황
④ 감사하는 상황

10

다음을 듣고, 무엇에 대한 설명인지 고르시오.
····························· (　　　)

① 　　②

③ 　　④

11

다음 대화를 듣고, 여자의 자동차 색깔을 고르시오. ································ (   )

① 초록색   ② 노란색

③ 흰색   ④ 푸른색

14

다음 대화를 듣고, 두 사람의 대화가 <u>어색한</u> 것을 고르시오. ···················· (   )

①   ②   ③   ④

12

다음 대화를 듣고, 두 아이가 좋아하는 운동을 바르게 짝지은 것을 고르시오. ····· (   )

	여자 아이	남자 아이
①	테니스	축구
②	축구	테니스
③	배구	농구
④	농구	축구

13

다음 대화를 듣고, 민지가 오후에 할 일을 고르시오. ································ (   )

①    ②

③    ④

15

다음 대화를 듣고, 여자가 찾는 물건을 고르시오. ································ (   )

①   ②

③    ④

16

다음 대화를 듣고, 상대방에게 축하하는 대화를 고르시오. ···················· (   )

①   ②   ③   ④

17

다음 대화를 듣고, 대화가 이루어지는 장소를 고르시오. ····················· (   )

① 제과점   ② 옷 가게
③ 학교   ④ 서점

18

다음 대화를 듣고, 이어질 말로 알맞은 것을 고르시오. ···················· (   )

M _____

① My dad is busy.
② I feel good.
③ That's a good idea.
④ Did you catch many fish?

19

다음 대화를 듣고, 이어질 말로 알맞은 것을 고르시오. ···················· (   )

M _____

① Okay. I'll take them.
② They are not my shoes.
③ Sorry. I don't have money.
④ I'd like to, but I can't.

20

다음 대화를 듣고, 이어질 말로 적절하지 않은 것을 고르시오. ···················· (   )

W _____

① No, I can't.
② Yes, I can speak Chinese a little bit.
③ No, but I want to learn.
④ Yes, China is a big country.

Dictation 영어 듣기 모의고사

 보통 속도 빠른 속도

정답 및 해석 p. 12

| 학습일 | 월 일 | 부모님 확인 | | 점수 |

● 잘 듣고, 빈칸에 알맞은 말을 쓰세요.

1

다음 그림을 보고, 남자 아이가 할 말로 알맞은 것을 고르시오. ·············· ( )

① ② ③ ④

B: ❶ Do you like reading books?

❷ Can I _____ your _____?

❸ Can you lend me some money?

❹ Can I use your _____?

borrow 빌리다 | umbrella 우산 | lend 빌려주다 | money 돈 | phone 전화기

2

다음을 듣고, 상대방에게 음식을 권할 때 쓰는 표현을 고르시오. ·············· ( )

① ② ③ ④

W: ❶ That's too bad.

❷ What a nice car!

❸ _____ _____.

❹ Have a nice day.

too 무척 | bad 좋지 않은 | nice 멋진

TIPS Help yourself.는 '많이 드세요.'라는 의미로 뒤에 음식을 이용해서 Help yourself to this pizza.(이 피자 좀 드세요.)라고 표현할 수 있습니다.

3

다음 대화를 듣고, 도서관의 위치로 알맞은 것을 고르시오. ·············· ( )

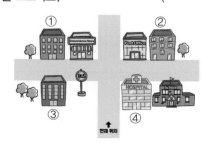

① ② ③ ④

M: Excuse me. Where is the library?

W: The library? Do you see the _____?

M: That hospital?

W: Yes, go straight and _____ _____ at the hospital. The library is _____ _____ the post office.

M: Thank you.

library 도서관 | hospital 병원 | straight 곧장 | turn right 오른쪽으로 돌다 | next to ~ 옆에 | post office 우체국

TIPS 위치와 관련된 전치사

behind ~ 뒤에   in front of ~ 앞에   across from ~ 건너편에

4

다음 대화를 듣고, 무엇에 관해 이야기하고 있는지 고르시오. ·················· (   )

① 학교 숙제   ② 장래 희망
③ 방학 계획   ④ 좋아하는 음악

G: Mike, what are you doing?

B: I'm writing about my _____ _____.

G: Do you still want to be a police officer?

B: No, I have a _____ _____ now.

G: What is it?

B: I want to be a _____.

future job 장래 직업 | still 여전히 | police officer 경찰관 | new 새로운 | dream 꿈 |
now 지금 | singer 가수

TIPS What is it?에서 it은 a new dream을 의미합니다. 경찰관은 policeman
이라고도 하지만 요즘에는 police officer를 더 많이 사용합니다.

5

다음 대화를 듣고, 여자 아이가 저녁식사 후 하는 것을 고르시오. ·················· (   )

①   ②   ③   ④

G: I get up at 7. I go to school at 8:30.

School _____ _____ at 3.

I do my homework after school.

I have dinner at 6:30. I usually _____

_____. _____ _____ after dinner.

get up 일어나다 | go to school 학교에 가다 | be over 끝나다 | usually 보통 |
go for a walk 산책하다

TIPS 방과 후에는 숙제를 하고 저녁식사 후에는 산책을 합니다.

6

다음 대화를 듣고, 내용과 일치하지 <u>않는</u> 것을 고르시오. ·················· (   )

① 민수는 12시 30분에 점심식사를 한다.
② 민수는 점심식사 후 축구를 한다.
③ 수업은 3시에 끝난다.
④ 방과 후 민수는 태권도 수업을 듣는다.

G: Minsu, what time do you have lunch?

B: I have lunch at _____.
   After lunch, I usually _____ _____
   with my classmates.

G: What time do you finish your class?

B: School is over at 3.

G: What do you do after school?

B: After school, I have a _____ _____
   at 4.

play soccer 축구하다 | classmate 반 친구 | finish 끝나다 | lesson 수업

TIPS breakfast(아침식사), lunch(점심식사), dinner(저녁식사) 앞에는 관사를
붙이지 않습니다. have는 '가지다' 외에 '먹다'라는 의미도 있습니다.
I have a computer. 나는 컴퓨터가 있다.
I usually have lunch at noon. 나는 보통 정오에 점심식사를 한다.

7

다음 대화를 듣고, 오이 한 개의 가격을 고르시오. ·············· ( )

① 100원   ② 200원
③ 400원   ④ 1,000원

M: May I help you?

W: I need some cucumbers. _____ _____ is this cucumber?

M: We are selling cucumbers for _____ won _____.

W: Okay. Can I get five?

cucumber 오이 | how much (가격) 얼마 | sell 팔다 | each 각각

TIPS a, one, two, several 등과 함께 hundred를 쓸 때에는 hundred끝에 s를 붙이지 않습니다. 200원은 two hundred won이라고 씁니다.

8

다음 대화를 듣고, 여자가 부탁을 거절한 이유를 고르시오. ·············· ( )

① 잡지가 너무 재미없어서
② 잡지를 반납해야 해서
③ 집에 가야해서
④ 다른 친구에게 잡지를 빌려줘야 해서

M: Jennie, what are you doing?

W: I'm reading a _____.

M: Is it interesting?

W: Yes, it is.

M: Can I _____ your magazine?

W: Sorry, I can't lend it to you. I have to _____ _____ to the library today.

magazine 잡지 | interesting 재미있는 | borrow 빌리다 | lend 빌려주다 | return 돌려주다

TIPS return it에서 it은 magazine을 의미합니다. return(돌려주다)의 의미를 알면 문제를 쉽게 해결 할 수 있습니다.

9

다음 대화를 듣고, 어떤 상황에서 이루어지는 대화인지 고르시오. ·············· ( )

① 사과하는 상황
② 헤어지는 상황
③ 오랜만에 만난 상황
④ 감사하는 상황

M: Hi, Alice. _____ _____ no see.

W: Hi, Mike. _____ to _____ you again. How are you?

M: I'm good. How was your vacation?

W: It was great.

see 보다 | vacation 휴가 | great 좋은, 훌륭한

TIPS Long time no see. 는 오랜만에 만날 때 하는 인사말로 Good to see you. 대신 Nice to see you again.(다시 만나서 반가워.)으로 답할 수 있습니다.

10

다음을 듣고, 무엇에 대한 설명인지 고르시오. ·············· ( )

M: This is a sport. We play this on a _____. There is a net in the _____ _____ the table. We need a racket and a small and _____ _____.

sport 스포츠 | net 네트 | in the middle of ~의 가운데에 | racket 라켓 | light 가벼운

TIPS a small and light ball은 '작고 가벼운 공' 이란 뜻입니다. 명사 ball을 두 개의 형용사가 수식하고 있습니다. 이와 같이 한 개의 명사를 다수의 형용사가 수식 할 수 있습니다.

11

다음 대화를 듣고, 여자의 자동차 색깔을 고르시오. ·········· (   )

① 초록색   ② 노란색
③ 흰색   ④ 푸른색

M: Where did you _____ your car?

W: My car is over there.

M: Do you mean the white car _____ _____ the tree?

W: No, the _____ _____ is mine.

M: What a nice car!

park 주차하다 | over there 저쪽에 | mean 의미하다 | next to ~ 옆에 | green 초록의 | mine 나의 것

TIPS the green one에서 one은 car를 의미하고, mine은 '나의 것'이라는 의미의 소유대명사로 뒤에 명사가 오지 않습니다.

yours 너의 것   hers 그녀의 것   his 그의 것

12

다음 대화를 듣고, 두 아이가 좋아하는 운동을 바르게 짝지은 것을 고르시오. ······ (   )

	여자 아이	남자 아이
①	테니스	축구
②	축구	테니스
③	배구	농구
④	농구	축구

B: Do you like sports?

G: Yes, I do. I usually _____ _____ every Sunday. How about you?

B: I like sports, _____.

G: What sport do you like most?

B: I like _____ _____.
I want to be a soccer player.

usually 보통 | play tennis 테니스를 치다 | every Sunday 일요일마다 | most 가장

TIPS 운동 경기 앞에는 관사를 붙이지 않습니다.

I play a volleyball.(x)   I play volleyball.(o) 나는 배구를 한다.

13

다음 대화를 듣고, 민지가 오후에 할 일을 고르시오. ·········· (   )

① ② ③ ④

B: Minji, are you free this afternoon?

G: Yes, I am. Why?

B: I'll _____ _____ _____ at the park. Will you come with me?

G: Sure.

B: Then, _____ _____ at the park at 5.

free 한가한 | this afternoon 오늘 오후 | walk 산책시키다 | park 공원

TIPS • walk는 '걷다'라는 의미 이외에 '(동물을) 산책시키다'라는 의미도 있습니다.
• [Let's + 동사원형]은 '~하자'라는 의미입니다. 전치사 at은 시각과 장소 앞에 위치합니다.

14

다음 대화를 듣고, 두 사람의 대화가 어색한 것을 고르시오. ········· (   )

①   ②   ③   ④

❶ B: Hi, Mary. _____ _____

    _____ doing?

  G: I'm doing my homework.

❷ B: What's your favorite season?

  G: I like _____ _____.

❸ B: Let's play baseball after school.

  G: Sounds great!

❹ B: How do you go to school?

  G: I usually go to school _____

    _____.

homework 숙제 | season 계절 | autumn 가을 | baseball 야구 | by bus 버스로

TIPS How are you doing?은 '어떻게 지내니?'라는 뜻으로 I am good! / I am great! 등으로 대답할 수 있습니다. How are you doing? 대신 How are you? / How is it going? / What's up? 등을 사용할 수 있습니다.

15

다음 대화를 듣고, 여자가 찾는 물건을 고르시오. ········· (   )

①   ②

③   ④

M: What's wrong?

W: I can't find _____ _____.

M: Your cellphone?

W: Yes. Did you see it?

M: It's on the chair _____ _____

  the TV.

wrong 잘못된 | cellphone 휴대폰 | next to ~ 옆에

16

다음 대화를 듣고, 상대방에게 축하하는 대화를 고르시오. ········· (   )

①   ②   ③   ④

❶ M: See you tomorrow.

  W: Bye. See you.

❷ M: What's the problem?

  W: I _____ _____ _____.

❸ M: Thank you for your kindness.

  W: It's my pleasure.

❹ M: I won a _____ in a writing contest.

  W: That's great. _____.

tomorrow 내일 | problem 문제 | have a cold 감기에 걸리다 | kindness 친절 | pleasure 즐거움 | contest 대회 | win 타다, 이기다 | prize 상 | congratulations 축하해

TIPS Congratulations!는 '축하해!'라는 의미입니다, 반드시 끝에 –s를 붙여야 합니다. Congratulations on your exam results! 시험 결과[시험 잘 본 거] 축하해!

17

다음 대화를 듣고, 대화가 이루어지는 장소를 고르시오. ··········· (   )

① 제과점　　　② 옷 가게
③ 학교　　　　④ 서점

M: What can I do for you?

W: I'm looking for a skirt.

M: How about this _____ _____?

W: Hmm... Do you have _____ _____ in pink?

M: Yes, we have _____ _____ over there.

look for ~을 찾다 | skirt 치마 | another 다른 | over there 저쪽에

18

다음 대화를 듣고, 이어질 말로 알맞은 것을 고르시오. ··········· (   )

M _____

① My dad is busy.
② I feel good.
③ That's a good idea.
④ Did you catch many fish?

W: How was your weekend?

M: It was fun. I _____ _____ with my family. What did you do last weekend?

W: I _____ _____ with my dad.

M: _____

weekend 주말 | go camping 캠핑을 가다 | family 가족 | go fishing 낚시하러 가다 | busy 바쁜 | idea 생각 | catch 잡다

19

다음 대화를 듣고, 이어질 말로 알맞은 것을 고르시오. ··········· (   )

M _____

① Okay. I'll take them.
② They are not my shoes.
③ Sorry. I don't have money.
④ I'd like to, but I can't.

W: May I help you?

M: I want _____ _____. How much are they?

W: They are _____ _____.

M: _____

shoes 신발 | how much (가격) 얼마 | take 사다 | money 돈

TIPS 동사 take는 '물건을 구매하다'라는 의미입니다.
I'll take the black jacket. 검정 재킷을 사겠어요.

20

다음 대화를 듣고, 이어질 말로 적절하지 <u>않은</u> 것을 고르시오. ··········· (   )

W _____

① No, I can't.
② Yes, I can speak Chinese a little bit.
③ No, but I want to learn.
④ Yes, China is a big country.

W: Jim, can you _____ _____?

M: Yes, I can. _____ _____?

W: _____

speak 말하다 | Chinese 중국어 | a little bit 조금 | learn 배우다 | country 나라

TIPS Can you?는 Can you speak Chinese?를 줄여 말한 것입니다.
can을 이용해 묻고 있으므로 can 또는 can't를 이용해 대답해야 합니다.

● 다음 들려주는 단어의 의미를 쓰세요.

	단어	의미
01	lend	빌려주다
02	straight	
03	still	
04	cucumber	
05	each	
06	magazine	
07	return	
08	light	
09	walk	
10	kindness	
11	another	
12	catch	
13	country	
14	congratulations	
15	pleasure	

● 앞에 모의고사에 나오는 문장들을 잘 듣고, 빈칸을 완성하세요.

01 __Help__ __yourself__.

02 Go straight and _____ _____ at the hospital.

03 I'm writing about my _____ _____.

04 I have a _____ _____ now.

05 I usually _____ _____ _____ _____ after dinner.

06 We are selling cucumbers for _____ _____ _____.

07 I have to _____ _____ to the library today.

08 _____ _____ _____ you again.

09 There is a net _____ _____ _____ of the table.

10 What a _____ _____!

11 I usually play tennis _____ _____.

12 I _____ _____ _____ at the park.

13 Thank you for _____ _____.

14 I won a prize in a _____ _____.

15 I _____ _____ with my family.

영어 듣기 모의고사

보통 속도

빠른 속도

| 학습일 | 월 일 | 부모님 확인 | 점수 |

1

다음 그림을 보고, 남자 아이가 할 말로 알맞은 것을 고르시오. ················· (   )

①   ②   ③   ④

2

다음을 듣고, 아침에 친구를 만났을 때 쓰는 표현을 고르시오. ················· (   )

①   ②   ③   ④

3

다음 대화를 듣고, 현재 시각을 고르시오.
································· (   )

① 10시 3분   ② 10시 10분
③ 3시 10분   ④ 3시 20분

4

다음 대화를 듣고, 남자 아이가 주말에 한 일을 고르시오. ···················· (   )

①    ②

③    ④

5

다음 대화를 듣고, 대화가 일어나는 장소를 고르시오. ···················· (   )

① 병원   ② 식당
③ 학교   ④ 도서관

6

다음 대화를 듣고, 여자 아이가 할 수 있는 운동을 고르시오. ····························· (   )

①

②

③

④

7

다음 대화를 듣고, 두 아이가 좋아하는 과목을 고르시오. ····························· (   )

① 수학   ② 과학
③ 역사   ④ 미술

8

다음 대화를 듣고, 오늘이 무슨 요일인지 고르시오. ····························· (   )

① 화요일   ② 목요일
③ 금요일   ④ 토요일

9

다음 대화를 듣고, 남자 아이의 장래 희망을 고르시오. ····························· (   )

① 제빵사   ② 의사
③ 선생님   ④ 변호사

10

다음 대화를 듣고, 어떤 상황에서 이루어지는 대화인지 고르시오. ····················· (   )

① 사과하는 상황
② 헤어지는 상황
③ 오랜만에 만난 상황
④ 부탁하는 상황

11

다음 대화를 듣고, 대화의 내용과 <u>다른</u> 것을 고르시오. ·· (   )

① 다음 주 일요일이 Amy의 생일이다.
② Amy는 생일선물로 컴퓨터를 원한다.
③ Amy는 생일에 친구를 초대할 예정이다.
④ Amy는 현재 컴퓨터가 없다.

12

다음 대화를 듣고, Susie가 하고 있는 것을 고르시오. ································· (   )

①
②

③
④

13

다음 그림을 보고, 그림과 일치하는 대화를 고르시오. ·································· (   )

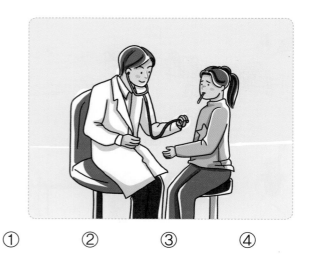

①   ②   ③   ④

14

다음 대화를 듣고, 남자가 늦은 이유를 고르시오. ······································· (   )

① 늦잠을 자서
② 버스를 놓쳐서
③ 교통사고가 나서
④ 약속시간을 몰라서

15

다음 대화를 듣고, 여자가 찾는 시계를 고르시오. ·························· (   )

①   ②

③   ④

16

다음 대화를 듣고, 상대방에게 위로하는 대화를 고르시오. ······················ (   )

①   ②   ③   ④

17

다음 대화를 듣고, 무엇에 관해 이야기하고 있는지 고르시오. ······················ (   )

① 점심시간   ② 학교 생활
③ 점심 메뉴   ④ 아침식사

18

다음 대화를 듣고, 이어질 말로 알맞은 것을 고르시오. ·························· (   )

B _____

① It's not my book.
② I usually finish at 4.
③ It's Monday.
④ I go to bed at 10.

19

다음 대화를 듣고, 이어질 말로 알맞은 것을 고르시오. ·························· (   )

M _____

① I ate pizza for lunch.
② I want a new computer.
③ I don't like Korean food.
④ I want fried chicken.

20

다음 대화를 듣고, 이어질 말로 적절하지 않은 것을 고르시오. ·························· (   )

W _____

① Oh, that's too bad.
② What does your bike look like?
③ Where is your bike?
④ Really? Let's find it together.

● 잘 듣고, 빈칸에 알맞은 말을 쓰세요.

1

다음 그림을 보고, 남자 아이가 할 말로 알맞은 것을 고르시오. ················· (   )

① ② ③ ④

B: ❶ How much is the chair?

❷ _____ _____ do you want?

❸ Can I have some water?

❹ I would like to _____ a _____.

how much (가격) 얼마 | size 크기 | would like to ~하고 싶다 | have a haircut 머리를 자르다

TIPS 남자 아이가 이발소에 있는 그림으로 이와 연관된 단어는 haircut입니다.

2

다음을 듣고, 아침에 친구를 만났을 때 쓰는 표현을 고르시오. ················· (   )

① ② ③ ④

M: ❶ Here you are.

❷ That's _____ _____.

❸ How can I help you?

❹ _____ _____ _____ doing today?

here you are 여기 있다 | news 소식 | help 돕다 | today 오늘

TIPS How are you doing?은 How are you?와 같은 뜻이면서 가장 많이 쓰이는 인사말입니다.

3

다음 대화를 듣고, 현재 시각을 고르시오.
················· (   )

① 10시 3분   ② 10시 10분
③ 3시 10분   ④ 3시 20분

W: What time is it now?

M: It's _____ _____ _____.

W: You mean it's _____?

M: Yes, it is.

what time 몇 시 | now 지금 | past ~을 지나서 | mean 의미하다

TIPS 시간을 말할 때는 '시'와 '분' 순서로 기수로 말할 수 있습니다. 또한 past[after]나 to 를 이용해서 '분'을 먼저 말할 수도 있습니다.

4

다음 대화를 듣고, 남자 아이가 주말에 한 일을 고르시오. ·········· ( )

① ②

③ ④

B: How was your weekend, Cathy?

G: It was _____ _____.

B: What did you do?

G: I went to the zoo. How about you?

B: I stayed home and _____ _____.

weekend 주말 | **pretty** 꽤, 무척 | **zoo** 동물원 | **stay** 머무르다

TIPS 주말에 한 일을 얘기해야 하므로 동사를 과거형으로 해야 합니다.

5

다음 대화를 듣고, 대화가 일어나는 장소를 고르시오. ·········· ( )

① 병원   ② 식당
③ 학교   ④ 도서관

W: Are you ready to _____?

M: Yes, please. I'd like the spaghetti.

W: Would you like _____ _____ _____ with that?

M: I'd like a Coke, please.

ready 준비된 | **order** 주문하다 | **something** 무언가

TIPS I'd like는 I would like의 줄임말로 '~하고 싶다'라는 의미입니다.

6

다음 대화를 듣고, 여자 아이가 할 수 있는 운동을 고르시오. ·········· ( )

① ②

③ ④

G: Tom, can you play table tennis?

B: Yes, I can. Can you?

G: No, I can't, but I'm _____ _____ _____ during summer vacation.

B: What sports can you play?

G: I can _____ _____.

table tennis 탁구 | **learn** 배우다 | **during** ~ 동안 | **vacation** 방학 | **tennis** 테니스

TIPS [be going to + 동사원형]은 '~ 할 예정이다'라는 가까운 미래에 예정된 일을 표현할 때 사용합니다.

7

다음 대화를 듣고, 두 아이가 좋아하는 과목을 고르시오. ·········· ( )

① 수학   ② 과학
③ 역사   ④ 미술

G: Minsu, what are you doing?

B: I'm doing my _____ _____.

G: Do you like math?

B: No, I don't.

G: What's your favorite subject?

B: I _____ _____.

G: I like it, _____.

math 수학 | **favorite** 좋아하는 | **subject** 과목 | **science** 과학

TIPS I like it, too.에서 it은 science를 의미합니다.

8

다음 대화를 듣고, 오늘이 무슨 요일인지 고르시오. ·············· (   )

① 화요일   ② 목요일
③ 금요일   ④ 토요일

B: Jennie, where are you going?

G: I'm going to the swimming pool. I have a swimming lesson _____ _____.

B: Friday? It's Thursday today.

G: Really?

B: Yes, _____ _____ _____.

swimming pool 수영장 | lesson 수업 | every Friday 금요일마다 | Thursday 목요일

TIPS 요일은 다음과 같습니다.
Monday 월요일, Tuesday 화요일, Wednesday 수요일, Thursday 목요일, Friday 금요일, Saturday 토요일, Sunday 일요일

9

다음 대화를 듣고, 남자 아이의 장래 희망을 고르시오. ·············· (   )

① 제빵사   ② 의사
③ 선생님   ④ 변호사

B: Would you like some cookies?

G: Yes, thanks. Where did you get them?

B: I made _____ _____.

G: Really?

B: Yes, I want to _____ _____ _____ in the future.

cookie 쿠키 | get 얻다 | myself 나 자신, 직접 | baker 제빵사 | in the future 장래에

TIPS 직업을 나타내는 단어는 다음과 같은 것들이 있습니다.
cook 요리사   lawyer 변호사   nurse 간호사
musician 음악가   writer 작가   scientist 과학자

10

다음 대화를 듣고, 어떤 상황에서 이루어지는 대화인지 고르시오. ·············· (   )

① 사과하는 상황
② 헤어지는 상황
③ 오랜만에 만난 상황
④ 부탁하는 상황

M: Alice, do you have _____ _____ tomorrow?

W: I don't have anything special to do. Why?

M: Can you _____ _____? I'm going to paint my house.

W: Okay.

plan 계획 | tomorrow 내일 | special 특별한 | paint 페인트칠하다 | house 집

TIPS [be going to + 동사원형]은 '~ 할 예정이다'라는 예정된 가까운 미래에 예정된 일을 표현할 때 사용합니다.

11

다음 대화를 듣고, 대화의 내용과 <u>다른</u> 것을 고르시오. ································· (   )

① 다음 주 일요일이 Amy의 생일이다.
② Amy는 생일선물로 컴퓨터를 원한다.
③ Amy는 생일에 친구를 초대할 예정이다.
④ Amy는 현재 컴퓨터가 없다.

B: Amy, your birthday is _____ _____, isn't it?

G: Yes, it is. I'm going to invite my friends on my birthday.

B: What do you want for your birthday?

G: I want a _____ _____.

B: You don't have a computer?

G: I have a computer, but it's _____ _____.

next Sunday 다음 주 일요일 | invite 초대하다 | old 오래된, 낡은

12

다음 대화를 듣고, Susie가 하고 있는 것을 고르시오. ································· (   )

B: Susie, what are you doing?

G: I'm _____ _____ of flowers.

B: Can I see them?

G: Sure.

B: Wow. You are _____ _____ taking photos.

G: Thanks.

take photos 사진을 찍다 | flower 꽃 | sure 물론, 그럼 | be good at ~을 잘하다
TIPS take photos는 '사진을 찍다'라는 의미입니다.

13

다음 그림을 보고, 그림과 일치하는 대화를 고르시오. ································· (   )

①   ②   ③   ④

❶ M: What's wrong?

　G: I _____ _____ _____ and a headache.

❷ M: How was your vacation?

　G: It was great.

❸ M: What do you want for lunch?

　G: I'd like to have fried chicken.

❹ M: _____ _____ do you have dinner?

　G: I have dinner at 7.

fever 열 | headache 두통 | vacation 휴가 | fried chicken 프라이드치킨
TIPS 병원에서 진찰을 받는 그림이므로 이와 관련된 단어를 알고 있는 것이 문제 해결의 열쇠입니다.

14

다음 대화를 듣고, 남자가 늦은 이유를 고르시오. ·························· (   )

① 늦잠을 자서
② 버스를 놓쳐서
③ 교통사고가 나서
④ 약속시간을 몰라서

M: I'm sorry I'm late.

W: _____ were you late today?

M: I had a _____ _____.

W: Really? Are you okay?

M: Yes, I am.

late 늦은 | today 오늘 | car accident 자동차 사고

TIPS had는 have의 과거형입니다. 여기서 have는 '경험하다'라는 의미입니다.
We had a good time at the party. 우리는 파티에서 좋은 시간을 보냈다.

15

다음 대화를 듣고, 여자가 찾는 시계를 고르시오. ·························· (   )

①   ②
③   ④

M: What are you doing here, Cindy?

W: I'm looking for _____ _____.

M: Your watch? Is this your watch?

W: No, it isn't.

M: What does your watch look like?

W: It is _____ and its color is _____.

here 여기 | watch 손목시계 | look like ~처럼 생기다 | round 둥근

TIPS 모양을 묘사하는 영어 표현
triangle 삼각형   square 정사각형   cone 원뿔   pentagon 오각형   circle 원

16

다음 대화를 듣고, 상대방에게 위로하는 대화를 고르시오. ·························· (   )

①   ②   ③   ④

❶ W: Sam, _____ _____ the party?
   M: It was great.

❷ M: I got a C on the math test.
   W: _____ _____!
      You'll do better next time.

❸ M: Can I ask you a question?
   W: Sure. What is it?

❹ M: Did you see the soccer game yesterday?
   W: Yes, it was _____ _____.

party 파티 | math test 수학 시험 | cheer up 기운 내다 | better 더 나은 |
next time 다음번 | question 질문 | exciting 흥미진진한

17

다음 대화를 듣고, 무엇에 관해 이야기하고 있는지 고르시오. ·················· (　　)

① 점심시간　　② 학교 생활
③ 점심 메뉴　　④ 아침식사

W: Jim, do you _____ _____ every day?

M: Yes, I do.

W: What do you have for breakfast?

M: I _____ _____ cereal. How about you?

W: I don't have breakfast.

breakfast 아침(식사) | every day 매일 | usually 보통 | cereal 시리얼

TIPS 동사 have는 '~을 먹다'라는 의미가 있습니다.

18

다음 대화를 듣고, 이어질 말로 알맞은 것을 고르시오. ·················· (　　)

B _____

① It's not my book.
② I usually finish at 4.
③ It's Monday.
④ I go to bed at 10.

G: Hi, John. _____ _____ does your first class start?

B: It starts _____ _____.

G: Really? My first class starts at 8:40. Then, what time does your school finish?

B: _____

first 처음의 | class 수업 | really 정말 | finish 끝나다

TIPS what time으로 질문하면 정확한 시각으로 답해야 합니다.

19

다음 대화를 듣고, 이어질 말로 알맞은 것을 고르시오. ·················· (　　)

M _____

① I ate pizza for lunch.
② I want a new computer.
③ I don't like Korean food.
④ I want fried chicken.

W: I'm hungry. _____ _____ some pizza.

M: Sorry. I don't like pizza.

W: Then, _____ do you want to _____?

M: _____

hungry 배고픈 | order 주문하다 | Korean food 한국 음식 | fried chicken 프라이드치킨

TIPS What do you want to have? 대신 What do you want to eat? 으로 표현할 수 있으며, 의문사 what으로 질문하면, yes나 no로 답변할 수 없습니다.

20

다음 대화를 듣고, 이어질 말로 적절하지 않은 것을 고르시오. ·················· (　　)

W _____

① Oh, that's too bad.
② What does your bike look like?
③ Where is your bike?
④ Really? Let's find it together.

W: You _____ _____. What's wrong?

M: I _____ my bike.

W: _____

sad 슬픈 | wrong 잘못된 | lost 잃어버리다(lose)의 과거분사형 | together 함께

TIPS 자전거를 잃어버렸다고 했는데 Where is your bike?(자전거 어디에 있니?)는 어울리지 않습니다.

5 회 Word Check

● 다음 들려주는 단어의 의미를 쓰세요.

	단어	의미
01	news	소식
02	past	
03	accident	
04	during	
05	table tennis	
06	myself	
07	special	
08	invite	
09	sure	
10	headache	
11	better	
12	cereal	
13	exciting	
14	really	
15	together	

● 앞에 모의고사에 나오는 문장들을 잘 듣고, 빈칸을 완성하세요.

01 I would like to ___have___ ___a___ ___haircut___.

02 That's _____ _____.

03 I _____ _____ and watched TV.

04 I'm going to learn _____ summer _____.

05 I have a swimming lesson _____ _____.

06 I _____ them _____.

07 I'm going to _____ _____ _____.

08 I have a computer, but it's _____ _____.

09 I'm _____ _____ of flowers.

10 I _____ _____ _____ and a headache.

11 I had a _____ _____.

12 I got a C on the _____ _____.

13 My first class _____ _____ 8:40.

14 _____ _____ some pizza.

15 I _____ _____ _____.

영어 듣기 모의고사

 보통 속도 빠른 속도

| 학습일 | 월 일 | 부모님 확인 | 점수 |

1

다음 대화를 듣고, 남자가 산 것을 고르시오.
·· (   )

①  ②

③   ④

2

다음 그림을 보고, 남자 아이가 할 말로 알맞은 것을 고르시오. ······················ (   )

①   ②   ③   ④

3

다음 대화를 듣고, 여자 아이가 산책을 할 수 없는 이유를 고르시오. ·············· (   )

① 숙제를 해야 해서
② 청소를 해야 해서
③ 피아노 연습을 해야 해서
④ 어머니를 도와야 해서

4

다음 대화를 듣고, Bob이 하고 있는 운동을 고르시오. ···························· (   )

①  ②

③  ④

5

다음 대화를 듣고, 남자의 여동생을 고르시오.
.... ( )

① 　②

③ 　④

7

다음 대화를 듣고, 남자 아이가 살 물건을 고르시오. .... ( )

① 　②

③  　④

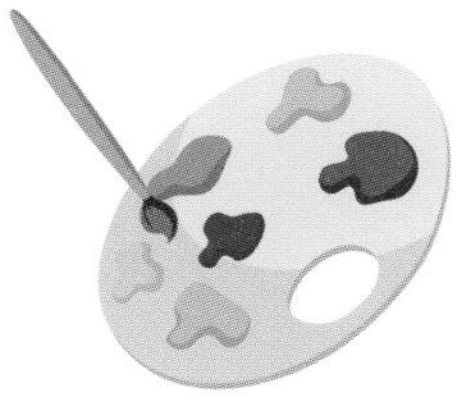

6

다음 그림을 보고, 여자 아이가 할 말로 알맞은 것을 고르시오. .... ( )

① ② ③  ④

8

다음을 듣고, 대화가 자연스러운 것을 고르시오. .... ( )

① ② ③ ④

9

다음 대화를 듣고, 무엇에 관해 이야기하고 있는지 고르시오. .... ( )

① 아침식사 메뉴 　② 좋아하는 음식
③ 좋아하는 계절 　④ 아침 먹는 시간

10

다음 대화를 듣고, 어떤 상황에서 이루어지는 대화인지 고르시오. ················ (   )

① 부탁을 거절하는 상황
② 헤어지는 상황
③ 오랜만에 만난 상황
④ 칭찬하는 상황

11

다음 대화를 듣고, 대화의 내용과 <u>다른</u> 것을 고르시오. ···························· (   )

① Amy는 몸상태가 좋지 않다.
② Amy는 두통이 있다.
③ Amy는 두통약을 먹지 않았다.
④ Amy는 두통약이 있다.

12

다음을 듣고, 그림과 일치하는 설명을 고르시오. ···························· (   )

①   ②   ③   ④

13

다음 대화를 듣고, 여자가 있는 장소를 고르시오. ···························· (   )

① 정원   ② 공원
③ 꽃 가게   ④ 우체국

14

다음 대화를 듣고, 여자가 어젯밤에 한 일을 고르시오. ···························· (   )

① 축구 경기   ② TV 시청
③ 컴퓨터게임   ④ 시험공부

15

다음 대화를 듣고, 누구에 대해 말하고 있는지 고르시오. ···························· (   )

① 여자 아이의 사촌
② 여자 아이의 이모
③ 여자 아이의 여동생
④ 여자 아이의 삼촌

16

다음 대화를 듣고, 남자가 전화를 건 목적을 고르시오. ····································· (   )

① 약속을 취소하려고
② 함께 캠핑 가려고
③ 텐트를 돌려주려고
④ 텐트를 빌리려고

17

다음을 듣고, 이어질 말로 알맞은 것을 고르시오. ····································· (   )

M _____

① It sounds good.
② I don't have any plans.
③ Yes, I'm busy.
④ It's not my idea.

18

다음을 듣고, 이어질 말로 알맞은 것을 고르시오. ····································· (   )

W _____

① It's not my T-shirt.
② I like that blue T-shirt.
③ I bought it on the Internet.
④ It's 10 dollars.

19

다음 대화를 듣고, 이어질 말로 알맞은 것을 고르시오. ····································· (   )

M _____

① I don't like noodles.
② No, thanks. I'm full.
③ No, that's all.
④ I have something for you.

20

다음 대화를 듣고, 이어질 말로 적절하지 <u>않은</u> 것을 고르시오. ····································· (   )

G _____

① Okay. What time shall we meet?
② Yes, I went shopping yesterday.
③ I'd like to, but I have to do my homework.
④ I'm sorry, but I can't.

학습일 | 월 일 | 부모님 확인 | 점수

● 잘 듣고, 빈칸에 알맞은 말을 쓰세요.

1

다음 대화를 듣고, 남자가 산 것을 고르시오.
····················( )

① ②

③ ④

W: May I help you?

M: I need some cucumbers.

W: Sorry. We _____ _____ any cucumbers now.

M: Then, do you _____ _____?

W: Yes, we do. _____ _____ onions do you want?

M: Five.

need 필요하다 | cucumber 오이 | now 지금 | onion 양파

TIPS [How many + 복수명사 ~?]나 [How much + 셀 수 없는 명사 ~?] 형태로 사용합니다.

2

다음 그림을 보고, 남자 아이가 할 말로 알맞은 것을 고르시오. ····················( )

① ② ③ ④

B: ❶ Excuse me. Where is the bank?

❷ I'm _____ to hear that.

❸ I'm _____.
Can I have _____ _____?

❹ No, thanks. I'm full.

bank 은행 | hear 듣다 | thirsty 목마른 | full 배부른

TIPS 갈증이 나서 물을 마시고 싶은 그림에 어울리는 문장이 필요합니다.
I'm sorry to hear that.은 상대방의 불행에 대해 슬픔이나 유감을 나타내는 표현으로 '그 소식을 듣게 되어서 정말 유감이다.'라는 뜻입니다. 여기서 sorry는 '미안한'이 아니라 '유감스러운'의 의미입니다.

3

다음 대화를 듣고, 여자 아이가 산책을 할 수 없는 이유를 고르시오. ····················( )

① 숙제를 해야 해서
② 청소를 해야 해서
③ 피아노 연습을 해야 해서
④ 어머니를 도와야 해서

G: How is the weather today?

B: It's sunny. Let's _____ _____ _____ after lunch.

G: Sorry, I can't. I have to _____ _____ _____.

B: Oh, I see.

weather 날씨 | sunny 맑은 | take a walk 산책하다 | practice 연습하다

TIPS [have to + 동사원형]은 '~해야 한다'라는 의미입니다.

4

다음 대화를 듣고, Bob이 하고 있는 운동을 고르시오. ················· ( )

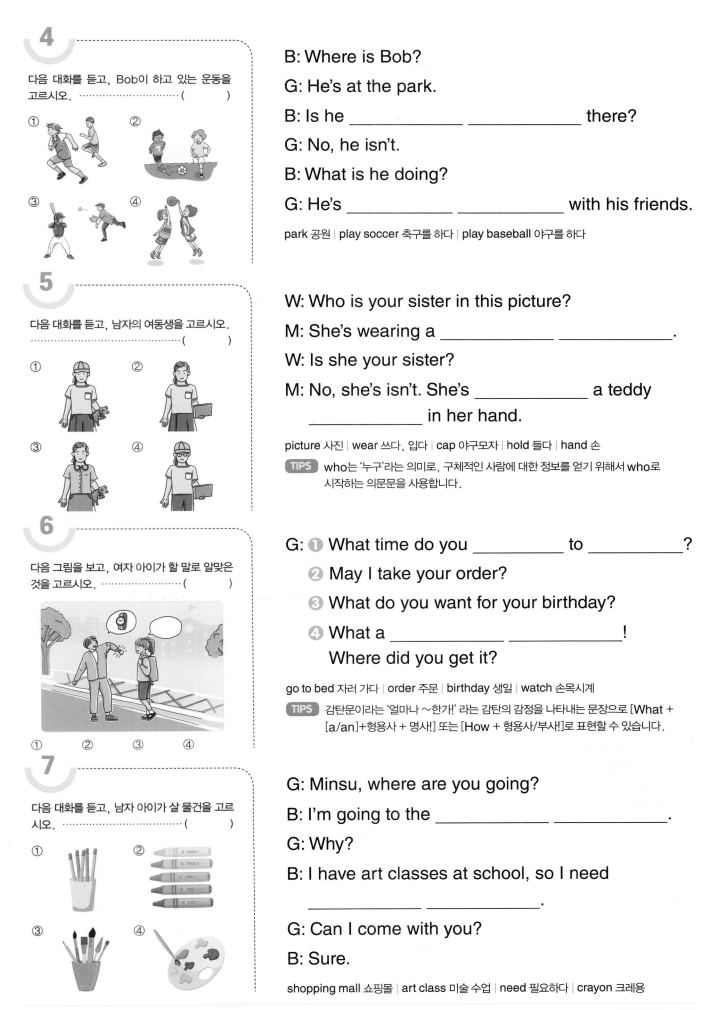

① ② ③ ④

B: Where is Bob?

G: He's at the park.

B: Is he _____ _____ there?

G: No, he isn't.

B: What is he doing?

G: He's _____ _____ with his friends.

park 공원 | play soccer 축구를 하다 | play baseball 야구를 하다

5

다음 대화를 듣고, 남자의 여동생을 고르시오.
················· ( )

① ② ③ ④

W: Who is your sister in this picture?

M: She's wearing a _____ _____.

W: Is she your sister?

M: No, she's isn't. She's _____ a teddy
_____ in her hand.

picture 사진 | wear 쓰다, 입다 | cap 야구모자 | hold 들다 | hand 손

TIPS who는 '누구'라는 의미로, 구체적인 사람에 대한 정보를 얻기 위해서 who로 시작하는 의문문을 사용합니다.

6

다음 그림을 보고, 여자 아이가 할 말로 알맞은 것을 고르시오. ················· ( )

① ② ③ ④

G: ❶ What time do you _____ to _____?

❷ May I take your order?

❸ What do you want for your birthday?

❹ What a _____ _____!
Where did you get it?

go to bed 자러 가다 | order 주문 | birthday 생일 | watch 손목시계

TIPS 감탄문이라는 '얼마나 ~한가!' 라는 감탄의 감정을 나타내는 문장으로 [What + [a/an]+형용사 + 명사!] 또는 [How + 형용사/부사!]로 표현할 수 있습니다.

7

다음 대화를 듣고, 남자 아이가 살 물건을 고르시오. ················· ( )

① ② ③ ④

G: Minsu, where are you going?

B: I'm going to the _____ _____.

G: Why?

B: I have art classes at school, so I need
_____ _____.

G: Can I come with you?

B: Sure.

shopping mall 쇼핑몰 | art class 미술 수업 | need 필요하다 | crayon 크레용

8

다음을 듣고, 대화가 자연스러운 것을 고르시오. ········· (   )

①   ②   ③   ④

❶ M: _____ _____ is it now?

W: It's Saturday.

❷ M: _____ _____ is this?

W: It's my mom's car.

❸ M: Who is the man over there?

W: Nice to meet you.

❹ M: I have a fever and a headache.

W: Have a good time.

now 지금 | Saturday 토요일 | whose 누구의 | over there 저쪽에 | meet 만나다 | fever 열 | headache 두통

TIPS 답변이 It's Saturday.가 되기 위해서는 질문이 What day is it today?가 되어야 합니다. Who로 질문하면, 사람과 연관된 대답이 와야 합니다.

9

다음 대화를 듣고, 무엇에 관해 이야기하고 있는지 고르시오. ··············· (   )

① 아침식사 메뉴   ② 좋아하는 음식
③ 좋아하는 계절   ④ 아침 먹는 시간

W: James, what do you eat _____ _____?

M: I eat bread. How about you?

W: I _____ _____ cereal and eggs.

M: Eggs?

W: Yes. I like scrambled eggs.

breakfast 아침(식사) | bread 빵 | usually 보통 | scrambled egg 스크램블 에그

TIPS How about you?(너는 어때?)는 상대방에 대한 질문으로, 여기서는 What do you eat for breakfast?를 상대방에 묻고 있는 것입니다.

10

다음 대화를 듣고, 어떤 상황에서 이루어지는 대화인지 고르시오. ··············· (   )

① 부탁을 거절하는 상황
② 헤어지는 상황
③ 오랜만에 만난 상황
④ 칭찬하는 상황

B: Guess what, Mom?

W: What?

B: I won _____ _____ in the essay contest.

W: Really?

B: Yes, I did.

W: _____ _____! I'm proud of you.

guess 추측하다 | first prize 1등 | essay 에세이 | contest 대회 | be proud of ~이 자랑스럽다

TIPS Good job!은 '잘했어!', '훌륭해!'라는 의미로 You did a good job.의 줄임말입니다.

11

다음 대화를 듣고, 대화의 내용과 <u>다른</u> 것을 고르시오. ·························· (   )

① Amy는 몸상태가 좋지 않다.
② Amy는 두통이 있다.
③ Amy는 두통약을 먹지 않았다.
④ Amy는 두통약이 있다.

M: Are you okay, Amy?

W: No, I don't ＿＿＿＿＿＿ ＿＿＿＿＿＿.
I have a headache.

M: Sorry to hear that. Did you ＿＿＿＿＿＿
＿＿＿＿＿＿ ＿＿＿＿＿＿?

W: No, I didn't. I don't have medicine for a headache.

M: Really? I'll ＿＿＿＿＿＿ ＿＿＿＿＿＿ some medicine.

feel well 건강이 좋다 | headache 두통 | take some medicine 약을 좀 먹다

TIPS [get + 사람 + 사물]의 문장은 '사람에게 사물을 가져다주다'라는 의미입니다.
Can I get you something? 뭐 좀 가져다 줄까요?

12

다음을 듣고, 그림과 일치하는 설명을 고르시오. ·························· (   )

①   ②   ③   ④

M: ❶ A boy is catching a ball.

   ❷ A boy is ＿＿＿＿＿＿ fish.

   ❸ A boy is swimming in the river.

   ❹ A boy is ＿＿＿＿＿＿ ＿＿＿＿＿＿.

catch 잡다 | ball 공 | fish 생선, 물고기 | river 강

TIPS [be동사 + -ing] 형태는 진행시제로 진행 중인 동작을 나타냅니다.

13

다음 대화를 듣고, 여자가 있는 장소를 고르시오. ·························· (   )

① 정원   ② 공원
③ 꽃 가게   ④ 우체국

M: Jennifer, what are you doing?

W: I'm watering the flowers ＿＿＿＿＿＿
＿＿＿＿＿＿ ＿＿＿＿＿＿.

M: How often do you water the flowers?

W: ＿＿＿＿＿＿ ＿＿＿＿＿＿ ＿＿＿＿＿＿.

water 물을 주다 | garden 정원 | how often 얼마나 자주 | twice 두 번

TIPS 여자가 정원에서 꽃에 물을 주고 있습니다. How often은 '얼마나 자주'라는 의미로 다음과 같이 대답할 수 있습니다.
A: How often do you play baseball? 얼마나 자주 야구를 하니?
B: Once a week. 일주일에 한 번. / Twice a month. 한 달에 두 번.

14

다음 대화를 듣고, 여자가 어젯밤에 한 일을 고르시오. ·························· (　　　)

① 축구 경기　　② TV 시청
③ 컴퓨터게임　　④ 시험공부

M: Amy, how are you doing today?

W: I'm not good.

M: Why?

W: I _____ _____ _____
　 last night.

M: Did you play computer games?

W: No, I _____ a soccer game
　 _____ _____ .

today 오늘 | stay up late 늦게까지 안 자다 | last night 지난밤 | soccer game 축구 경기

TIPS Did로 물었으므로, 대답도 과거형으로 해야 합니다. watch의 과거형은 watched 입니다.

15

다음 대화를 듣고, 누구에 대해 말하고 있는지 고르시오. ·························· (　　　)

① 여자 아이의 사촌
② 여자 아이의 이모
③ 여자 아이의 여동생
④ 여자 아이의 삼촌

B: Who is the woman in the picture?

G: She's _____ _____ , Ann.

B: Do you have a cousin?

G: Yes, she _____ _____ Canada.

B: She's very tall. How old is she?

G: She's 14 years old.

woman 여자 | cousin 사촌 | tall 키가 큰

TIPS 가족 호칭
sister / older sister 누나(언니)　　sister / younger sister 여동생
aunt 고모, 이모　　nephew 조카(남자)　　niece 조카(여자)

16

다음 대화를 듣고, 남자가 전화를 건 목적을 고르시오. ·························· (　　　)

① 약속을 취소하려고
② 함께 캠핑 가려고
③ 텐트를 돌려주려고
④ 텐트를 빌리려고

[Cellphone rings.]

W: Hello.

M: Hi, Amy. _____ _____ Tom.

W: Oh, hi, Tom. What's up?

M: I'm going camping tomorrow, but I don't have a
　 tent. Will you lend me _____ _____ ?

W: Sure. I'll _____ it to your house.

cellphone 휴대폰 | go camping 캠핑 가다 | tent 텐트 | lend 빌려주다 | bring 가져다주다

TIPS 통화에서 '누구세요?'라는 표현은 Who is this?라고 합니다. 이에 대답도 this를 이용하여 This is Brian.(브라이언입니다.)이라고 합니다. 전화 통화에서는 Who are you?라고 하지 않습니다.

17

다음을 듣고, 이어질 말로 알맞은 것을 고르시
오. ·· (   )

M _____

① It sounds good.
② I don't have any plans.
③ Yes, I'm busy.
④ It's not my idea.

W: What _____ _____ _____
about my plan?

M: _____

think 생각하다 | plan 계획 | idea 생각

TIPS What do you think of[about] ~?은 '~에 대해 어떻게 생각하세요?'라는
의미로 상대방의 의견을 물을 때 사용합니다.

18

다음을 듣고, 이어질 말로 알맞은 것을 고르시
오. ·· (   )

W _____

① It's not my T-shirt.
② I like that blue T-shirt.
③ I bought it on the Internet.
④ It's 10 dollars.

M: _____ _____ _____ get
that T-shirt? It's so cool.

W: _____

where 어디 | get 얻다 | cool 멋진 | bought 사다(buy)의 과거형 |
on the Internet 인터넷에서, 온라인에서

TIPS 의문사 Where(어디에서)로 묻고 있으므로, 구체적인 장소로 대답합니다.

19

다음 대화를 듣고, 이어질 말로 알맞은 것을 고
르시오. ······································· (   )

M _____

① I don't like noodles.
② No, thanks. I'm full.
③ No, that's all.
④ I have something for you.

W: _____ would you like to have?

M: I'll have fried rice and a Coke.

W: _____ _____?

M: _____

fried rice 볶음밥 | anything else 그밖에 다른 것 | noodles 국수 | full 배부른 |
that's all 그뿐이다 | something 무언가

TIPS [would like to + 동사원형]은 '~하고 싶다'라는 의미입니다.
I would like to talk to her. 나는 그녀와 얘기하고 싶다.
I would like to stay here. 나는 이곳에 머물고 싶다.

20

다음 대화를 듣고, 이어질 말로 적절하지 <u>않은</u>
것을 고르시오. ····························· (   )

G _____

① Okay. What time shall we meet?
② Yes, I went shopping yesterday.
③ I'd like to, but I have to do my
   homework.
④ I'm sorry, but I can't.

B: Hi, Jessie?

G: Oh, Mike. _____ _____?

B: I'm going to the shopping mall this afternoon.
   Do you want to _____ _____
   _____?

B: _____

shopping mall 쇼핑몰 | this afternoon 오후에 | meet 만나다 | homework 숙제

TIPS What's up?은 How are you?보다 덜 격식을 갖춘 안부를 묻는 말입니다.
대답은 Good.(좋아.) / Nothing.[Not much.] (별일 없어.) 등으로 답합니다.

● 다음 들려주는 단어의 의미를 쓰세요.

단어	의미
01 onion	양파
02 thirsty	
03 practice	
04 stay up	
05 hold	
06 crayon	
07 guess	
08 essay	
09 contest	
10 catch	
11 twice	
12 cousin	
13 bring	
14 idea	
15 noodles	

● 앞에 모의고사에 나오는 문장들을 잘 듣고, 빈칸을 완성하세요.

01 I have to ___practice___ ___the___ ___piano___.

02 She's _____ a _____ _____ in her hand.

03 _____ a nice _____!

04 I have _____ _____ at school.

05 I _____ a fever and _____ _____.

06 I _____ _____ cereal and eggs.

07 I won _____ _____ in the essay contest.

08 I don't have _____ _____ a headache.

09 A boy _____ _____ fish.

10 I'm _____ the flowers in the _____.

11 I'm _____ _____ today.

12 I'll _____ _____ to your house.

13 I don't have _____ _____.

14 I bought it _____ _____ _____.

15 I'm going to the shopping mall _____ _____.

보통 속도 빠른 속도

| 학습일 | 월   일 | 부모님 확인 | 점수 |

1

다음 그림을 보고, 여자가 할 말로 알맞은 것을 고르시오. ·························· (   )

①   ②   ③   ④

2

다음 대화를 듣고, 두 사람이 만날 시각을 고르시오. ································· (   )

① 7시 10분   ② 7시 20분
③ 7시 30분   ④ 7시 40분

3

다음 대화를 듣고, 여자 아이의 물건을 고르시오. ································· (   )

① 휴대전화기   ② 자전거
③ 컴퓨터   ④ 사진기

4

다음 대화를 듣고, 여자 아이가 해변에 가지 못하는 이유를 고르시오. ·············· (   )

① 숙제를 해야 해서
② 청소를 해야 해서
③ 피아노 연습을 해야 해서
④ 어머니를 도와야 해서

5

다음을 듣고, 그림과 일치하는 설명을 고르시오. ······································ (   )

①   ②   ③   ④

6

다음 대화를 듣고, 남자가 가장 좋아하는 과일을 고르시오. ························ (   )

① 사과   ② 오렌지
③ 멜론   ④ 딸기

7

다음을 듣고, John이 하고 있는 것을 고르시오. ······························ (   )

①    ②

③    ④

8

다음 그림을 보고, 그림과 일치하는 대화를 고르시오. ························ (   )

①   ②   ③   ④

9

다음 대화를 듣고, 여자 아이가 사려는 가방의 색을 고르시오. ·················· (   )

① 보라색   ② 파란색
③ 빨간색   ④ 노란색

10

다음 대화를 듣고, 대화가 자연스럽지 <u>않은</u> 것을 고르시오. ·················· (   )

①   ②   ③   ④

11

다음 대화를 듣고, 무엇에 관해 이야기하고 있는지 고르시오. ………………… (　　)

① 좋아하는 영화
② 좋아하는 운동
③ 좋아하는 계절
④ 좋아하는 음식

14

다음 대화를 듣고, 어떤 상황에서 이루어지는 대화인지 고르시오. ………………… (　　)

① 제안을 거절하는 상황
② 헤어지는 상황
③ 오랜만에 만난 상황
④ 칭찬하는 상황

12

다음 대화를 듣고, 두 사람이 이용할 교통수단을 고르시오. ………………… (　　)

① 택시　　　　② 지하철
③ 버스　　　　④ 자전거

13

다음 대화를 듣고, 남자 아이가 주말에 집에 있었던 이유를 고르시오. ………… (　　)

① 숙제를 해야 해서
② 개를 산책시켜야 해서
③ 부모님을 도와드려야 해서
④ 개를 돌봐야 해서

15

다음 대화를 듣고, 대화의 내용과 다른 것을 고르시오. ………………… (　　)

① 수잔은 동물을 좋아한다.
② 수잔은 수의사가 되고 싶어 한다.
③ 수잔은 두 마리의 개를 기르고 있다.
④ 남자 아이는 고양이를 기르고 있다.

16

다음 대화를 듣고, 남자가 지불할 금액으로 알맞은 것을 고르시오. ·················· (   )

① $25   ② $28
③ $38   ④ $40

17

다음 대화를 듣고, 두 사람의 대화가 이루어지는 장소를 고르시오. ·············· (   )

① 도서관   ② 옷 가게
③ 서점   ④ 박물관

18

다음 대화를 듣고, 이어질 말로 알맞은 것을 고르시오. ·················· (   )

G _____

① Then, how about 4:30?
② It sounds good.
③ That's too bad.
④ I feel good today.

19

다음 대화를 듣고, 이어질 말로 알맞은 것을 고르시오. ·················· (   )

B _____

① I play tennis after school.
② No, thanks.
③ Yes, I like it.
④ No, I'm not.

20

다음 대화를 듣고, 이어질 말로 적절하지 <u>않은</u> 것을 고르시오. ·················· (   )

G _____

① It's tomorrow.
② It's not my dad's.
③ It's next Monday.
④ It's July 10.

보통 속도 빠른 속도

정답 및 해석 p. 23

Dictation 영어 듣기 모의고사

| 학습일 | 월 | 일 | 부모님 확인 | | 점수 |

● 잘 듣고, 빈칸에 알맞은 말을 쓰세요.

1

다음 그림을 보고, 여자가 할 말로 알맞은 것을 고르시오. ·················· (　　)

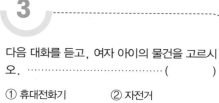

①　　②　　③　　④

W: ❶ Let's _____ _____ together.

❷ Wait here, please.

❸ It's time to _____ _____.

❹ Do you want some more?

have dinner 저녁식사를 하다 | together 함께 | here 여기 | wake up 일어나다

TIPS wake up은 '일어나다'는 의미로 그림과 가장 관련된 표현입니다.

2

다음 대화를 듣고, 두 사람이 만날 시각을 고르시오. ·················· (　　)

① 7시 10분　　② 7시 20분
③ 7시 30분　　④ 7시 40분

M: Alice, are you going to the swimming pool tonight?

W: Yes, I am. Why?

M: I want to take the _____ _____ with you. Is it okay?

W: Sure. The lesson starts at 7:30. Let's meet in front of the pool _____ _____.

M: Okay.

swimming pool 수영장 | tonight 오늘 저녁, 오늘 밤 | lesson 수업 | meet 만나다 | in front of ~ 앞에

TIPS 시각을 말할 때 '시간', '분' 순서로 말을 합니다. 그러나 past와 to를 이용할 때에는 '분', '시간' 순으로 말합니다.
It's 10:50. 10시 50분이다.　It's ten to eleven. 10분 전 11시이다.

3

다음 대화를 듣고, 여자 아이의 물건을 고르시오. ·················· (　　)

① 휴대전화기　　② 자전거
③ 컴퓨터　　④ 사진기

B: Amy, is this your camera?

G: No, it isn't. It's my mom's.

B: Oh, I see. _____ _____ is this?

G: It's _____.

B: Can I use it for a minute?

G: Of course.

camera 카메라 | whose 누구의 | cellphone 휴대폰 | use 사용하다 | for a minute 잠깐 | of course 물론

4

다음 대화를 듣고, 여자 아이가 해변에 가지 못하는 이유를 고르시오. ·············· (　　)

① 숙제를 해야 해서
② 청소를 해야 해서
③ 피아노 연습을 해야 해서
④ 어머니를 도와야 해서

G: How is the weather today?

B: It's _____. Let's go to the beach.

G: Sorry, I can't. I _____ _____
_____ my room.

B: Oh, I see.

weather 날씨 | sunny 맑은 | beach 해변 | clean 청소하다

TIPS [have to + 동사원형]은 '~해야 한다'라는 의미입니다.

5

다음을 듣고, 그림과 일치하는 설명을 고르시오. ·························· (　　)

① ② ③ ④

W: ❶ There are some _____ on the
_____ _____.

❷ There is a book on the _____.

❸ There are some pencils on the round table.

❹ There are some apples on the table.

round 둥근 | table 탁자 | floor 바닥, 마루

6

다음 대화를 듣고, 남자가 가장 좋아하는 과일을 고르시오. ·························· (　　)

① 사과　　② 오렌지
③ 멜론　　④ 딸기

W: Donovan, what do you eat for breakfast?

M: I usually have _____ _____.

W: What kind of fruit do you eat?

M: I eat _____.

W: Do you like apples?

M: Yes, but I like _____ the most.

breakfast 아침(식사) | usually 보통 | fruit 과일 | strawberry 딸기

TIPS most는 '가장 (많이)', '최고로'라는 의미로 much와 many의 최상급입니다.
*many/much – more(비교급) – most(최상급)

7

다음을 듣고, John이 하고 있는 것을 고르시오. ·························· (　　)

① ② ③ ④

G: Jessie, did you see John?

B: Yes, he is in the _____.

G: Is he reading a book there?

B: No, he isn't.

G: _____ is he doing there?

B: He's _____ some books.

see 보다 | library 도서관 | read 읽다 | borrow 빌리다

TIPS some은 셀 수 없는 명사나 복수명사와 함께 쓰여 '조금', '약간의', '몇몇의' 등의 의미를 가지고 있습니다.
some cheese 약간의 치즈　　some coins 몇 개의 동전

8

다음 그림을 보고, 그림과 일치하는 대화를 고르시오. ·········· (   )

① ② ③ ④

❶ M: What are you doing?

W: I'm playing a computer game.

❷ M: May I help you?

W: I'm _____ _____ a computer.

❸ M: Can I help you?

W: I think there is _____ _____ with my computer.

❹ M: Whose computer is this?

W: It's _____ _____.

play a computer game 컴퓨터 게임을 하다 | look for ~을 찾다 | wrong 잘못된

TIPS 컴퓨터 수리점에서 일어나는 대화로 가장 어울리는 것을 고르세요.

9

다음 대화를 듣고, 여자 아이가 사려는 가방의 색을 고르시오. ·········· (   )

① 보라색　　　② 파란색
③ 빨간색　　　④ 노란색

M: May I help you?

G: Yes, I'm looking for a bag.

M: How about this red one?

G: It's nice, but I already have a red bag. Can you show me a _____ _____?

M: Then, how about this _____ _____?

G: I like it. _____ _____ is it?

nice 멋진 | already 이미, 벌써 | show 보여주다 | different 다른 | color 색

10

다음 대화를 듣고, 대화가 자연스럽지 않은 것을 고르시오. ·········· (   )

① ② ③ ④

❶ G: What do you want to be in the future?

B: I'd like to be _____ _____.

❷ G: Hi, Paul. How was your trip to Korea?

B: It was good.

❸ G: How are you doing?

B: _____ _____.

❹ G: Would you like some pizza?

B: _____, _____. I like it very much.

in the future 장래에 | singer 가수 | trip 여행 | pretty 꽤

TIPS No, thanks.는 상대방의 제안을 거절할 때 사용하는 표현이므로 이어지는 말로 I like it very much.보다는 I don't like it.이 더 어울립니다.

11

다음 대화를 듣고, 무엇에 관해 이야기하고 있는지 고르시오. ·················· (   )

① 좋아하는 영화
② 좋아하는 운동
③ 좋아하는 계절
④ 좋아하는 음식

M: Mira, what do you think about this movie?

W: It's a lot of fun.

Do you like _____ _____?

M: Yes, I love comedy. What about you?

W: I like comedy, too.

But I love _____ _____ the most.

movie 영화 | fun 재미 | comedy movie 코미디 영화 | romance movie 로맨스 영화 | the most 가장

TIPS 이외에도 영화 종류에는 다음과 같은 것들이 있습니다.
horror movie 공포 영화   war movie 전쟁 영화
animated movie 만화 영화

12

다음 대화를 듣고, 두 사람이 이용할 교통수단을 고르시오. ·················· (   )

① 택시   ② 지하철
③ 버스   ④ 자전거

M: Hurry up. We are _____ _____ the concert.

W: All right. Should we take the subway?

M: No, the subway station is _____ _____ from here.

W: Well, how about _____ _____ _____?

M: Okay. Let's go!

hurry up 서두르다 | late 늦은 | concert 음악회 | subway 지하철 | station 역 | far 먼

TIPS 동사 take는 '교통수단 · 도로 등을 타다(이용하다)'라는 의미입니다.
take a bus 버스를 타다   take a train 기차를 타다

13

다음 대화를 듣고, 남자 아이가 주말에 집에 있었던 이유를 고르시오. ·················· (   )

① 숙제를 해야 해서
② 개를 산책시켜야 해서
③ 부모님을 도와드려야 해서
④ 개를 돌봐야 해서

G: Hi, Mike. What did you do last weekend?

B: I just stayed home. I couldn't _____ _____.

G: Really? Why?

B: My dog was sick. I had to _____ _____ _____ him.

G: I'm _____ to hear that.

weekend 주말 | stay 머무르다 | anything 아무것 | sick 아픈 | take care of ~을 돌보다

TIPS • had to는 have to의 과거형으로 '~해야 했다'라는 의미입니다.
• I'm sorry to hear that.은 상대방의 불행에 대해 슬픔이나 유감을 나타내는 표현으로 '그 소식을 듣게 되어서 정말 유감이다.'라는 뜻으로 That's too bad. (그것 참 안됐다, (그렇다니) 유감이다.)로 바꿔 쓸 수 있습니다.

14

다음 대화를 듣고, 어떤 상황에서 이루어지는 대화인지 고르시오. ·········· (   )

① 제안을 거절하는 상황
② 헤어지는 상황
③ 오랜만에 만난 상황
④ 칭찬하는 상황

[Cellphone rings.]

M: Hello.

W: Hi, Ted. Where are you?

M: I'm at home. _____ _____?

W: I'm going to play basketball with Jane and Tony today. Will you _____ _____?

M: I'd like to, but _____ _____.
I have to visit my uncle.

cellphone 휴대폰 | basketball 농구 | join 함께하다 | visit 방문하다 | uncle 삼촌

TIPS I'd like to, but I can't.는 제안을 거절할 때 사용하는 표현입니다.

15

다음 대화를 듣고, 대화의 내용과 <u>다른</u> 것을 고르시오. ············· (   )

① 수잔은 동물을 좋아한다.
② 수잔은 수의사가 되고 싶어 한다.
③ 수잔은 두 마리의 개를 기르고 있다.
④ 남자 아이는 고양이를 기르고 있다.

B: Susan, do you have a pet?

G: Oh, yes, I have two cats and _____ _____.

B: Wow. I think you really like animals.

G: Yes, I do. I want to be _____ _____ in the future. Do you have any pets?

B: Yes, I have _____ _____.

pet 반려동물 | think 생각하다 | really 정말 | veterinarian(= vet) 수의사

TIPS any는 복수명사 또는 셀 수 없는 명사 앞에 와서 '얼마간의', '조금의', '몇몇의' 등의 의미로 사용합니다. any는 부정문과 의문문에서 사용합니다.
I don't want any more vegetables. 난 채소 더 안 먹을래.

16

다음 대화를 듣고, 남자가 지불할 금액으로 알맞은 것을 고르시오. ·········· (   )

① $25   ② $28
③ $38   ④ $40

W: May I help you?

M: Yes, I'm looking for a pair of blue jeans.
How much are these?

W: They are $40.

M: Do you have any _____ _____?

W: Those ones are _____.

M: Oh, that's good, I'll _____ them.

help 돕다 | how much (가격) 얼마 | cheap 싼 | take 사다

TIPS ones는 one의 복수형으로 앞에서 언급한 blue jeans를 대신해서 사용한 대명사입니다.

17

다음 대화를 듣고, 두 사람의 대화가 이루어지는 장소를 고르시오. ·············· (   )

① 도서관　　　　② 옷 가게
③ 서점　　　　　④ 박물관

M: Good evening. May I help you?

G: Yes, I'm looking for a _____.

M: How about this one? It's very popular _____ _____.

G: Can I _____ _____ _____?

M: Sure, the fitting room is right over there.

evening 저녁 | skirt 치마 | popular 인기 있는 | among ~ 사이에 | teens 십대 | fitting room 탈의실

TIPS　try something on은 '(옷 따위를) 입어[신어] 보다'라는 의미입니다.

18

다음 대화를 듣고, 이어질 말로 알맞은 것을 고르시오. ·············· (   )

G _____

① Then, how about 4:30?
② It sounds good.
③ That's too bad.
④ I feel good today.

G: John, let's go to the park after school.

B: Okay. _____ _____ shall we meet? My class _____ at 3 today.

G: _____

park 공원 | meet 만나다 | finish 끝나다 | feel good 기분이 좋다

TIPS　What time shall we meet?에 어울리는 대답은 '시간'을 언급하는 것입니다.

19

다음 대화를 듣고, 이어질 말로 알맞은 것을 고르시오. ·············· (   )

B _____

① I play tennis after school.
② No, thanks.
③ Yes, I like it.
④ No, I'm not.

B: What's your _____ _____?

G: I like baseball. How about you?

B: I like tennis.

G: Are you _____ _____ tennis?

B: _____

favorite 좋아하는 | sport 운동 | tennis 테니스 | like 좋아하다

TIPS　be good at은 '~을 잘하다'라는 의미입니다.
　　　A: Are you good at taking photos? 사진을 잘 찍니?
　　　B: Yes, I am. / No, I'm not. 그래, 잘 찍어. / 아니, 그렇지 않아.

20

다음 대화를 듣고, 이어질 말로 적절하지 않은 것을 고르시오. ·············· (   )

G _____

① It's tomorrow.
② It's not my dad's.
③ It's next Monday.
④ It's July 10.

B: Hi, Jessie. _____ are you going?

G: I'm going to the shopping center. I'll _____ _____ _____ for my dad's birthday.

B: _____ is your dad's birthday?

G: _____

shopping center 쇼핑센터 | buy 사다 | gift 선물 | birthday 생일

TIPS　when(언제)으로 질문을 했으므로, 구체적인 시각이나 날짜 등으로 대답을 해야 합니다.

● 다음 들려주는 단어의 의미를 쓰세요.

단어	의미
01 together	함께
02 strawberry	
03 already	
04 different	
05 trip	
06 concert	
07 station	
08 subway	
09 far	
10 anything	
11 round	
12 pet	
13 cheap	
14 popular	
15 teens	

● 앞에 모의고사에 나오는 문장들을 잘 듣고, 빈칸을 완성하세요.

01 It's time to _____wake_____ _____up_____.

02 I want to _____ the swimming _____ with you.

03 Can I use it _____ _____ _____?

04 _____ _____ to the beach.

05 I usually have _____ _____.

06 He's _____ _____ _____.

07 I think there is _____ _____ with my computer.

08 I love _____ _____ the most.

09 The subway station is too _____ _____ _____.

10 I had to _____ _____ _____ him.

11 I'd _____ _____, but I can't.

12 I want to be a veterinarian _____ _____ _____.

13 It's very popular _____ _____.

14 The _____ _____ is right over there.

15 My class _____ _____ _____ today.

영어 듣기 모의고사

 보통 속도   빠른 속도

학습일   월   일   부모님 확인   점수

1

다음 대화를 듣고, 여자 아이가 슬픈 이유를 고르시오. ······················· (   )

① 지갑을 잃어버려서
② 시계를 잃어버려서
③ 시험을 못 봐서
④ 개를 잃어버려서

2

다음 그림을 보고, 남자가 할 말로 알맞은 것을 고르시오. ···························· (   )

①   ②   ③   ④

3

다음 대화를 듣고, 사과하는 상황의 대화로 알맞은 것을 고르시오. ················· (   )

①   ②   ③   ④

4

다음 대화를 듣고, 남자 아이의 사촌을 고르시오. ······························· (   )

①    ②

③    ④

5

다음 대화를 듣고, 남자 아이가 주말에 한 일을 고르시오. ···························· (   )

① 숙제   ② 동물원 방문
③ 병문안   ④ 독서

6

다음 대화를 듣고, 여자가 산 과일과 개수가 바르게 짝지어진 것을 고르시오. …… (   )

① 오렌지 – 6개   ② 오렌지 – 5개

③ 배 – 5개   ④ 배 – 6개

7

다음 대화를 듣고, 남자 아이가 좋아하는 과목을 고르시오. ………………………… (   )

① 과학   ② 수학

③ 체육   ④ 미술

8

다음 그림을 보고, 그림과 일치하는 대화를 고르시오. ……………………………… (   )

①   ②   ③   ④

9

다음 대화를 듣고, Jane이 있는 곳을 고르시오. ……………………………………… (   )

① 도서관   ② 학교 식당

③ 체육관   ④ 교실

10

다음 대화를 듣고, 현재 시각을 고르시오.
…………………………………………… (   )

① 5시 30분   ② 5시 45분

③ 5시 55분   ④ 6시

11

다음 대화를 듣고, 아이들이 하려고 하는 것을 고르시오. ·································· (   )

①

②

③

④

12

다음 대화를 듣고, 무엇에 관한 내용인지 고르시오. ······························· (   )

① 크리스마스 계획
② 생일 선물
③ 크리스마스 선물
④ 크리스마스 파티

13

다음 대화를 듣고, 내용과 일치하지 <u>않는</u> 것을 고르시오. ······························· (   )

① 수잔 어머니가 케이크를 만들었다.
② 케이크는 어제 만들었다.
③ 수잔 어머니는 제빵사다.
④ 남자 아이는 배가 부르다.

14

다음을 듣고, 대화가 자연스럽지 <u>않은</u> 것을 고르시오. ························· (   )

①   ②   ③   ④

15

다음 대화를 듣고, 어떤 상황에서 이루어지는 대화인지 고르시오. ················ (   )

① 음식을 주문하는 상황
② 예약을 변경하는 상황
③ 음식점 예약을 하는 상황
④ 안부 전화를 하는 상황

16

다음을 듣고, 그림과 일치하는 설명을 고르시오. ································· (   )

①   ②   ③   ④

17

다음 대화를 듣고, 남자 아이가 할 일로 알맞은 것을 고르시오. ·················· (　　　)

① 저녁식사 만들기
② 쓰레기 버리기
③ 청소하기
④ 설거지하기

19

다음 대화를 듣고, 이어질 말로 알맞은 것을 고르시오. ·················· (　　　)

M _____

① It's not my camera.
② I'm sorry to hear that.
③ Okay. Here they are.
④ What kind of flowers do you like?

18

다음 대화를 듣고, 이어질 말로 알맞은 것을 고르시오. ·················· (　　　)

W _____

① I'll have a chicken salad.
② I don't like sandwiches.
③ That's not my sandwich.
④ I'll go to the park after lunch.

20

다음 대화를 듣고, 이어질 말로 적절하지 <u>않은</u> 것을 고르시오. ·················· (　　　)

G _____

① No, I can't.
② Of course. Open it!
③ Sure.
④ Yes, I hope you like it.

Dictation 영어 듣기 모의고사

| 학습일 | 월 일 | 부모님 확인 | 점수 |

● 잘 듣고, 빈칸에 알맞은 말을 쓰세요.

1

다음 대화를 듣고, 여자 아이가 슬픈 이유를 고르시오. ·················· (   )

① 지갑을 잃어버려서
② 시계를 잃어버려서
③ 시험을 못 봐서
④ 개를 잃어버려서

B: Are you okay? You don't look happy.

G: I _____ _____ _____.

B: Really?

G: Yes, I put my watch on the desk, but I can't find it.

B: Don't be _____. Let's find it together.

lost 잃어버리다(lose)의 과거형 | really 정말 | put 놓다 | find 찾다 | together 함께

TIPS 부정명령문은 [Don't + 동사원형] 형태로 '~하지 마'라는 의미입니다.

2

다음 그림을 보고, 남자가 할 말로 알맞은 것을 고르시오. ·················· (   )

①   ②   ③   ④

M: ❶ How many _____ do you have?

❷ Wow, what a nice _____ you have!

❸ Who is the man in the room?

❹ Wow, you're very _____ _____
_____.

cap 야구모자 | room 방 | be good at ~을 잘하다 | painting 그림 그리기

3

다음 대화를 듣고, 사과하는 상황의 대화로 알맞은 것을 고르시오. ·················· (   )

①   ②   ③   ④

❶ W: James, what's wrong?

M: I have a cold.

❷ W: I'm _____ _____ not calling
you yesterday.

M: It's okay.

❸ W: I won first prize in the singing contest.

M: Wow! _____!

❹ W: Can I borrow your pencil?

M: Sure. _____ _____ _____.

wrong 잘못된 | have a cold 감기 걸리다 | call 전화하다 | yesterday 어제 |
first prize 1등 | contest 대회 | congratulations 축하해 | borrow 빌리다

TIPS I'm sorry for는 '~에 대해 유감이다', '~해서 미안하다'라는 의미입니다.
I'm sorry for the mistake. 실수한 거 미안해요.

4

다음 대화를 듣고, 남자 아이의 사촌을 고르시
오. ·· (   )

①
②
③
④

G: James, who is your cousin in this picture?

B: She's wearing a _____ _____.

G: Is she wearing glasses?

B: No, she's _____ _____

_____.

G: Oh, I see.

cousin 사촌 | picture 사진 | skirt 치마 | glasses 안경 | hold 들다 | flower 꽃

TIPS 동사 wear는 '입다, 쓰다'라는 의미와 장신구 등을 '착용하다'라는 의미가 있습니다.

5

다음 대화를 듣고, 남자 아이가 주말에 한 일을
고르시오. ································ (   )

① 숙제
② 동물원 방문
③ 병문안
④ 독서

B: Susan, how was your weekend?

G: It was great. I went to the zoo with my family.
What did you do _____ _____?

B: I went to the hospital.

G: Were you sick?

B: No, I _____ my grandmother. She is

_____ _____ _____.

weekend 주말 | zoo 동물원 | family 가족 | hospital 병원 | sick 아픈 | visit 방문하다

6

다음 대화를 듣고, 여자가 산 과일과 개수가 바
르게 짝지어진 것을 고르시오. ······ (   )

① 오렌지 – 6개
② 오렌지 – 5개
③ 배 – 5개
④ 배 – 6개

M: May I help you?

W: Yes, I want some oranges.

M: Sorry. We don't have any oranges now.
How about _____ _____?

W: Okay.

M: _____ _____ pears do you want?

W: _____.

orange 오렌지 | pear 배 | how many 얼마나 많이

TIPS 정확한 수를 알기 위해서는 [How many + 복수명사 ~?] 형태로 물어야 합니다.

7

다음 대화를 듣고, 남자 아이가 좋아하는 과목
을 고르시오. ···························· (   )

① 과학
② 수학
③ 체육
④ 미술

B: What's your _____ _____?

G: I like science. How about you?

B: I like P.E.

G: Why do you _____ _____?

B: I like playing sports.

favorite 좋아하는 | subject 과목 | science 과학 | P.E. 체육

TIPS P.E.는 physical education의 약자입니다.

8

다음 그림을 보고, 그림과 일치하는 대화를 고르시오. ·· (　　　)

① 　　② 　　③ 　　④

❶ M: How can I ＿＿＿＿＿＿ ＿＿＿＿＿＿?

W: I want ＿＿＿＿＿＿ ＿＿＿＿＿＿ for my mom.

❷ M: Do you have any hobbies?

W: I like drawing flowers.

❸ M: What ＿＿＿＿＿＿ of flowers do you like?

W: I like ＿＿＿＿＿＿.

❹ M: Are you ready to order?

W: Yes, I'd like the chicken salad.

flower 꽃 | hobby 취미 | draw 그리다 | kind 종류 | ready 준비된 | order 주문하다

TIPS 꽃 가게에서 꽃을 사려는 그림이므로 ①번이 가장 어울립니다.

9

다음 대화를 듣고, Jane이 있는 곳을 고르시오. ·· (　　　)

① 도서관　　　　② 학교 식당
③ 체육관　　　　④ 교실

B: Alice, did you see Jane?

G: Yes, she is ＿＿＿＿＿＿ ＿＿＿＿＿＿ ＿＿＿＿＿＿ now.

B: Really?

G: Yes, she is ＿＿＿＿＿＿ ＿＿＿＿＿＿ there.

B: Oh, I see. Thanks.

see 보다 | cafeteria 구내식당 | now 지금 | have lunch 점심을 먹다

TIPS cafeteria는 '구내식당'을 의미합니다.

10

다음 대화를 듣고, 현재 시각을 고르시오. ·· (　　　)

① 5시 30분　　② 5시 45분
③ 5시 55분　　④ 6시

B: Mary, what are you doing?

G: I'm eating some snacks.

B: What time does your ＿＿＿＿＿＿ ＿＿＿＿＿＿ start?

G: It starts at 6 o'clock.

B: Hurry up! It's ＿＿＿＿＿＿ to ＿＿＿＿＿＿.

G: Really? I'm going to be late!

snack 과자 | swimming lesson 수영 수업 | hurry up 서두르다 | late 늦은

TIPS 특정 시간을 '분'을 강조해서 말할 때는 after(후에), past(지난), to(~ 전)를 사용해서 '분'을 먼저 말하고 '시간'은 뒤에 말합니다.

ten to eleven 10분 전 11시　　　　twenty after three 3시 20분

11

다음 대화를 듣고, 아이들이 하려고 하는 것을 고르시오. ·············· (   )

① CINEMA
② (swimming)
③ (baseball)
④ (snowman)

B: It's hot today. How about swimming in the river?

G: I don't like swimming.

B: Then, how about _____ to _____ _____?

G: Sounds good! Let me check what movies are _____ _____.

hot 더운 | **river** 강 | **movie** 영화 | **check** 확인하다

TIPS go to the movies 대신 see a movie(영화 보다)라고 해도 됩니다.

12

다음 대화를 듣고, 무엇에 관한 내용인지 고르시오. ·············· (   )

① 크리스마스 계획
② 생일 선물
③ 크리스마스 선물
④ 크리스마스 파티

G: How was your Christmas?

B: It was great.

G: _____ _____ did you get?

B: I got a _____. What about you?

G: I got a _____ from my uncle.

B: Really? That's cool.

Christmas 크리스마스 | **gift** 선물 | **backpack** 배낭 | **smartphone** 스마트폰

TIPS 동사 get은 '~을 받다, 얻다'라는 의미입니다.
get a gift 선물을 받다   get a letter from ~에게서 편지를 받다

13

다음 대화를 듣고, 내용과 일치하지 <u>않는</u> 것을 고르시오. ·············· (   )

① 수잔 어머니가 케이크를 만들었다.
② 케이크는 어제 만들었다.
③ 수잔 어머니는 제빵사다.
④ 남자 아이는 배가 부르다.

B: Wow, Susan. This cake is really good.

G: Thanks, my mom _____ _____ for me yesterday.

B: Really? Is your mom a baker?

G: No, she's a _____.
Will you have some more cake?

B: No, thanks. I'm _____ _____.

yesterday 어제 | **baker** 제빵사 | **full** 배부른

TIPS some은 '조금', '약간의' 등의 의미를 가지고 있으며, 긍정적인 대답을 기대하는 경우에는 의문문에서도 some을 사용합니다.
Would you like some coffee? 커피 좀 드릴까요?

14

다음을 듣고, 대화가 자연스럽지 <u>않은</u> 것을 고르시오. ············· ( )

①   ②   ③   ④

❶ W: Tony, do you have _____ _____ this weekend?

M: No, I don't have any special plans.

❷ W: Bob, how was the party?

M: It was great.

❸ W: Chris, what _____ you _____ _____ do today?

M: I went to the park _____ _____.

❹ W: Hi, Mike. How are you doing?

M: I'm doing very well. Thanks.

plan 계획 | **special** 특별한 | **last night** 지난밤

TIPS [be going to + 동사원형]은 '~할 예정이다'라는 의미로 가까운 미래의 계획을 표현할 때 사용합니다. What are you going to do today?에 대한 대답은 [be 동사 현재형 + going to + 동사원형]을 이용해서 I'm going to stay home. (집에 있을 거야.) 등으로 답합니다.

15

다음 대화를 듣고, 어떤 상황에서 이루어지는 대화인지 고르시오. ············· ( )

① 음식을 주문하는 상황
② 예약을 변경하는 상황
③ 음식점 예약을 하는 상황
④ 안부 전화를 하는 상황

[Telephone rings.]

W: Hello, Star Pizza. May I help you?

B: I'd like to make _____ _____.

W: What would you like?

B: I want a medium–sized potato pizza.

W: _____ _____?

B: No, that's all.

order 주문하다 | **kind** 종류 | **medium–sized** 중간 크기의 | **potato** 감자

TIPS Anything else?는 Do you need anything else?의 줄임말입니다. 이때 대답으로 That's it.(그게 다예요.)을 사용해도 됩니다.

16

다음을 듣고, 그림과 일치하는 설명을 고르시오. ············· ( )

①   ②   ③   ④

W: ❶ A man is talking on the phone.

❷ A man is lying on the _____.

❸ A man _____ _____ on the sofa.

❹ A man is sitting on the _____.

talk 말하다 | **phone** 전화기 | **lie** 눕다 | **floor** 바닥 | **sit** 앉다

17

다음 대화를 듣고, 남자 아이가 할 일로 알맞은
것을 고르시오. ·················· (   )

① 저녁식사 만들기
② 쓰레기 버리기
③ 청소하기
④ 설거지하기

W: Sam, can you help me?

B: Sure. What can I do for you?

W: Can you _____ _____
_____ after dinner?

B: Sure, Mom. Anything else?

W: _____ _____. Thank you.

wash the dishes 설거지하다 | **after dinner** 저녁식사 후에 | **anything else** 뭐 다른 것

TIPS wash the dishes 대신 do the dishes(설거지하다)라고 해도 됩니다.

18

다음 대화를 듣고, 이어질 말로 알맞은 것을 고
르시오. ·················· (   )

W _____

① I'll have a chicken salad.
② I don't like sandwiches.
③ That's not my sandwich.
④ I'll go to the park after lunch.

W: What are you going to have for lunch?

M: _____ _____ a tuna sandwich.
_____ _____ you?

W: _____

lunch 점심(식사) | **tuna sandwich** 참치 샌드위치 | **salad** 샐러드 | **park** 공원

TIPS 여기서 How about you?는 What are you going to have for lunch?라는
의미입니다.

19

다음 대화를 듣고, 이어질 말로 알맞은 것을 고
르시오. ·················· (   )

M _____

① It's not my camera.
② I'm sorry to hear that.
③ Okay. Here they are.
④ What kind of flowers do you like?

W: What did you do yesterday?

M: I went to the park and _____ many
_____ of flowers.

W: Wow, that's cool. Can you _____
_____ the photos you took?

M: _____

take photos 사진을 찍다 | **flower** 꽃 | **cool** 멋진 | **show** 보여주다

TIPS 사진을 보여 달라고 했을 때 가장 어울리는 대답을 고르세요.

20

다음 대화를 듣고, 이어질 말로 적절하지 <u>않은</u>
것을 고르시오. ·················· (   )

G _____

① No, I can't.
② Of course. Open it!
③ Sure.
④ Yes, I hope you like it.

G: Happy birthday, Mike.

B: Thank you for coming to my birthday party.

G: _____ _____ your present.

B: Oh, thanks. _____ _____ open it now?

G: _____

birthday party 생일 파티 | **present** 선물 | **open** 열다

TIPS 상대방에게 허락을 구할 때 조동사 can이나 may를 이용합니다.
Can I come in? 들어가도 돼요?   May I sit here? 이곳에 앉아도 돼요?

● 다음 들려주는 단어의 의미를 쓰세요.

	단어	의미
01	really	정말
02	call	
03	tuna	
04	congratulations	
05	backpack	
06	weekend	
07	favorite	
08	cafeteria	
09	snack	
10	check	
11	order	
12	photo	
13	medium-sized	
14	floor	
15	lie	

8 Sentence Check

● 앞에 모의고사에 나오는 문장들을 잘 듣고, 빈칸을 완성하세요.

01 You don't _____ look _____ happy _____.

02 You're very _____ _____ _____.

03 _____ _____ _____ not calling you yesterday.

04 She's holding _____ _____.

05 She is _____ _____ _____.

06 I want _____ _____ for my mom.

07 Let me check _____ _____ are on today.

08 I _____ a smartphone _____ my uncle.

09 I don't have any _____ _____.

10 I'm _____ very _____.

11 A man _____ _____ on the phone.

12 A man is sleeping _____ _____ _____.

13 What are you going to _____ _____ _____?

14 I _____ many _____ of flowers.

15 _____ _____ _____ coming to my birthday party.

모의고사8회 **101**

보통 속도

빠른 속도

| 학습일 | 월 일 | 부모님 확인 | 점수 |

1

다음 그림을 보고, 여자 아이가 할 말로 알맞은 것을 고르시오. ······························ ( )

① ② ③ ④

2

다음을 듣고, 상대방에게 음식을 권할 때 쓰는 표현을 고르시오. ····················· ( )

① ② ③ ④

3

다음 그림을 보고, 그림에 알맞은 대화를 고르시오. ································· ( )

① ② ③ ④

4

다음 대화를 듣고, 남자 아이의 상태로 알맞은 것을 고르시오. ······················· ( )

①  ②

③  ④

5

다음 대화를 듣고, 두 사람이 먹을 음식을 고르시오. ················· (   )

①

②

③

④

6

다음 대화를 듣고, 대화의 내용과 <u>다른</u> 것을 고르시오. ····················· (   )

① 여자 아이의 여동생 이름은 Amy이다.
② Amy는 11살이다.
③ 여자 아이와 Amy는 같은 학교에 다닌다.
④ Amy는 걸어서 학교에 간다.

7

다음 대화를 듣고, 남자 아이가 어제 한 일을 고르시오. ···················· (   )

① 낚시   ② 축구
③ 농구   ④ 시험공부

8

다음 대화를 듣고, 남자 아이의 삼촌을 고르시오. ····················· (   )

①

②

③

④

9

다음 대화를 듣고, 무엇에 관해 이야기하고 있는지 고르시오. ················· (   )

① 학교 가는 방법
② 좋아하는 과목
③ 방과 후 활동
④ 좋아하는 운동

10

다음을 듣고, 설명하는 운동을 고르시오.
··· (   )

①  ②

③  ④

12

다음 대화를 듣고, David가 엄마를 도울 수 <u>없는</u> 이유를 고르시오. ············· (   )

① 책을 읽어야 해서

② 청소를 해야 해서

③ 온라인 수업을 들어야 해서

④ 숙제를 해야 해서

13

다음 대화를 듣고, 두 사람의 대화가 이루어지는 장소를 고르시오. ················· (   )

① 들판   ② 산
③ 공원   ④ 비행기

11

다음 대화를 듣고, 남자가 가리키는 표지판으로 알맞은 것을 고르시오. ········ (   )

①  ②

③  ④

14

다음 대화를 듣고, 대화가 자연스럽지 <u>않은</u> 것을 고르시오. ·························· (   )

①   ②   ③   ④

15

다음 대화를 듣고, 남자 아이 동생의 나이와 학년이 바르게 짝지어진 것을 고르시오.
·· (   )

① 8살 – 2학년   ② 9살 – 2학년
③ 9살 – 3학년   ④ 10살 – 4학년

16

다음 대화를 듣고, 여자 아이가 오늘 밤 할 일을 고르시오. ·························· (   )

① 동생 돌보기
② 동생 숙제 도와주기
③ 영화 보기
④ 친구와 산책하기

17

다음 대화를 듣고, 어떤 상황에서 이루어지는 대화인지 고르시오. ·················· (   )

① 선물을 고르는 상황
② 물건을 빌리는 상황
③ 물건을 교환하는 상황
④ 친구에게 선물을 전달하는 상황

18

다음 대화를 듣고, 이어질 말로 알맞은 것을 고르시오. ······················· (   )

B _____

① I don't like baseball.
② It was windy last night.
③ It was exciting.
④ We will do it again.

19

다음 대화를 듣고, 이어질 말로 알맞은 것을 고르시오. ······························· (   )

M _____

① Yes, that's all. Thank you.
② Are you all right?
③ I'm tired today.
④ Yes, I love it.

20

다음을 듣고, 이어질 말로 적절하지 않은 것을 고르시오. ··························· (   )

W _____

① You can get there by subway.
② Go straight one block and turn right.
③ Sorry, I'm new here, too.
④ It opens on Sundays.

Dictation 영어 듣기 모의고사

| 학습일 | 월 | 일 | 부모님 확인 | | 점수 |

● 잘 듣고, 빈칸에 알맞은 말을 쓰세요.

1

다음 그림을 보고, 여자 아이가 할 말로 알맞은 것을 고르시오. ·············· (　　)

① ② ③ ④

G: ❶ How much is it?

　❷ It's _____ today.

　❸ Let's take a walk.

　❹ _____ your _____!

sunny 맑은 | take a walk 산책하다 | watch 지켜보다

TIPS Watch your step! 대신 Watch out!(조심해!)라고 말할 수 있습니다.

2

다음을 듣고, 상대방에게 음식을 권할 때 쓰는 표현을 고르시오. ·············· (　　)

① ② ③ ④

M: ❶ Can I help you?

　❷ _____ _____ _____

　some cookies?

　❸ Can I have some cake?

　❹ _____ _____ is this cheese?

cookie 쿠키 | cake 케이크 | how much 얼마 | cheese 치즈

TIPS [Would you like some + 음식?]은 '~ 좀 드시겠습니까?'라는 의미입니다. would는 '정중한 제의나 초대'를 할 때 사용합니다.

3

다음 그림을 보고, 그림에 알맞은 대화를 고르시오. ·············· (　　)

① ② ③ ④

❶ B: May I help you?

　G: Yes, I want some cookies.

❷ B: Where are you from?

　G: I'm _____ _____.

❸ B: What are you doing here?

　G: I'm doing _____ _____.

❹ B: What is your favorite subject?

　G: I like music.

where 어디 | from ~로 부터 | here 여기 | favorite 좋아하는 | subject 과목

4

다음 대화를 듣고, 남자 아이의 상태로 알맞은 것을 고르시오. ················ (   )

① ② ③ ④

G: What's wrong, Mike?

B: I have a _____.

G: Did you go to the dentist?

B: Yes, I did.

G: I think you should _____ _____ candy.

wrong 잘못된 | **toothache** 치통 | **dentist** 치과의사 | **candy** 사탕

TIPS [stop + 동명사]는 '~하는 것을 멈추다'라는 의미입니다.
stop smoking 금연하다
stop playing computer games 컴퓨터 게임하는 것을 그만두다

5

다음 대화를 듣고, 두 사람이 먹을 음식을 고르시오. ················ (   )

① ② ③ ④

M: Susan, what do you want to have for lunch?

W: I want to eat pizza.

M: Again? We had pizza yesterday. How about chicken _____ _____?

W: That sounds good. It's _____ _____.

again 또, 다시 | **yesterday** 어제 | **fried rice** 볶음밥 | **favorite** 좋아하는 것

TIPS · had는 have의 과거형으로 '먹었다'라는 의미입니다.
· That sounds good.은 상대방의 제안에 동의할 때 사용합니다.
Sounds good.이라고 줄여서 말해도 됩니다.

6

다음 대화를 듣고, 대화의 내용과 <u>다른</u> 것을 고르시오. ················ (   )

① 여자 아이의 여동생 이름은 Amy이다.
② Amy는 11살이다.
③ 여자 아이와 Amy는 같은 학교에 다닌다.
④ Amy는 걸어서 학교에 간다.

B: Who is that girl over there?

G: She's my _____ _____, Amy.

B: She's very lovely. How old is she?

G: She's _____ _____ _____.

B: Does she go to the _____ _____ as you?

G: Yes, we _____ to school together.

over there 저쪽에 | **younger sister** 여동생 | **lovely** 사랑스러운 | **same** 같은 | **together** 함께

TIPS younger sister는 '여동생'으로 10살입니다.

7

다음 대화를 듣고, 남자 아이가 어제 한 일을 고르시오. ············ (   )

① 낚시   ② 축구
③ 농구   ④ 시험공부

G: James, did you see the _____ _____ on TV yesterday?

B: No, I didn't.

G: Then, what did you do yesterday?

B: I _____ _____ with my dad.

G: Really? Did you catch lots of fish?

B: Yes, we did.

soccer game 축구 경기 | go fishing 낚시 가다 | catch 잡다 | lots of 많은 | fish 물고기

TIPS went는 go(가다)의 과거형으로 went fishing은 '낚시를 갔다'는 의미입니다.

8

다음 대화를 듣고, 남자 아이의 삼촌을 고르시오. ············ (   )

① ② ③ ④

B: Look! There is my uncle on the stage.

G: Really? What musical instrument is he playing?

B: He's _____ _____ _____.

G: Is he wearing a baseball cap?

B: No, he's wearing _____.

uncle 삼촌 | stage 무대 | musical instrument 악기 | play 연주하다 | guitar 기타 | baseball cap 야구모자 | sunglasses 선글라스

TIPS 동사 play, practice와 악기 이름이 오면 악기 이름 앞에 정관사를 써야 합니다.
play the piano 피아노를 연주하다   practice the violin 바이올린 연습을 하다

9

다음 대화를 듣고, 무엇에 관해 이야기하고 있는지 고르시오. ············ (   )

① 학교 가는 방법
② 좋아하는 과목
③ 방과 후 활동
④ 좋아하는 운동

B: Mary, _____ do you go to school?

G: I usually _____ my _____ to school.

B: How long does it take from your house to your school?

G: It takes about ten minutes. What about you?

B: My school is near my house, so I _____ _____ _____.

go to school 학교에 가다 | usually 보통 | minute 분 | near 가까운 | walk 걷다

TIPS [How long ~ ?]은 시간이나 사물의 길이를 물어볼 때 사용합니다. 여기서 사용하는 동사 take는 '시간이 걸리다'라는 의미입니다.

10

다음을 듣고, 설명하는 운동을 고르시오.
················( )

① ② ③ ④

M: This is a very popular sport. Players cannot use their hands. Players have to _____ _____ _____ and heads. Players _____ a round _____.

popular 인기 있는 | use 사용하다 | hand 손 | head 머리 | kick 차다 | ball 공
TIPS feet은 foot(발)의 복수형입니다.

11

다음 대화를 듣고, 남자가 가리키는 표지판으로 알맞은 것을 고르시오. ········( )

① ② ③ ④

M: Susan, are you _____ _____?
W: Yes. Do you want to see the photos?
M: Look at _____ _____. You can't take photos here.
W: Oh! I see. I didn't know that.

take photos 사진을 찍다 | sign 표지판 | here 여기 | know 알다

12

다음 대화를 듣고, David가 엄마를 도울 수 없는 이유를 고르시오. ········( )

① 책을 읽어야 해서
② 청소를 해야 해서
③ 온라인 수업을 들어야 해서
④ 숙제를 해야 해서

W: David, what are you doing?
B: I'm reading a book.
W: Can you _____ _____? I'm cleaning the living room.
B: Sorry, Mom. I'm going to _____ _____ _____ soon.

clean 청소하다 | living room 거실 | online 온라인의 | class 수업 | soon 곧
TIPS have online classes은 '온라인 수업을 듣다'라는 의미입니다.

13

다음 대화를 듣고, 두 사람의 대화가 이루어지는 장소를 고르시오. ········( )

① 들판   ② 산
③ 공원   ④ 비행기

M: Jane, _____ _____ at the sky.
W: Wow, there are so many stars.
M: Yeah. Let's _____ _____ the tent over there.
W: Okay. Can we make a _____ here?
M: No, we can't make a campfire _____ _____ _____.
W: Oh, I see.

look up 올려 보다 | set up 세우다 | tent 텐트 | campfire 모닥불 | mountain 산

14

다음 대화를 듣고, 대화가 자연스럽지 않은 것을 고르시오. ·········· (   )

①   ②   ③   ④

❶ M: Where did you buy the bag?

   W: I bought it at the mall.

❷ M: How was your _____?

   W: It will _____ _____ tomorrow.

❸ M: What happened to your leg?

   W: I broke it last week.

❹ M: Do you like movies?

   W: Yes, I _____ _____ movies.

mall 쇼핑몰 | vacation 휴가 | happen 일어나다 | leg 다리 | broke 부러지다(break)의
과거형 | last week 지난주 | movie 영화

TIPS It will be sunny tomorrow.가 올바른 대답이 되기 위해서는 What's the
weather like tomorrow?(내일 날씨는 어때?)로 질문해야 합니다.

15

다음 대화를 듣고, 남자 아이 동생의 나이와 학년이 바르게 짝지어진 것을 고르시오.
·········· (   )

① 8살 – 2학년   ② 9살 – 2학년
③ 9살 – 3학년   ④ 10살 – 4학년

G: Mike, do you have any brothers?

B: Yes, I have a younger brother.

G: How old is he?

B: He's _____ _____ _____.

G: Is he in the second grade?

B: No, he's in the _____ _____.

brother 형제 | younger brother 남동생 | second 두 번째 | grade 학년 |
third 세 번째

TIPS 학년을 표현 할 때에는 서수를 이용합니다.

16

다음 대화를 듣고, 여자 아이가 오늘 밤 할 일을 고르시오. ·········· (   )

① 동생 돌보기
② 동생 숙제 도와주기
③ 영화 보기
④ 친구와 산책하기

[Cellphone rings.]

G: Hello.

B: Hello, Alice. Where are you?

G: I'm at home. Why?

B: I have movie tickets. Do you want to _____ _____ _____ _____ with me tonight?

G: I'm sorry, but I can't. I have to take care of my _____ _____.

cellphone 휴대폰 | ring 울리다 | movie ticket 영화표 | tonight 오늘 저녁, 오늘 밤 |
take care of ~을 돌보다

17

다음 대화를 듣고, 어떤 상황에서 이루어지는 대화인지 고르시오. ·············· (　　)

① 선물을 고르는 상황
② 물건을 빌리는 상황
③ 물건을 교환하는 상황
④ 친구에게 선물을 전달하는 상황

G: Sam, what's wrong?

B: I lost my pencil case.

G: Really?

B: Yes, I left it on my desk, but it's gone.

_____ _____ _____

your pencil?

G: Sure. _____ _____ _____.

pencil case 필통 | **left** 두다(leave)의 과거형 | **be gone** 사라지다 | **borrow** 빌리다 | **here you are** 여기 있다

TIPS Can I borrow your pencil? 대신 Can you lend me your pencil? 이라고 표현해도 됩니다. borrow는 '빌리다', lend는 '빌려주다'라는 의미입니다.

18

다음 대화를 듣고, 이어질 말로 알맞은 것을 고르시오. ·············· (　　)

B _____

① I don't like baseball.
② It was windy last night.
③ It was exciting.
④ We will do it again.

G: What did you do last night?

B: I watched a _____ _____ at the gym.

G: _____ _____ the game?

B: _____

last night 지난밤 | **basketball** 농구 | **gym** 체육관

TIPS How was the game? 대한 대답으로 It was exciting. / It was boring. (지루했어.) / It was fun.(재미있었어.) 등으로 대답할 수 있습니다.

19

다음 대화를 듣고, 이어질 말로 알맞은 것을 고르시오. ·············· (　　)

M _____

① Yes, that's all. Thank you.
② Are you all right?
③ I'm tired today.
④ Yes, I love it.

W: May I help you?

M: Can I get three potatoes?

W: Sure. Here you are. _____ _____?

M: I need four carrots, too.

W: Okay. _____ _____ _____?

M: _____

potato 감자 | **anything else** 또 다른 것 | **carrot** 당근 | **too** 역시 | **all right** 괜찮은

20

다음을 듣고, 이어질 말로 적절하지 <u>않은</u> 것을 고르시오. ·············· (　　)

W _____

① You can get there by subway.
② Go straight one block and turn right.
③ Sorry, I'm new here, too.
④ It opens on Sundays.

M: Excuse me. How can I _____ _____ _____ _____ from here?

W: _____

get to ~에 도착하다 | **by subway** 지하철로 | **go straight** 곧장 가다

TIPS It opens on Sundays.가 정답이 되려면 When does the museum open?(박물관은 언제 여니?) 등으로 물어야 합니다.

● 다음 들려주는 단어의 의미를 쓰세요.

단어	의미
01 subject	과목
02 toothache	
03 again	
04 lovely	
05 same	
06 stage	
07 sunglasses	
08 carrot	
09 near	
10 kick	
11 soon	
12 campfire	
13 happen	
14 second	
15 grade	

● 앞에 모의고사에 나오는 문장들을 잘 듣고, 빈칸을 완성하세요.

01 ___Watch___ your ___step___!

02 I think you should _____ _____ candy.

03 I _____ _____ _____.

04 It's _____ _____.

05 We _____ _____ _____ together.

06 I _____ _____ with my dad.

07 He's _____ _____.

08 I usually _____ my _____ to school.

09 It _____ about _____ _____.

10 Players _____ _____ their hands.

11 You can't _____ _____ here.

12 I'm going to _____ _____ _____ soon.

13 We can't _____ _____ _____ in the mountains.

14 He's _____ _____ _____.

15 I have to _____ _____ _____ my younger brother.

영어 듣기 모의고사

보통 속도   빠른 속도

| 학습일 | 월 일 | 부모님 확인 | 점수 |

1

다음 그림을 보고, 여자 아이가 할 말로 알맞은 것을 고르시오. ·············· (   )

①   ②   ③   ④

2

다음을 듣고, 감탄하는 표현을 고르시오.
································· (   )

①   ②   ③   ④

3

다음 그림을 보고, 그림과 일치하는 대화를 고르시오. ···················· (   )

①   ②   ③   ④

4

다음 대화를 듣고, 남자 아이가 주말에 한 일을 고르시오. ···················· (   )

①    ②

③    ④

5

다음 대화를 듣고, 남자가 가을을 좋아하는 이유를 고르시오. ···················· (   )

① 날씨가 좋아서

② 단풍을 볼 수 있어서

③ 휴가를 갈 수 있어서

④ 낙엽을 볼 수 있어서

정답 및 해석 p. 34

6

다음 대화를 듣고, 여자가 찾고 있는 물건을 고르시오. ······················· (   )

①

②

③

④

8

다음 대화를 듣고, 두 사람이 할 수 있는 운동을 고르시오. ······················· (   )

①

②

③

④

7

다음 대화를 듣고, 남자 아이가 원하는 선물을 고르시오. ······················· (   )

①

②

③

④

9

다음 대화를 듣고, 여자가 가고자 하는 곳을 고르시오. ······················· (   )

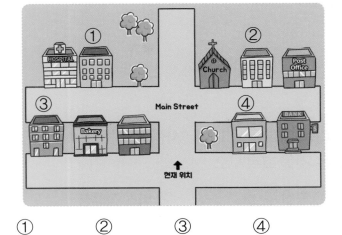

①   ②   ③   ④
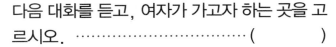

10

다음을 듣고, 설명하는 동물을 고르시오.
·· (   )

①    ②

③    ④

11

다음 대화를 듣고, 남자가 어젯밤에 한 일을 고르시오. ··························· (   )

① 개 돌보기   ② 컴퓨터 게임
③ 숙제하기   ④ 개 산책 시키기

12

다음 대화를 듣고, 두 사람이 있는 장소로 알맞은 것을 고르시오. ····················· (   )

① 공원   ② 버스 정류장
③ 공항   ④ 버스 안

13

다음 대화를 듣고, 대화가 자연스럽지 않은 것을 고르시오. ························· (   )

①   ②   ③   ④

14

다음 대화를 듣고, 대화의 내용과 일치하지 않는 것을 고르시오. ···················· (   )

① 어제는 Mike 여동생 생일이었다.
② Mike는 여동생을 위해 점심식사를 만들었다.
③ Mike는 요리 수업을 받았다.
④ Mike는 파스타를 만들었다.

15

다음 대화를 듣고, 여자 아이가 외출할 수 없는 이유를 고르시오. ···················· (   )

① 동생을 돌봐야 해서
② 숙제를 해야 해서
③ 청소를 해야 해서
④ 다른 약속이 있어서

16

다음 대화를 듣고, 무엇에 관해 이야기하고 있는지 고르시오. ···························· (   )

① 주말 계획   ② 휴가 계획
③ 좋아하는 장소   ④ 좋아하는 음식

17

다음 대화를 듣고, 오늘이 무슨 요일인지 고르시오. ···························· (   )

① 월요일   ② 화요일
③ 수요일   ④ 금요일

18

다음 대화를 듣고, 이어질 말로 알맞은 것을 고르시오. ···························· (   )

B _____

① I like dancing.
② It's at the corner.
③ It is very fun.
④ It's this Saturday.

19

다음 대화를 듣고, 이어질 말로 알맞은 것을 고르시오. ···························· (   )

M _____

① Okay. No problem.
② No, it's not my book.
③ I'm sorry to hear that.
④ What a nice book!

20

다음 대화를 듣고, 이어질 말로 적절하지 <u>않은</u> 것을 고르시오. ···························· (   )

G _____

① I bought it last week.
② My dad bought it for me.
③ I borrowed it from my friend.
④ It's on the table.

보통 속도 빠른 속도

학습일   월   일   부모님 확인   점수

● 잘 듣고, 빈칸에 알맞은 말을 쓰세요.

1

다음 그림을 보고, 여자 아이가 할 말로 알맞은 것을 고르시오. ·················· (   )

① ② ③ ④

G: ❶ Nice to meet you.

❷ Wash your hands.

❸ Please _____ _____ the light.

❹ Let's _____ _____ the trash.

meet 만나다 | turn on (불 등을) 켜다 | pick up 줍다 | trash 쓰레기

TIPS 아이들이 쓰레기를 줍고 있는 그림에 어울리는 문장을 고르세요.
garbage는 음식물 찌꺼기나 다른 물기 있는 쓰레기를 주로 가리키고, 반면에 trash는 종이나 판지 등과 같은 물기 없는 쓰레기를 말합니다.

2

다음을 듣고, 감탄하는 표현을 고르시오.
·················· (   )
① ② ③ ④

M: ❶ How is the weather?

❷ _____ _____ she is!

❸ How old are you?

❹ _____ _____ is this?

weather 날씨 | beautiful 아름다운 | old 나이 든

TIPS 감탄문은 '얼마나 ~한가!'라는 감탄의 감정을 나타내는 문장으로 [What + [a/an] + 형용사 + 명사!] 또는 [How + 형용사/부사!]로 표현할 수 있습니다.

3

다음 그림을 보고, 그림과 일치하는 대화를 고르시오. ·················· (   )

① ② ③ ④

❶ M: Who is that man?

W: He's my dad.

❷ M: Nice to meet you.

W: Nice to _____ _____, too.

❸ M: May I help you?

W: Yes, I'm looking for a cake.

❹ M: _____ _____ _____ you something?

W: Sure. What is it?

look for ~을 찾다 | ask 묻다 | something 무언가 | sure 물론, 그럼

TIPS 만나서 인사하는 그림이므로 그에 가장 어울리는 대화를 골라보세요.

4

다음 대화를 듣고, 남자 아이가 주말에 한 일을 고르시오. ·················· (　　)

①
②
③
④

B: What did you do last weekend, Cindy?

G: I _____ _____ with my family.

B: Oh, that's cool. Was it fun?

G: Yes, it was. What did you do?

B: I _____ my dad's _____.

last weekend 지난 주말 | go camping 캠핑 가다 | cool 멋진 | wash one's car 세차하다

TIPS cool은 '시원한'이란 의미 이외에 '멋진, 끝내 주는'이라는 의미가 있습니다.

5

다음 대화를 듣고, 남자가 가을을 좋아하는 이유를 고르시오. ·················· (　　)

① 날씨가 좋아서
② 단풍을 볼 수 있어서
③ 휴가를 갈 수 있어서
④ 낙엽을 볼 수 있어서

M: Susan, what's your favorite season?

W: I like summer because I can swim in the sea.
_____ _____ you?

M: I like fall.

W: Why do you like it?

M: I love the _____ _____ in fall.

season 계절 | because 왜냐하면 | sea 바다 | fall 가을 | colorful leaf 단풍

6

다음 대화를 듣고, 여자가 찾고 있는 물건을 고르시오. ·················· (　　)

①
②
③
④

M: Susie, what are you doing?

W: I'm looking for the _____ _____.
Did you see it?

M: No, I didn't. Did you look under the sofa?

W: No, I'll _____ _____ now.

remote control 리모컨 | under ~ 아래에 | check 확인하다 | now 지금

TIPS Did로 질문하면 did나 didn't를 이용하여 답합니다.
on the sofa 소파 위에　　behind the sofa 소파 뒤에

7

다음 대화를 듣고, 남자 아이가 원하는 선물을 고르시오. ·················· (　　)

①
②
③
④

G: Sam, your birthday is _____ _____.

B: Yeah. Can you come to my birthday party?

G: Of course. _____ do you want
_____ your parents?
Do you want a smartphone?

B: No, I don't. I want _____ _____.

soon 곧 | birthday party 생일 파티 | parents 부모 | smartphone 스마트폰 |
puppy 강아지

8

다음 대화를 듣고, 두 사람이 할 수 있는 운동을 고르시오. .... (　　)

①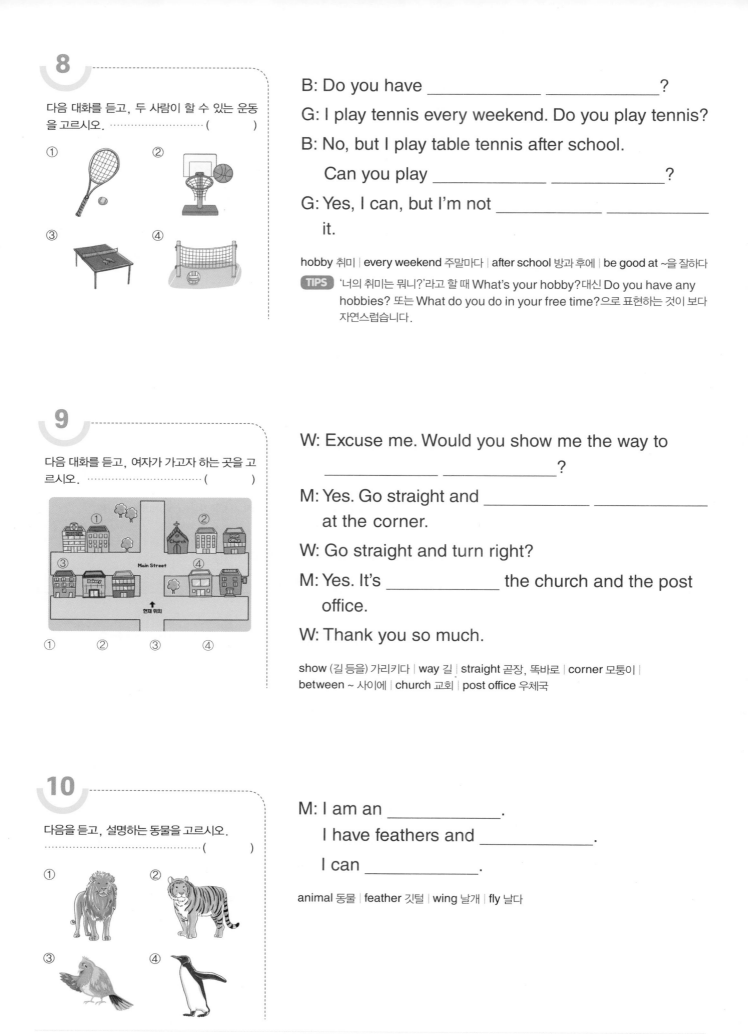
②
③
④

B: Do you have _____ _____?

G: I play tennis every weekend. Do you play tennis?

B: No, but I play table tennis after school.

　　Can you play _____ _____?

G: Yes, I can, but I'm not _____ _____ it.

hobby 취미 | every weekend 주말마다 | after school 방과 후에 | be good at ~을 잘하다

TIPS '너의 취미는 뭐니?'라고 할 때 What's your hobby?대신 Do you have any hobbies? 또는 What do you do in your free time?으로 표현하는 것이 보다 자연스럽습니다.

9

다음 대화를 듣고, 여자가 가고자 하는 곳을 고르시오. .... (　　)

Main Street
① ② ③ ④
현재 위치

W: Excuse me. Would you show me the way to _____ _____?

M: Yes. Go straight and _____ _____ at the corner.

W: Go straight and turn right?

M: Yes. It's _____ the church and the post office.

W: Thank you so much.

show (길 등을) 가리키다 | way 길 | straight 곧장, 똑바로 | corner 모퉁이 | between ~ 사이에 | church 교회 | post office 우체국

10

다음을 듣고, 설명하는 동물을 고르시오.
.... (　　)

① ② ③ ④

M: I am an _____.
　　I have feathers and _____.
　　I can _____.

animal 동물 | feather 깃털 | wing 날개 | fly 날다

11

다음 대화를 듣고, 남자가 어젯밤에 한 일을 고르시오. ·············· ( )

① 개 돌보기　　② 컴퓨터 게임
③ 숙제하기　　④ 개 산책 시키기

W: John, you _____ _____.
　　What's wrong?
M: I didn't sleep well _____ _____.
W: Did you play computer games again?
M: No, my dog was _____, so I _____
　　_____ of him until late at night.
W: I'm sorry to hear that.

tired 피곤한 | **last night** 지난밤 | **again** 또 | **sick** 아픈 | **take care of** ~을 돌보다 | **until late** 늦게까지 | **at night** 밤에

TIPS I'm sorry to hear that.은 상대방의 불행에 대해 슬픔이나 유감을 나타내는 표현으로 '그 소식을 듣게 되어서 정말 유감이다.'라는 뜻입니다.

12

다음 대화를 듣고, 두 사람이 있는 장소로 알맞은 것을 고르시오. ·············· ( )

① 공원　　② 버스 정류장
③ 공항　　④ 버스 안

G: Jason, long time no see.
B: Hi, Cindy, How are you?
G: I'm good. Where are you going?
B: I'm going to _____ _____.
　　How about you?
G: I'm going to the _____. Oh, I have to get
　　off _____ _____. See you.

bookstore 서점 | **museum** 박물관 | **get off** 내리다 | **stop** 정거장

TIPS ・get off(내리다), this stop(이번 정류장) 등의 표현에서 두 사람이 버스 안에서 대화하고 있다는 것을 알 수 있습니다.
・See you.는 헤어질 때 하는 인사말로 See you around.(잘 가.) / Take care.(몸 건강히 지내.) / See you next time.(다음에 봐.) 등이 있습니다.

13

다음 대화를 듣고, 대화가 자연스럽지 <u>않은</u> 것을 고르시오. ·············· ( )

①　　②　　③　　④

❶ W: Where are you from?
　　M: I'm from India.
❷ W: What do you want to have _____
　　_____?
　　M: I had sandwiches _____ _____.
❸ W: Peter, I have something to ask you.
　　M: What is that?
❹ W: When is your birthday?
　　M: It's _____ 10.

India 인도 | **something** 무언가 | **ask** 묻다 | **November** 11월

TIPS What do you want to have for dinner?에 대한 대답으로는 [I want to have + 음식.]의 형태가 어울립니다.

14

다음 대화를 듣고, 대화의 내용과 일치하지 않는 것을 고르시오. ·············· (   )

① 어제는 Mike 여동생 생일이었다.
② Mike는 여동생을 위해 점심식사를 만들었다.
③ Mike는 요리 수업을 받았다.
④ Mike는 파스타를 만들었다.

W: Mike, what did you do yesterday?

M: I _____ _____ for my sister. Yesterday was her birthday.

W: Really? Can you cook?

M: Yes, I took a _____ _____ last year.

W: What kind of food did you make?

M: I made some tomato _____.

W: Wow, that's cool.

make dinner 저녁을 만들다 | cook 요리하다 | class 수업 | last year 작년 | cool 멋진
TIPS 마이크는 저녁식사를 만들었습니다.

15

다음 대화를 듣고, 여자 아이가 외출할 수 없는 이유를 고르시오. ·············· (   )

① 동생을 돌봐야 해서
② 숙제를 해야 해서
③ 청소를 해야 해서
④ 다른 약속이 있어서

[Cellphone rings.]

G: Hello.

B: Hello, Alice. Where are you?

G: I'm _____ _____.

B: How about _____ _____ this afternoon?

G: Sorry, but I can't.

B: Do you have to do your homework?

G: No, I have to _____ my _____.

cellphone 휴대폰 | go swimming 수영하러 가다 | afternoon 오후 | clean 청소하다
TIPS [How/What about + 명사/동명사?]는 상대방에게 제안할 때 사용합니다.
How about pizza for lunch? 점심식사로 피자 먹을래?
What about playing soccer after school? 방과 후 축구할래?

16

다음 대화를 듣고, 무엇에 관해 이야기하고 있는지 고르시오. ·············· (   )

① 주말 계획   ② 휴가 계획
③ 좋아하는 장소   ④ 좋아하는 음식

W: What are you going to do during _____ _____?

M: I'm going to Busan.

W: I love it there. That's a great choice.

M: _____ _____ you?

W: I don't have any _____ _____ yet.

summer vacation 여름방학 | choice 선택 | special 특별한 | plan 계획 | yet 아직
TIPS any는 '아무것도', '조금도', '무슨' 등의 의미로 부정문과 의문문에 사용합니다.
Do you have any questions? 무슨 질문이 있나요?

17

다음 대화를 듣고, 오늘이 무슨 요일인지 고르시오. ·············· (   )

① 월요일   ② 화요일
③ 수요일   ④ 금요일

G: Jason, where are you going?

B: I'm going to my piano lesson.

G: Do you have a _____ _____ today?

B: Yes, I have piano lessons on Tuesdays and Fridays.

G: I thought today was Wednesday.

B: No, _____ is _____.

lesson 수업 | Tuesday 화요일 | Friday 금요일 | thought 생각하다(think)의 과거형

18

다음 대화를 듣고, 이어질 말로 알맞은 것을 고르시오. ·············· (   )

B _____

① I like dancing.
② It's at the corner.
③ It is very fun.
④ It's this Saturday.

G: Peter, you _____ _____.
   What did you do last night?

B: I practiced dancing for the festival.

G: _____ _____ the festival?

B: _____

tired 피곤한 | last night 지난밤 | practice 연습하다 | festival 축제 | corner 모퉁이

TIPS when(언제)으로 질문했으므로 구체적인 시각이나, 날짜 등으로 대답해야 합니다.

19

다음 대화를 듣고, 이어질 말로 알맞은 것을 고르시오. ·············· (   )

M _____

① Okay. No problem.
② No, it's not my book.
③ I'm sorry to hear that.
④ What a nice book!

W: Brian, what are you doing?

M: Why? Do you need something?

W: Yes. Can you _____ _____ move this box? It's _____ _____ for me.

M: _____

need 필요하다 | something 무언가 | move 옮기다 | too 너무 | heavy 무거운

TIPS 여자가 상자를 옮겨 달라고 부탁하고 있으므로 ①번이 가장 어울립니다.
      No, it's not my book.에 어울리는 질문은 Is this your book?입니다.

20

다음 대화를 듣고, 이어질 말로 적절하지 않은 것을 고르시오. ·············· (   )

G _____

① I bought it last week.
② My dad bought it for me.
③ I borrowed it from my friend.
④ It's on the table.

B: Amy, is this _____ _____?

G: Yes, it is.

B: It's very nice. Where did you _____ _____?

G: _____

camera 카메라 | nice 멋진 | get 얻다

TIPS Where did you get it?에서 get은 '~을 얻다[받다]'라는 의미이며, it은 camera를 의미합니다. It's on the table.에 어울리는 질문은 Where is your camera?입니다.

● 다음 들려주는 단어의 의미를 쓰세요.

단어	의미
01 animal	동물
02 season	
03 colorful	
04 straight	
05 practice	
06 show	
07 remote control	
08 corner	
09 trash	
10 feather	
11 wing	
12 heavy	
13 choice	
14 yet	
15 festival	

10^회 Sentence Check

● 앞에 모의고사에 나오는 문장들을 잘 듣고, 빈칸을 완성하세요.

01 Let's ___pick___ ___up___ the trash.

02 _____ _____ she is!

03 Can I _____ you _____?

04 I _____ my dad's _____.

05 I like summer _____ I can _____ in the sea.

06 I love the _____ _____ in fall.

07 I'm looking for the _____ _____.

08 I play tennis _____ _____.

09 Go straight and _____ _____ at the corner.

10 I have _____ and _____.

11 I took care of him until late _____ _____.

12 I have to _____ _____ this stop.

13 I have _____ _____ _____ you.

14 I don't have _____ _____ _____ yet.

15 I _____ _____ for the festival.

보통 속도 빠른 속도

| 학습일 | 월 일 | 부모님 확인 | 점수 |

1

다음을 듣고, 상대방을 위로하는 표현을 고르시오. ·························· (   )

①   ②   ③   ④

2

다음 그림을 보고, 남자 아이가 할 말로 알맞은 것을 고르시오. ··················· (   )

①   ②   ③   ④

3

다음 대화를 듣고, 무엇에 관해 이야기하고 있는지 고르시오. ···················· (   )

① 취미 생활   ② 점심 메뉴
③ 좋아하는 음식   ④ 요리 수업

4

다음 그림을 보고, 그림에 알맞은 설명을 고르시오. ·························· (   )

①   ②   ③   ④

5

다음 대화를 듣고, 남자 아이의 상태로 알맞은 것을 고르시오. ···················· (   )

①    ②

③    ④

6

다음 대화를 듣고, 내일 날씨를 고르시오.
·· (   )

① 　　②

③ 　　④

8

다음 대화를 듣고, 남자가 산 물건과 개수를 고르시오. ······································· (   )

산 물건	개수
①	3상자
② 	2상자
③	3상자
④ 	2상자

9

다음 그림을 보고, 그림과 일치하는 대화를 고르시오. ······································· (   )

①　　　②　　　③　　　④

7

다음 대화를 듣고, 남자 아이가 방과 후에 할 일을 고르시오. ···························· (   )

① 수영하기　　② 영어 숙제하기
③ 영화보기　　④ 영어 수업 참석하기

10

다음 대화를 듣고, 내용과 일치하지 <u>않는</u> 것을 고르시오. ················· (   )

① John은 7시에 일어난다.
② John은 매일 아침식사를 한다.
③ John은 학교에 걸어서 간다.
④ John의 학교는 9시 20분에 시작한다.

11

다음 대화를 듣고, 여자가 어제 한 일을 고르시오. ···································· (   )

① 쇼핑하기   ② 숙제하기
③ 요리하기   ④ 청소하기

12

다음 대화를 듣고, 두 사람이 만날 시각과 장소를 고르시오. ························· (   )

① 2시 – 버스 정류장
② 2시 – 지하철 역
③ 3시 – 버스 정류장
④ 3시 – 지하철 역

13

다음 대화를 듣고, 두 사람이 좋아하는 운동을 고르시오. ························· (   )

①    ②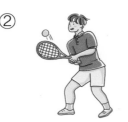

③    ④

14

다음 대화를 듣고, 대화가 자연스럽지 <u>않은</u> 것을 고르시오. ····················· (   )

①   ②   ③   ④

15

다음 대화를 듣고, 남자 아이가 전화한 목적을 고르시오. ························· (   )

① 집에 초대하려고
② 병원에 함께 가려고
③ 약속 장소를 알아보려고
④ 약속을 취소하려고

16

다음 대화를 듣고, 남자 아이의 아버지가 있는 장소를 고르시오. ················· ( )

① 차고　　　　　　② 정원
③ 부엌　　　　　　④ 거실

17

다음 대화를 듣고, 남자 아이가 구입할 물건을 고르시오. ······················ ( )

① 모자　　　　　　② 양말
③ 인형　　　　　　④ 가방

18

다음 대화를 듣고, 이어질 말로 알맞은 것을 고르시오. ······················ ( )

M _____

① They are not my cats.
② I don't have cats.
③ Yes, I want the cat.
④ I like cats very much.

19

다음 대화를 듣고, 이어질 말로 알맞은 것을 고르시오. ······················ ( )

G _____

① He is sick in bed.
② He likes science.
③ I'll visit him after school.
④ He's my best friend.

20

다음 대화를 듣고, 이어질 말로 적절하지 <u>않은</u> 것을 고르시오. ······················ ( )

B _____

① Yes, reading is my hobby.
② Yes, I like reading fairy tales.
③ No, I don't go to the library.
④ No, I don't like reading books.

보통 속도   빠른 속도

학습일   월   일   부모님 확인   점수

● 잘 듣고, 빈칸에 알맞은 말을 쓰세요.

1

다음을 듣고, 상대방을 위로하는 표현을 고르시오. ·················· (   )

① ② ③ ④

W: ❶ I'm sorry, but I can't help you.

　 ❷ Thank you ＿＿＿＿＿＿ ＿＿＿＿＿＿ me.

　 ❸ Don't worry. Everything will ＿＿＿＿＿＿ ＿＿＿＿＿＿.

　 ❹ Let's have dinner together.

worry 걱정하다 | everything 모든 것 | together 함께

TIPS Everything is going to be okay.(모든 것이 잘 될 거야.) / Cheer up.(기운 내.) 등이 위로하는 표현입니다.

2

다음 그림을 보고, 남자 아이가 할 말로 알맞은 것을 고르시오. ············ (   )

① ② ③ ④

B: ❶ Where is your notebook?

　 ❷ ＿＿＿＿＿＿ ＿＿＿＿＿＿ is this book?

　 ❸ I don't play computer games.

　 ❹ ＿＿＿＿＿＿ I ＿＿＿＿＿＿ your phone?

notebook 공책 | use 사용하다

TIPS 남자 아이가 전화기를 쓸 수 있는지 허락을 구하는 표현이 그림과 가장 어울립니다.

3

다음 대화를 듣고, 무엇에 관해 이야기하고 있는지 고르시오. ············ (   )

① 취미 생활　　② 점심 메뉴
③ 좋아하는 음식　④ 요리 수업

M: Alice, what did you have for lunch?

W: I had pasta.

M: ＿＿＿＿＿＿?

W: Yes, it's my favorite. What's your ＿＿＿＿＿＿ ＿＿＿＿＿＿?

M: I like gimbap.

pasta 파스타 | again 또 | favorite 좋아하는 (것) | food 음식 | gimbap 김밥

4

다음 그림을 보고, 그림에 알맞은 설명을 고르시오. ············ (   )

① ② ③ ④

B: ❶ Do not jump here.

　 ❷ Do not ＿＿＿＿＿＿ ＿＿＿＿＿＿.

　 ❸ Do not run here.

　 ❹ Do not ＿＿＿＿＿＿ ＿＿＿＿＿＿.

jump 뛰어오르다 | park 주차하다

TIPS Do not run here.　 Do not park here.

5

다음 대화를 듣고, 남자 아이의 상태로 알맞은 것을 고르시오. ·············· ( )

① ② 1..10 ③ ④

B: How are you, Susie?

G: I'm fine. Thanks. How are you?

B: I don't feel good today.

　I'm _____ and _____.

G: Why?

B: I did my homework _____ _____.

feel good 기분이 좋다 | tired 피곤한 | sleepy 졸린 | until midnight 자정까지

TIPS 감정을 나타내는 형용사로 다음과 같은 것들이 있습니다.
angry 화가 난	sad 슬픈	lonely 외로운
depressed 우울한	surprised 놀란	bored 심심한

6

다음 대화를 듣고, 내일 날씨를 고르시오.
·············· ( )

① ② ③ ④

M: Cathy, what are you going to do tomorrow?

W: I'm going to the beach with my friends.

M: Did you check the _____ _____?

W: No, I didn't.

M: It said it would _____ _____ tomorrow.

W: Oh, no.

tomorrow 내일 | beach 해변 | check 확인하다 | weather report 일기예보 | rainy 비 오는

TIPS 날씨를 나타내는 표현에는 다음과 같은 것들이 있습니다.
cold 추운	cool 시원한	sunny 맑은	cloudy 흐린
foggy 안개 낀	windy 바람 부는	hot 더운	

7

다음 대화를 듣고, 남자 아이가 방과 후에 할 일을 고르시오. ·············· ( )

① 수영하기　　② 영어 숙제하기
③ 영화보기　　④ 영어 수업 참석하기

G: James do you like pizza?

B: Yes, I do. It's my _____.

G: I'm going to the pizza store with Jane after school.
　Do you want to _____ _____ _____?

B: Sorry, I can't. I have to take an _____ language _____ after school.

favorite 좋아하는 (것) | pizza store 피자 가게 | language 언어 | program 프로그램

8

다음 대화를 듣고, 남자가 산 물건과 개수를 고르시오. ·············· (　　)

산 물건	개수
① 🍎	3상자
② 🍌	2상자
③ 🍓	3상자
④ 🥒	2상자

W: Good afternoon. May I help you?

M: Good afternoon. I want to buy ＿＿＿＿＿＿＿ ＿＿＿＿＿＿＿ and strawberries.

W: Sorry, we don't have any apples today.

M: Then, I'll just ＿＿＿＿＿＿＿ ＿＿＿＿＿＿＿.

W: How many boxes of strawberries do you want?

M: ＿＿＿＿＿＿＿.

strawberry 딸기 | box 상자

TIPS · [How many + 복수명사는 ~?] 는 셀 수 있는 것의 수에 대해 질문할 때 사용합니다.
· strawberry의 복수형은 strawberries입니다.

9

다음 그림을 보고, 그림과 일치하는 대화를 고르시오. ·············· (　　)

① ② ③ ④

❶ B: How much is this toy car?

　 G: It's 20 dollars.

❷ B: I won ＿＿＿＿＿＿＿ ＿＿＿＿＿＿＿ in the contest.

　 G: Wow, ＿＿＿＿＿＿＿.

❸ B: Where did you get that?

　 G: I ＿＿＿＿＿＿＿ ＿＿＿＿＿＿＿ last week.

❹ B: What are you doing?

　 G: I'm looking for my bag.

toy car 장난감 자동차 | first prize 1등 | contest 대회 | congratulations 축하해

TIPS 아이가 대회에서 일등을 했고, 이에 축하의 말을 건네는 대화가 가장 어울립니다.

10

다음 대화를 듣고, 내용과 일치하지 <u>않는</u> 것을 고르시오. ·············· (　　)

① John은 7시에 일어난다.
② John은 매일 아침식사를 한다.
③ John은 학교에 걸어서 간다.
④ John의 학교는 9시 20분에 시작한다.

G: John, what time do you get up?

B: I ＿＿＿＿＿＿＿ get up at 7.

G: Do you have breakfast ＿＿＿＿＿＿ ＿＿＿＿＿＿?

B: Yes, I have scrambled eggs and milk for breakfast.

G: How do you go to school?

B: My school is near my house, so I ＿＿＿＿＿＿＿ ＿＿＿＿＿＿＿ ＿＿＿＿＿＿＿.

G: What time does your school start?

B: It starts at 9:30.

get up 일어나다 | usually 보통 | every day 매일 | scrambled eggs 스크램블 에그 | near 가까운 | walk 걷다 | start 시작하다

11

다음 대화를 듣고, 여자가 어제 한 일을 고르시오. ·························· ( )

① 쇼핑하기   ② 숙제하기
③ 요리하기   ④ 청소하기

M: Hi, Cindy, did you _____ _____ yesterday?

W: No, I didn't.

M: Then, what did you do?

W: I _____ _____ for my family.

M: Oh, that's great.

go shopping 쇼핑 가다 | yesterday 어제 | cook 요리하다 | great 훌륭한
TIPS cook dinner는 '저녁식사를 만들다'라는 의미입니다.

12

다음 대화를 듣고, 두 사람이 만날 시각과 장소를 고르시오. ·························· ( )

① 2시 – 버스 정류장
② 2시 – 지하철 역
③ 3시 – 버스 정류장
④ 3시 – 지하철 역

M: Jennifer, are you busy tomorrow?

W: No, I'm not.

M: _____ _____ going to the museum?

W: Sounds good.

M: Then, let's meet at _____ _____ _____ at 2 o'clock.

W: Okay. See you tomorrow.

busy 바쁜 | museum 박물관 | bus stop 버스 정류장
TIPS 여기서 then은 '그럼', '그러면'이란 의미로 대화의 시작이나 끝을 나타낼 때 사용합니다. 또한 then은 '그때에'라는 의미도 있습니다.
See you then. 그때 봐. (※ 전화로 만날 약속을 할 때)

13

다음 대화를 듣고, 두 사람이 좋아하는 운동을 고르시오. ·························· ( )

①   ②

③   ④

M: Jane, do you like tennis?

W: No, I don't.

M: What's your _____ _____?

W: I like bowling.

M: _____ _____.
I go bowling every weekend.
Let's _____ _____ together tomorrow.

W: Okay.

tennis 테니스 | bowling 볼링 | every weekend 주말마다 | together 함께
TIPS Me too.는 I like bowling, too.의 의미입니다.

14

다음 대화를 듣고, 대화가 자연스럽지 <u>않은</u> 것을 고르시오. ············· (   )

①   ②   ③   ④

❶ G: What's your favorite color?

    B: My _____ _____ is blue.

❷ G: Did you make this cake?

    B: Yes, I did.

❸ G: _____ does your father do?

    B: He is in the _____ _____.

❹ G: Is this your pencil?

    B: No, it's not _____.

color 색 | living room 거실 | mine 나의 것

TIPS What does your father do?에 대한 올바른 대답은 My father is a teacher. 등과 같이 아버지의 직업을 말하는 것입니다.

15

다음 대화를 듣고, 남자 아이가 전화한 목적을 고르시오. ························· (   )

① 집에 초대하려고
② 병원에 함께 가려고
③ 약속 장소를 알아보려고
④ 약속을 취소하려고

[Cellphone rings.]

G: Hello.

B: Hello, Alice. Where are you?

G: I'm at home. What's up?

B: I _____ _____ you today.

G: Why?

B: I _____ _____ _____

    and a headache.

G: Oh, that's too bad. Take care of yourself.

cellphone 휴대전화 | meet 만나다 | fever 열 | headache 두통 |
take care of ~을 돌보다

TIPS What's up?은 상황에 따라 '안녕하세요.' / '무슨 일이에요?' / '무슨 일로 오셨어요?' 등의 의미를 가지고 있습니다.

16

다음 대화를 듣고, 남자 아이의 아버지가 있는 장소를 고르시오. ·················· (   )

① 차고   ② 정원
③ 부엌   ④ 거실

B: Mom, where is Dad?

W: He's _____ _____ _____.

B: Is he washing the car there?

W: No, he's _____ the garage.

B: Okay. I will go and help him.

garage 차고 | wash the car 세차하다 | clean 청소하다

TIPS in the garage는 '차고에'라는 의미입니다.

17

다음 대화를 듣고, 남자 아이가 구입할 물건을 고르시오. ·················· (   )

① 모자　　　　② 양말
③ 인형　　　　④ 가방

G: Tomorrow is Jina's birthday.
   What are you going to buy for her?
B: I'm going to buy her a _____ _____.
G: Well... She _____ _____
   wearing baseball caps.
B: Then, how about _____?
G: Good. She told me she needed some socks.

baseball cap 야구모자 | wear 쓰다 | socks 양말 | need 필요하다
TIPS 짝을 이루는 명사는 복수형으로 씁니다.
　　　socks 양말　　shoes 신발　　gloves 장갑　　shorts 반바지

18

다음 대화를 듣고, 이어질 말로 알맞은 것을 고르시오. ·················· (   )

M _____

① They are not my cats.
② I don't have cats.
③ Yes, I want the cat.
④ I like cats very much.

M: Look at those cats over there.
   Do you _____ _____, Julie?
W: Yes, I love cats.
   _____ _____ _____?
M: _____

over there 저쪽에 | very much 무척
TIPS What about you?는 Do you like cats?라는 의미입니다.

19

다음 대화를 듣고, 이어질 말로 알맞은 것을 고르시오. ·················· (   )

G _____

① He is sick in bed.
② He likes science.
③ I'll visit him after school.
④ He's my best friend.

B: Hi, Sara. Did you see Mike today?
G: No, he _____ _____ to school.
B: Do you know why he was absent?
G: _____

today 오늘 | come to school 학교에 오다 | absent 결석한 | sick in bed 아파서 누워 있는
TIPS What's the matter 뒤에 전치사 [with + 명사]가 올 때는 [with + 명사]에게 '무슨 일이 있니?'라는 의미입니다.

20

다음 대화를 듣고, 이어질 말로 적절하지 <u>않은</u> 것을 고르시오. ·················· (   )

B _____

① Yes, reading is my hobby.
② Yes, I like reading fairy tales.
③ No, I don't go to the library.
④ No, I don't like reading books.

B: Amy, what do you do after school?
G: I read books and practice the piano.
B: Wow, you are _____ _____.
G: Thanks. Do you _____ _____
   books?
B: _____

practice 연습하다 | diligent 부지런한 | hobby 취미 | fairy tale 동화

● 다음 들려주는 단어의 의미를 쓰세요.

단어	의미
01 worry	걱정하다
02 everything	
03 park	
04 tomorrow	
05 contest	
06 usually	
07 midnight	
08 start	
09 bowling	
10 headache	
11 garage	
12 absent	
13 fever	
14 diligent	
15 hobby	

● 앞에 모의고사에 나오는 문장들을 잘 듣고, 빈칸을 완성하세요.

01 Everything will _____be_____ _____okay_____.

02 _____ not _____ here.

03 I did my homework _____ _____.

04 It said it would _____ _____ tomorrow.

05 I have to _____ an English language _____ after school.

06 I won _____ _____ in the contest.

07 My school is near my house, so I _____ _____ _____.

08 _____ _____ at the bus stop at 2 o'clock.

09 Let's _____ _____ together tomorrow.

10 I _____ _____ _____ and a headache.

11 _____ _____ yourself.

12 I will _____ _____ _____ him.

13 She told me she needed _____ _____.

14 Look at those cats _____ _____.

15 I _____ books and _____ the piano.

보통 속도
 빠른 속도

학습일   월   일   부모님 확인   점수

1

다음 대화를 듣고, 대화가 상대방을 초대하고 있는 것을 고르시오. ······················ (   )

①   ②   ③   ④

2

다음 그림을 보고, 여자가 할 말로 알맞은 것을 고르시오. ······················ (   )

①   ②   ③   ④

3

다음 그림을 보고, 그림과 일치하는 대화를 고르시오. ······················ (   )

①   ②   ③   ④

4

다음 대화를 듣고, 남자 아이가 내일 할 일을 고르시오. ······················ (   )

① 스케이트 타기   ② 시험 공부
③ 피아노 수업   ④ 청소

정답 및 해석 p. 41

5

다음 대화를 듣고, 여자 아이의 가방으로 알맞은 것을 고르시오. ····················· (   )

①

②

③

④

6

다음 대화를 듣고, 여자 아이가 좋아하는 과목을 고르시오. ····················· (   )

① 음악   ② 수학

③ 과학   ④ 미술

7

다음 그림을 보고, 이어질 응답으로 알맞은 것을 고르시오. ····················· (   )

①   ②   ③   ④

8

다음을 듣고, 무엇에 관한 설명인지 고르시오.
····················· (   )

①

②

③

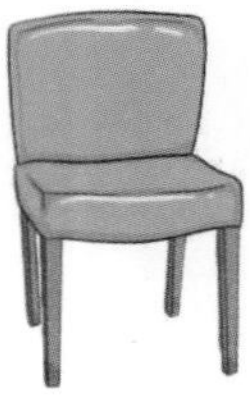

④

9

다음 대화를 듣고, 현재 시각을 고르시오.
····················· (   )

① 10시   ② 10시 30분

③ 11시   ④ 11시 30분

10

다음 대화를 듣고, 남자 아이 기분으로 알맞은 것을 고르시오. ·················· (   )

① 　②

③ 　④

11

다음 대화를 듣고, 대화가 이루어지는 장소를 고르시오. ······················· (   )

① 백화점　　　② 도서관
③ 동물원　　　④ 우체국

12

다음 대화를 듣고, 남자가 휴가 동안에 한 일을 고르시오. ······················· (   )

① 여행　　　　② 요리 수업
③ 영어 공부　　④ 수영

13

다음 대화를 듣고, 내용과 일치하지 <u>않는</u> 것을 고르시오. ·················· (   )

① 여자는 배구를 좋아한다.
② 여자는 배구팀 멤버이다.
③ 남자는 농구를 좋아한다.
④ 남자는 매일 농구를 한다.

14

다음 대화를 듣고, 대화가 자연스럽지 <u>않은</u> 것을 고르시오. ···················· (   )

①　　　②　　　③　　　④

15

다음 그림을 보고, 그림과 일치하지 <u>않는</u> 것을 고르시오. ···················· (   )

①　　　②　　　③　　　④

16

다음 대화를 듣고, 무엇에 관해 이야기하고 있는지 고르시오. ·········· (　　　)

① 방과 후 활동　　② 방과 후 운동
③ 장래 희망　　　④ 독서 모임

17

다음 대화를 듣고, 오늘이 무슨 요일인지 고르시오. ····························· (　　　)

① 수요일　　　② 목요일
③ 금요일　　　④ 토요일

18

다음 대화를 듣고, 이어질 말로 알맞은 것을 고르시오. ····························· (　　　)

B _____

① He's a farmer.
② He's tall and handsome.
③ He lives in Incheon.
④ He's 21 years old.

19

다음 대화를 듣고, 이어질 말로 알맞은 것을 고르시오. ····························· (　　　)

B _____

① She works at a bank.
② She's busy every day.
③ My mom doesn't have a car.
④ She is in the living room now.

20

다음 대화를 듣고, 이어질 말로 적절하지 <u>않은</u> 것을 고르시오. ····················· (　　　)

M _____

① Really good.
② The fried rice was amazing.
③ Very tasty.
④ It was very boring.

●잘 듣고, 빈칸에 알맞은 말을 쓰세요.

1

다음 대화를 듣고, 대화가 상대방을 초대하고 있는 것을 고르시오. ·········· (   )

① ② ③ ④

❶ M: What's your favorite color?
   W: I like green.
❷ M: Alice, where do you live?
   W: I live in Seoul.
❸ M: _____ _____ like to come to my house?
   W: Okay. I'd _____ _____.
❹ M: Thank you for your help.
   W: _____ _____.

green 초록색 | live in ~에 살다 | house 집 | pleasure 즐거움

TIPS Would you ~?는 상대방에게 뭔가를 해줄 의사가 있는지 물어볼 때 사용합니다.

2

다음 그림을 보고, 여자가 할 말로 알맞은 것을 고르시오. ·········· (   )

① ② ③ ④

W: ❶ Get up now. It's 8 o'clock.
   ❷ _____ _____. You're late.
   ❸ Come in, this is my room.
   ❹ _____. See you tomorrow.

get up 일어나다 | hurry up 서두르다 | goodbye 잘 가 | tomorrow 내일

3

다음 그림을 보고, 그림과 일치하는 대화를 고르시오. ·········· (   )

① ② ③ ④

❶ B: Do you want _____ _____?
   G: Yes, it's delicious.
❷ B: What are you doing?
   G: I'm _____ _____.
❸ B: What did you do after lunch?
   G: I played soccer.
❹ B: Let's have sandwiches for lunch.
   W: That's a _____ _____.

delicious 맛있는 | make dinner 저녁을 만들다 | sandwich 샌드위치 | idea 생각

TIPS more는 much / many의 비교급으로 '더 [많이]'의 의미입니다.

4

다음 대화를 듣고, 남자 아이가 내일 할 일을 고르시오. ·············· (　　)

① 스케이트 타기　② 시험 공부
③ 피아노 수업　④ 청소

B: Hi, Susan. What are you going to do tomorrow?

G: I'll _____ _____ with Sara.

B: Oh, that _____ _____.

G: Do you want to join us?

B: Sorry, I can't. I have a _____ _____.

go skating 스케이트 타러 가다 | sound ~인 것 같다 | join 함께하다 | lesson 수업

TIPS Sorry, I can't.는 상대방의 제안을 거절할 때 사용합니다.
Sorry, I can't. 대신 I'd like to, but I can't.로 표현할 수 있습니다.

5

다음 대화를 듣고, 여자 아이의 가방으로 알맞은 것을 고르시오. ·············· (　　)

① ② ③ ④

B: Susie, did you find your bag?

G: No, I didn't.

B: Is your bag yellow?

G: No, _____ _____, and there is a _____ on it.

B: Oh, _____ _____.

find 찾다 | yellow 노란 | green 초록의 | bear 곰 | I see 알다

TIPS 여자 아이의 가방은 초록색에 곰 그림이 있습니다.

6

다음 대화를 듣고, 여자 아이가 좋아하는 과목을 고르시오. ·············· (　　)

① 음악　② 수학
③ 과학　④ 미술

G: What's your favorite subject?

B: I like art because I like drawing. How about you?

G: I _____ _____.

B: Why do you like it?

G: It's _____, and I want to become a scientist in the future.

B: I think you will be a _____ _____.

subject 과목 | art 미술 | drawing 그리기 | interesting 재미있는 | become ~이 되다 |
in the future 장래에

7

다음 그림을 보고, 이어질 응답으로 알맞은 것을 고르시오. ·············· (　　)

① ② ③ ④

G: What _____ _____ your arm?

B: ❶ I got into a car accident.

❷ I fell down _____ _____.

❸ I slipped on ice.

❹ I _____ _____ from a tree.

happen 일어나다 | arm 팔 | car accident 자동차 사고 | fall down 넘어지다 |
stairs 계단 | slip 미끄러지다 | ice 얼음

TIPS 아이가 계단에서 넘어지는 그림에 가장 어울리는 답변을 고르세요.

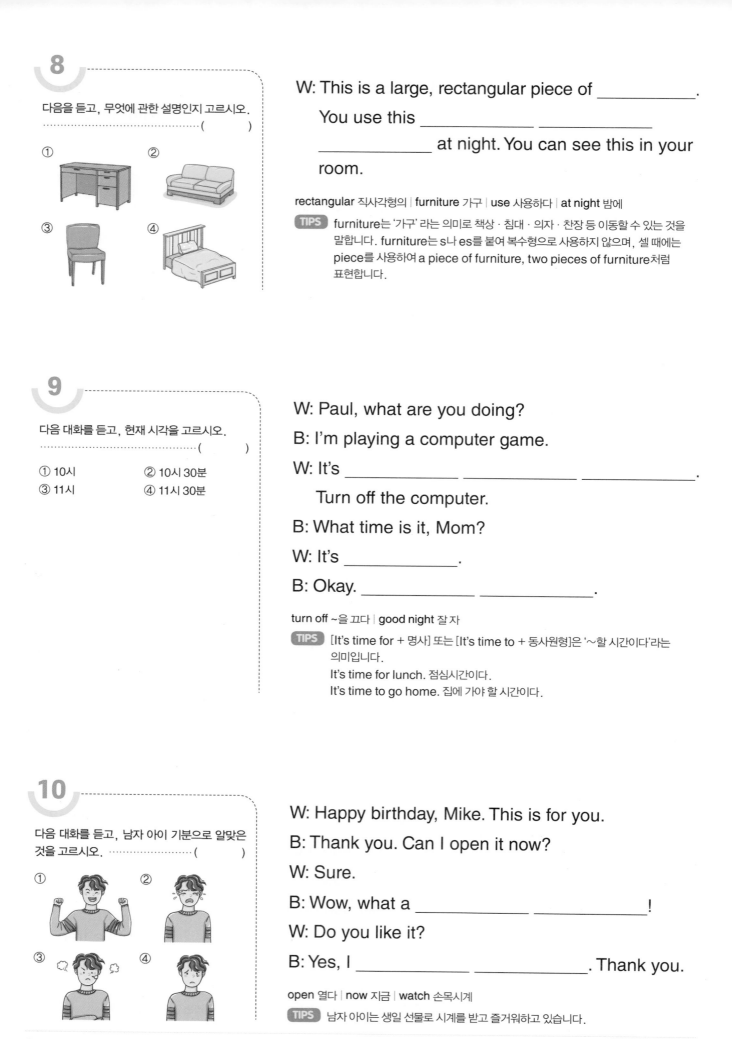

8

다음을 듣고, 무엇에 관한 설명인지 고르시오.
························· (   )

① ② ③ ④

W: This is a large, rectangular piece of _____.
You use this _____ _____
_____ at night. You can see this in your
room.

rectangular 직사각형의 | furniture 가구 | use 사용하다 | at night 밤에

TIPS furniture는 '가구'라는 의미로 책상 · 침대 · 의자 · 찬장 등 이동할 수 있는 것을
말합니다. furniture는 s나 es를 붙여 복수형으로 사용하지 않으며, 셀 때에는
piece를 사용하여 a piece of furniture, two pieces of furniture처럼
표현합니다.

9

다음 대화를 듣고, 현재 시각을 고르시오.
························· (   )

① 10시   ② 10시 30분
③ 11시   ④ 11시 30분

W: Paul, what are you doing?
B: I'm playing a computer game.
W: It's _____ _____ _____.
Turn off the computer.
B: What time is it, Mom?
W: It's _____.
B: Okay. _____ _____.

turn off ~을 끄다 | good night 잘 자

TIPS [It's time for + 명사] 또는 [It's time to + 동사원형]은 '~할 시간이다'라는
의미입니다.
It's time for lunch. 점심시간이다.
It's time to go home. 집에 가야 할 시간이다.

10

다음 대화를 듣고, 남자 아이 기분으로 알맞은
것을 고르시오. ························· (   )

① ② ③ ④

W: Happy birthday, Mike. This is for you.
B: Thank you. Can I open it now?
W: Sure.
B: Wow, what a _____ _____!
W: Do you like it?
B: Yes, I _____ _____. Thank you.

open 열다 | now 지금 | watch 손목시계

TIPS 남자 아이는 생일 선물로 시계를 받고 즐거워하고 있습니다.

11

다음 대화를 듣고, 대화가 이루어지는 장소를
고르시오. ·························· (   )

① 백화점　　　② 도서관
③ 동물원　　　④ 우체국

W: May I help you?

M: Yes, I'd like to send _____ _____ _____ to Seoul.

W: How do you want to send it?

M: _____ _____. How much is it?

W: It's 20 dollars.

send 보내다 | package 소포 | by airmail 항공우편으로

TIPS send, package, airmail 등의 표현으로 대화가 일어나는 장소를 알 수 있습니다.

12

다음 대화를 듣고, 남자가 휴가 동안에 한 일을
고르시오. ·························· (   )

① 여행　　　② 요리 수업
③ 영어 공부　　　④ 수영

M: Hi, Jennifer. What did you do _____ _____ _____ ?

W: I went to Hawaii with my family. It was so fun. What about you?

M: I took a _____ _____.

W: Really?

M: Yes, I learned to make many different kinds of food.

during ~ 동안 | vacation 휴가 | cooking class 요리 수업 | different 여러 가지의

TIPS take a cooking class는 '요리 수업을 듣다'라는 의미입니다.

13

다음 대화를 듣고, 내용과 일치하지 <u>않는</u> 것을
고르시오. ·························· (   )

① 여자는 배구를 좋아한다.
② 여자는 배구팀 멤버이다.
③ 남자는 농구를 좋아한다.
④ 남자는 매일 농구를 한다.

M: Jane, what sport do you like?

W: I _____ _____. I'm a member of the volleyball team.

M: That's cool.

W: What sport do you like?

M: I like _____. I play basketball in my _____ _____.

sport 스포츠 | volleyball 배구 | member 회원 | free time 여가 시간

TIPS 남자는 한가할 때 농구를 합니다. 의문사(what, when, why, how, where)로 물으면, Yes/No로 대답할 수 없습니다.

14

다음 대화를 듣고, 대화가 자연스럽지 <u>않은</u> 것을 고르시오. ·········· (　　)

① ② ③ ④

❶ M: May I have some water?

W: Sure. _____ _____

_____.

❷ M: Would you like some more chicken?

W: No, thanks. I'm full.

❸ M: What do you do in your _____

_____?

W: I want to be _____ _____.

❹ M: Good morning, everyone.

W: Good morning, Mr. Brown.

here you are 여기 있다 | full 배부른 | everyone 모두

TIPS I want to be a teacher.가 올바른 대답이 되려면 What do you want to be in the future?(장래 희망이 뭐니?)가 되어야 합니다.

15

다음 그림을 보고, 그림과 일치하지 <u>않는</u> 것을 고르시오. ·········· (　　)

① ② ③ ④

W: ❶ A boy is _____ _____.

❷ There is some water in the cup.

❸ A boy is _____ _____

_____.

❹ There is a clock on the wall.

food 음식 | hold 잡고 있다 | clock 시계 | on the wall 벽에

TIPS 소년은 수저를 들고 있으므로, A boy is holding a cup.이 아니라 A boy is holding a spoon.이 되어야 합니다.

16

다음 대화를 듣고, 무엇에 관해 이야기하고 있는지 고르시오. ·········· (　　)

① 방과 후 활동 　② 방과 후 운동
③ 장래 희망 　　④ 독서 모임

B: Jina, which after-school clubs do you want to join?

G: I want to join the _____ _____.
How about you?

B: I don't know yet.

G: How about joining the _____ _____?
You like reading books.

B: Oh, that's a _____ _____.

club 동아리 | join 가입하다 | yet 아직 | idea 생각

TIPS [How/What about + 명사/동명사?]는 상대방에게 제안할 때 사용합니다.
How about pizza for lunch? 점심식사로 피자 먹을래?
What about playing soccer after school? 방과 후 축구할래?

17

다음 대화를 듣고, 오늘이 무슨 요일인지 고르시오. ············· (   )

① 수요일　　　② 목요일
③ 금요일　　　④ 토요일

M: Alice, when are you going to the aquarium?

W: Tomorrow.

M: Oh, _____ _____ is it today? Is it Thursday?

W: No, _____ _____ .

M: Then, are you going there on Saturday?

W: Yes, I am.

aquarium 수족관, 아쿠아리움 | tomorrow 내일 | Thursday 목요일 | Saturday 토요일

18

다음 대화를 듣고, 이어질 말로 알맞은 것을 고르시오. ············· (   )

B _____

① He's a farmer.
② He's tall and handsome.
③ He lives in Incheon.
④ He's 21 years old.

G: What did you do _____ _____ ?

B: I visited my uncle.

G: Where does _____ _____ ?

B: _____

last weekend 지난 주말 | visit 방문하다 | farmer 농부 | handsome 잘생긴

TIPS　Where(어디)로 묻고 있으므로 구체적인 장소로 대답합니다.

19

다음 대화를 듣고, 이어질 말로 알맞은 것을 고르시오. ············· (   )

B _____

① She works at a bank.
② She's busy every day.
③ My mom doesn't have a car.
④ She is in the living room now.

G: Kevin, what does your mother do?

B: Do you mean _____ _____ ?

G: Yes.

B: _____

mean 의미하다 | job 직업 | bank 은행 | every day 매일

TIPS　She is in the living room now.가 정답이 되려면 'Where is your mother?'로 질문해야 합니다.

20

다음 대화를 듣고, 이어질 말로 적절하지 <u>않은</u> 것을 고르시오. ············· (   )

M _____

① Really good.
② The fried rice was amazing.
③ Very tasty.
④ It was very boring.

W: Did you _____ _____ last night?

M: Yes, I went to the new restaurant next to the bank.

W: Do you mean the Chinese _____ ?

M: Yes.

W: _____ _____ the food?

M: _____

eat out 외식하다 | last night 지난밤 | restaurant 식당 | next to ~ 옆에 | amazing 놀라운 | tasty 맛있는 | boring 지루한

TIPS　It was very boring.은 음식의 맛 표현에 어울리지 않습니다. It was very boring.은 How was the movie? / How was the soccer game? 등의 질문에 어울립니다.

● 다음 들려주는 단어의 의미를 쓰세요.

	단어	의미
01	pleasure	즐거움
02	delicious	
03	art	
04	interesting	
05	become	
06	stairs	
07	slip	
08	rectangular	
09	furniture	
10	package	
11	different	
12	member	
13	clock	
14	club	
15	aquarium	

● 앞에 모의고사에 나오는 문장들을 잘 듣고, 빈칸을 완성하세요.

01 __Thank__ __you__ __for__ your help.

02 That's a _____ _____.

03 I have a _____ _____.

04 I like art _____ I like _____.

05 _____ _____ you will be a great scientist.

06 I _____ _____ the stairs.

07 You use this _____ _____ _____ at night.

08 _____ _____ for bed.

09 I'd like to _____ _____ _____ to Seoul.

10 I learned to make _____ _____ _____ of food.

11 I'm a member of the _____ _____.

12 I _____ _____ in my free time.

13 A boy is _____ _____ _____.

14 _____ _____ your mother _____?

15 I went to the _____ _____ next to the bank.

보통 속도

빠른 속도

학습일   월   일   **부모님 확인**   점수

1

다음 그림을 보고, 남자가 할 말로 알맞은 것을 고르시오. ·· (   )

①   ②   ③   ④

2

다음 대화를 듣고, 무엇에 관해 이야기하고 있는지 고르시오. ····························· (   )

① 외국어   ② 영어 수업

③ 방과 후 활동   ④ 취미

3

다음 그림을 보고, 그림과 일치하는 대화를 고르시오. ·· (   )

①   ②   ③   ④

4

다음 대화를 듣고, 두 사람이 좋아하는 영화 종류를 고르시오. ····························· (   )

① 공포 영화   ② 만화 영화

③ 코미디 영화   ④ 탐정 영화

5

다음을 듣고, 그림과 일치하는 설명을 고르시오. ······················· (   )

① ② ③ ④

6

다음 대화를 듣고, 여자가 어젯밤에 한 일을 고르시오. ························ (   )

① 동생 돌보기 　　② 빨래하기
③ 강아지 산책시키기 　　④ 청소하기

7

다음 그림을 보고, 남자 아이의 형을 고르시오. ·························· (   )

8

다음 대화를 듣고, 대화와 일치하는 그림을 고르시오. ······················· (   )

9

다음 대화를 듣고, 여자 아이의 장래 희망을 고르시오. ······················· (   )

① 경찰관 　　② 작가
③ 의사 　　④ 요리사

10

다음 대화를 듣고, 남자 아이가 주말이 즐겁지 <u>않았던</u> 이유를 고르시오. ············ (   )

① 몸이 아파서 　　② 숙제가 많아서
③ 잠을 잘 못 자서 　　④ 청소를 많이 해서

11

다음 대화를 듣고, 여자 아이가 방과 후에 할
일을 고르시오. ································· (   )

① 테니스 수업   ② 독서

③ 숙제   ④ 피아노 연습

12

다음 대화를 듣고, 여자 아이가 전화한 목적을
고르시오. ····························· (   )

① 영화를 함께 보려고

② 숙제를 함께 하려고

③ 청소를 함께 하려고

④ 음악회에 함께 가려고

13

다음 대화를 듣고, 남자가 가려고 하는 곳을 고
르시오. ····························· (   )

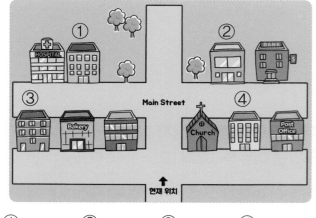

①   ②   ③   ④

14

다음을 듣고, 그림에 알맞은 설명을 고르시오.
································· (   )

①   ②   ③   ④

15

다음 대화를 듣고, 남자 아이가 할 일을 고르시
오. ································· (   )

① 숙제하기   ② 손 씻기

③ 청소하기   ④ 샤워하기

16

다음 대화를 듣고, 무엇에 관해 이야기하고 있는지 고르시오. ·························· (   )

① 좋아하는 달   ② 좋아하는 계절
③ 좋아하는 색   ④ 좋아하는 음식

17

다음을 듣고, 내용과 일치하지 않는 것을 고르시오. ······························ (   )

① 여자 아이는 싱가포르에 산다.
② 여자 아이는 12살이다.
③ 여자 아이는 수영하는 것을 좋아한다.
④ 여자 아이는 기타를 잘 친다.

18

다음 대화를 듣고, 이어질 말로 알맞은 것을 고르시오. ·························· (   )

M _____

① I went there by train.
② I stayed there for 4 days.
③ I stayed at a hotel.
④ I went swimming at the beach.

19

다음 대화를 듣고, 이어질 말로 알맞은 것을 고르시오. ·························· (   )

B _____

① Sure, no problem.
② No, I don't like reading books.
③ I'm glad you like it.
④ It's at seven in the evening.

20

다음 대화를 듣고, 이어질 말로 적절하지 않은 것을 고르시오. ·························· (   )

G _____

① I ride my bike to school.
② My mom gives me a ride.
③ I go to school by bus.
④ I am often late for school.

| 학습일 | 월 일 | 부모님 확인 | 점수 |

 잘 듣고, 빈칸에 알맞은 말을 쓰세요.

1

다음 그림을 보고, 남자가 할 말로 알맞은 것을 고르시오. .... (   )

① ② ③ ④

M: ❶ It's time to _____ _____.

❷ Let's have dinner together.

❸ Have a _____ _____, Sally.

❹ Turn on the light, please.

wake up 일어나다 | together 함께 | good night 잘 자 | turn on (불 등을) 켜다 | light 불

TIPS Have a good night. 대신 Good night. / Sweet dreams.(좋은 꿈 꿔.) 등으로 표현할 수 있습니다.

2

다음 대화를 듣고, 무엇에 관해 이야기하고 있는지 고르시오. .... (   )

① 외국어 　　② 영어 수업
③ 방과 후 활동 　④ 취미

M: Susan, can you speak any foreign languages?

W: Yes, I can _____ _____.
How about you?

M: I can _____ _____ and Spanish.

W: Wow, that's cool.

speak 말하다 | foreign language 외국어 | Chinese 중국어 | Spanish 스페인어 | cool 멋진

TIPS 외국어는 이외에도 Japanese(일본어), French(프랑스어) 등이 있습니다.

3

다음 그림을 보고, 그림과 일치하는 대화를 고르시오. .... (   )

① ② ③ ④

❶ M: Are there any strawberries in the box?

W: No, _____ _____.

❷ M: Where are you going?

W: I'm going to _____ _____.

❸ M: What's your favorite fruit?

W: I like apples.

❹ M: May I help you?

W: Yes, I want _____ _____.

strawberry 딸기 | market 시장 | fruit 과일

TIPS 과일 가게에서 물건을 사는 상황에 어울리는 대화를 고르세요.

4

다음 대화를 듣고, 두 사람이 좋아하는 영화 종류를 고르시오. ┈┈┈┈┈┈┈┈┈┈ (   )

① 공포 영화   ② 만화 영화
③ 코미디 영화   ④ 탐정 영화

M: Sara, what do you do in your free time?

W: I _____ _____.

M: What _____ of movie do you like?

W: I like comedy.

M: I like _____, _____.
They make me feel good.

free time 여가 시간 | **watch movies** 영화 보다 | **kind** 종류 | **comedy** 코미디

TIPS horror movie 공포 영화   war movie 전쟁 영화
animated movie 만화 영화

5

다음을 듣고, 그림과 일치하는 설명을 고르시오. ┈┈┈┈┈┈┈┈┈┈ (   )

①   ②   ③   ④

M: ❶ Do not run.

❷ Do not _____ and _____ here.

❸ Do not park here.

❹ Do not _____ here.

run 달리다 | **here** 여기 | **park** 주차하다

TIPS '~하라'고 상대방에게 지시하거나 명령하는 문장을 명령문이라고 합니다.
명령문은 주어(You)가 생략된 형태로 동사원형으로 시작합니다.
'~하지 마라'고 할 때는 [Do not + 동사원형] 을 사용합니다.

6

다음 대화를 듣고, 여자가 어젯밤에 한 일을 고르시오. ┈┈┈┈┈┈┈┈┈┈ (   )

① 동생 돌보기   ② 빨래하기
③ 강아지 산책시키기   ④ 청소하기

W: Sam, how was the party last night?

M: It was very fun. Why didn't you come to the party?

W: I _____ _____ last night.

M: Why?

W: My mom was sick, so I made dinner and
_____ _____ _____ my younger brother.

party 파티 | **last night** 지난밤 | **busy** 바쁜 | **sick** 아픈 | **take care of** ~을 돌보다 |
younger brother 남동생

TIPS take care of my younger brother는 '남동생을 돌보다'라는 의미입니다.

7

다음 그림을 보고, 남자 아이의 형을 고르시
오. ·············· Listening Mentor ·············· (   )

① ②  ③  ④

G: David, is your brother in the bookstore?

B: Yes, he's standing over there.

G: Is he _____ _____?

B: No, he isn't. He's _____ a white T-shirt
and _____ _____.

bookstore 서점 | stand 서다 | over there 저쪽에 | glasses 안경 | pants 바지

TIPS glasses는 '안경'으로 '안경을 쓰다'라고 할 때에는 동사 wear를 사용합니다.

8

다음 대화를 듣고, 대화와 일치하는 그림을 고
르시오. ·············· (   )

① ②  ③  ④

M: What's wrong?

G: I _____ _____ _____
and a runny nose.

M: Let me check.

G: I have a headache, too.

M: You _____ _____ _____,
so stay home and get some rest.

wrong 잘못된 | fever 열 | runny nose 콧물 | check 확인하다 | headache 두통 |
have a cold 감기 걸리다 | rest 휴식

TIPS a fever, a runny nose, check, have a cold 등의 표현으로 대화가 일어나는
장소를 알 수 있습니다.

9

다음 대화를 듣고, 여자 아이의 장래 희망을 고
르시오. ·············· (   )

① 경찰관 ② 작가
③ 의사 ④ 요리사

G: What do you want to be in the future?

B: I want to be a _____ _____.
What about you?

G: I really want to _____ _____
_____ like my dad.

B: I think you will be a great writer.

G: Thanks.

in the future 장래에 | police officer 경찰관 | writer 작가 | think 생각하다

10

다음 대화를 듣고, 남자 아이가 주말이 즐겁지 않았던 이유를 고르시오. ·········· (   )

① 몸이 아파서　　② 숙제가 많아서
③ 잠을 잘 못 자서　④ 청소를 많이 해서

G: Hi, Paul. How was your weekend?

B: It was not good.

G: Why?

B: I was _____ _____ _____.

G: Oh, I'm sorry to hear that. Are you okay now?

B: Yes, I _____ _____.

weekend 주말 | sick 아픈 | feel better (병, 기분) 나아지다

TIPS · be sick in bed는 '아파서 누워 있다'라는 의미입니다.
· better는 good의 비교급으로 '(몸 기분이) 나은, 더 좋은'이란 의미입니다.
I'm a lot better today. 나는 오늘 훨씬 나아졌다.

11

다음 대화를 듣고, 여자 아이가 방과 후에 할 일을 고르시오. ·········· (   )

① 테니스 수업　　② 독서
③ 숙제　　　　　④ 피아노 연습

G: Sam, what are you going to do after school?

B: I have a _____ _____ today.
How about you?

G: I'm going to _____ _____
_____.

B: Do you practice the piano every day?

G: Yes, the _____ _____ is next
Saturday.

B: Oh, I see.

tennis lesson 테니스 수업 | practice 연습하다 | every day 매일 | contest 대회

TIPS practice the piano는 '피아노 연습을 하다'라는 의미입니다.

12

다음 대화를 듣고, 여자 아이가 전화한 이유를 고르시오. ·········· (   )

① 영화를 함께 보려고
② 숙제를 함께 하려고
③ 청소를 함께 하려고
④ 음악회에 함께 가려고

[Cellphone rings.]

B: Hello.

G: Hi, Mike. This is Alice. What are you doing now?

B: I'm watching TV at home. Why?

G: I'm going to _____ _____ today.
Will you come with me?

B: Sure. What time shall we meet?

G: _____ _____ at the bus stop
at 5.

now 지금 | why 왜 | concert 음악회 | meet 만나다 | bus stop 버스 정류장

TIPS Will you come with me? 대신 Do you want to go with me?(나랑 함께 갈래?)라고 표현할 수 있습니다.

13

다음 대화를 듣고, 남자가 가려고 하는 곳을 고르시오. ················ ( )

①   ②   ③   ④

M: Excuse me. How can I get to the aquarium?

W: Let me see. _____ _____ one block and _____ _____.

M: Go straight one block and turn left?

W: Yes, it'll be on your right _____ _____ the hospital.

M: Oh, I see. Thank you very much.

aquarium 수족관 | **straight** 곧장 | **turn left** 왼쪽으로 돌다 | **on one's right** 오른쪽에 | **next to ~** 옆에 | **hospital** 병원

14

다음을 듣고, 그림에 알맞은 설명을 고르시오. ················ ( )

①   ②   ③   ④

W: ❶ He's dancing in the room.

   ❷ He's _____ _____ _____.

   ❸ He's passing a ball.

   ❹ He's _____ on the bench.

dance 춤추다 | **room** 방 | **catch** 잡다 | **pass** 건네다 | **bench** 벤치

TIPS 야구공을 잡고 있는 모습이므로 ②번이 가장 그림과 어울립니다.

15

다음 대화를 듣고, 남자 아이가 할 일을 고르시오. ················ ( )

① 숙제하기   ② 손 씻기

③ 청소하기   ④ 샤워하기

B: Mom, _____ _____.

W: How was your day at school?

B: It was a lot of fun today. I'm _____ _____ hungry. Can I have a snack?

W: Sure. But _____ _____ _____ first.

B: Okay, Mom.

fun 재미 | **a little** 조금 | **hungry** 배고픈 | **wash one's hands** 손을 씻다 | **first** 먼저

TIPS a little 은 '조금', '약간', '다소' 등의 의미를 가지고 있습니다.

16

다음 대화를 듣고, 무엇에 관해 이야기하고 있는지 고르시오. ················ ( )

① 좋아하는 달   ② 좋아하는 계절

③ 좋아하는 색   ④ 좋아하는 음식

B: Jessie, what's your _____ _____?

G: I like _____. I can see a lot of beautiful flowers in April. What's your favorite month?

B: I _____ _____.

G: Why?

B: My birthday is in October.

month 달 | **a lot of** 많은 | **beautiful** 아름다운 | **birthday** 생일

17

다음을 듣고, 내용과 일치하지 <u>않는</u> 것을 고르시오. ···················(   )

① 여자 아이는 싱가포르에 산다.
② 여자 아이는 12살이다.
③ 여자 아이는 수영하는 것을 좋아한다.
④ 여자 아이는 기타를 잘 친다.

G: Hello, everyone. My name is Alice Brown.
    I live in Singapore. I'm _____ years old.
    My favorite color is blue. I like _____.
    I'm good at playing _____ _____.

everyone 모두 | **Singapore** 싱가포르 | **color** 색 | **violin** 바이올린
TIPS be good at playing the violin은 '바이올린을 잘 연주한다'라는 의미입니다.

18

다음 대화를 듣고, 이어질 말로 알맞은 것을 고르시오. ···················(   )

M _____

① I went there by train.
② I stayed there for 4 days.
③ I stayed at a hotel.
④ I went swimming at the beach.

W: How was your _____ _____?
M: It was fun. I went to Busan.
W: _____ _____ _____ do
    there?
M: _____

summer vacation 여름 휴가 | **went** 가다(go)의 과거형 | **by train** 기차로 | **stay** 머무르다 | **beach** 해변
TIPS '부산에서 무엇을 했니?'라고 묻고 질문에 가장 알맞은 대답을 고르세요.
I went there by train.에 알맞은 질문은 How did you go there?이고,
I stayed there for 4 days.에 알맞은 질문은 How long did you stay there?
입니다.

19

다음 대화를 듣고, 이어질 말로 알맞은 것을 고르시오. ···················(   )

B _____

① Sure, no problem.
② No, I don't like reading books.
③ I'm glad you like it.
④ It's at seven in the evening.

G: Kevin, will you go to the library today?
B: Yes, I will. Why?
G: _____ _____ go with you?
    I want to _____ some _____.
B: _____

library 도서관 | **borrow** 빌리다 | **no problem** 문제없다 | **glad** 기쁜 | **evening** 저녁
TIPS Can I go with you?에 대한 대답으로 Sure, no problem. 대신 Of course.
(물론이지.)라고 말해도 됩니다.

20

다음 대화를 듣고, 이어질 말로 적절하지 <u>않은</u> 것을 고르시오. ···················(   )

G _____

① I ride my bike to school.
② My mom gives me a ride.
③ I go to school by bus.
④ I am often late for school.

B: Is your school near your house?
G: No, it isn't.
B: Then, how do you _____ _____
    _____?
G: _____

near 가까운 | **house** 집 | **ride a bike** 자전거를 타다 | **give a ride** 태워 주다 | **often** 종종

● 다음 들려주는 단어의 의미를 쓰세요.

	단어	의미
01	speak	말하다
02	language	
03	market	
04	comedy	
05	bookstore	
06	runny nose	
07	pass	
08	police officer	
09	future	
10	contest	
11	concert	
12	aquarium	
13	straight	
14	catch	
15	borrow	

● 앞에 모의고사에 나오는 문장들을 잘 듣고, 빈칸을 완성하세요.

01 Have a ___good___ ___night___.

02 I can _____ _____ and Spanish.

03 I'm _____ _____ the market.

04 They make me _____ _____.

05 I _____ _____ and took care of my younger brother.

06 _____ _____ over there.

07 I have a fever and a _____ _____.

08 You have a cold, so stay home and _____ _____ _____.

09 I want to be a _____ _____.

10 I was _____ _____ _____.

11 It'll be _____ _____ _____ next to the hospital.

12 I'm _____ _____ playing the violin.

13 I can see a lot of beautiful flowers _____ _____.

14 I want to _____ _____ _____.

15 I am _____ _____ for school.

영어 듣기 모의고사

 보통 속도
 빠른 속도

학습일	월 일	부모님 확인	점수

1

다음 그림을 보고, 남자가 할 말로 알맞은 것을 고르시오. ·························· (   )

①   ②   ③   ④

2

다음 대화를 듣고, 남자 아이가 어젯밤에 한 일을 고르시오. ··················· (   )

①    ②

③    ④

3

다음 대화를 듣고, 여자 아이가 좋아하는 색깔을 고르시오. ····················· (   )

① 노란색   ② 초록색

③ 분홍색   ④ 파란색

4

다음 그림을 보고, 그림과 일치하는 대화를 고르시오. ····························· (   )

①   ②   ③   ④

5

다음 대화를 듣고, 여자 아이가 겨울을 좋아하는 이유를 고르시오. ·················· (   )

① 눈사람을 만들 수 있어서

② 겨울 운동을 할 수 있어서

③ 눈싸움을 할 수 있어서

④ 바람이 많이 불어서

6

다음 대화를 듣고, 여자 아이가 사려는 선물을
고르시오. ································ (   )

①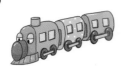

②

③

④

7

다음을 듣고, 남자 아이가 가려고 하는 곳을 고
르시오. ······························ (   )

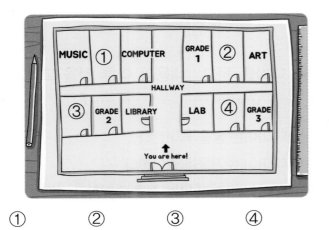

①   ②   ③   ④

8

다음 대화를 듣고, 음악회 날짜를 고르시오.
································ (   )

① 2월 10일   ② 2월 20일
③ 3월 20일   ④ 3월 22일

9

다음 대화를 듣고, 대화가 이루어지는 장소를
고르시오. ····························· (   )

① 꽃 가게   ② 서점
③ 도서관   ④ 편의점

10

다음 대화를 듣고, 남자 아이 삼촌의 나이를 고
르시오. ······························ (   )

① 18살   ② 21살
③ 28살   ④ 38살

11

다음 대화를 듣고, 여자 아이 아버지의 직업을 고르시오. ·················· (   )

①    ②

③    ④

12

다음 대화를 듣고, 대화가 자연스럽지 않은 것을 고르시오. ·························· (   )

①   ②   ③   ④

13

다음 대화를 듣고, 남자 아이가 이번 주 토요일에 할 일을 고르시오. ··············· (   )

① 생일 파티 참석   ② 결혼식 참석
③ 병원 방문   ④ 친척 방문

14

다음 대화를 듣고, 무엇에 관해 이야기하고 있는지 고르시오. ···················· (   )

① 좋아하는 TV 프로그램
② TV 드라마
③ 좋아하는 운동
④ 좋아하는 영화

15

다음 대화를 듣고, 어떤 상황에서 이루어지는 대화인지 고르시오. ················ (   )

① 축하하는 상황
② 도움을 요청하는 상황
③ 사과하는 상황
④ 제안을 거절하는 상황

16

다음 대화를 듣고, 내용과 다른 것을 고르시오. ······························· (   )

① 남자 아이는 봄을 좋아한다.
② 여자 아이는 겨울을 좋아한다.
③ 여자 아이는 스키 타는 것을 좋아한다.
④ 여자 아이는 겨울에 일주일에 2번 스키를 탄다.

17

다음을 듣고, 설명하는 운동을 고르시오.
.... (   )

①

②

③

④

19

다음 대화를 듣고, 이어질 말로 알맞은 것을 고르시오. .... (   )

B _____

① I took the subway.
② I built a sandcastle on the beach.
③ It was very fun.
④ It was very sunny.

18

다음 대화를 듣고, 이어질 말로 알맞은 것을 고르시오. .... (   )

W _____

① I like listening to the radio.
② I can play the violin.
③ I listen to music every day.
④ I like K-pop.

20

다음 대화를 듣고, 이어질 말로 적절하지 <u>않은</u> 것을 고르시오. .... (   )

B _____

① I got up late.
② I missed the bus.
③ It snowed a lot this morning.
④ I usually walk to school.

| 학습일 | 월 일 | 부모님 확인 | 점수 |

● 잘 듣고, 빈칸에 알맞은 말을 쓰세요.

1

다음 그림을 보고, 남자가 할 말로 알맞은 것을 고르시오. ·················· ( )

① ② ③ ④

M: ❶ Do you have a car?

❷ We will ＿＿＿＿＿＿＿ ＿＿＿＿＿＿＿ for the concert.

❸ How do you go to the market?

❹ Cindy, ＿＿＿＿＿＿＿ your ＿＿＿＿＿＿＿ ＿＿＿＿＿＿＿.

be late 늦다 | concert 음악회 | market 시장 | fasten one's seat belt 안전벨트를 매다

TIPS Fasten your seat belt. 대신 Will you please fasten your seat belt?라고 표현할 수 있습니다.

2

다음 대화를 듣고, 남자 아이가 어젯밤에 한 일을 고르시오. ·················· ( )

① ② ③ ④

G: Minsu, what's wrong? You ＿＿＿＿＿＿＿ ＿＿＿＿＿＿＿.

B: Do I? I exercised too much last night.

G: What did you do?

B: I ＿＿＿＿＿＿＿ ＿＿＿＿＿＿＿ at the park.

look tired 피곤해 보이다 | exercise 운동하다 | too much 너무 많이 | jog 조깅하다

TIPS go jogging 은 '조깅하러 가다'라는 의미입니다.
go swimming 수영하러 가다　　　　　go fishing 낚시하러 가다
go shopping 쇼핑하러 가다

3

다음 대화를 듣고, 여자 아이가 좋아하는 색깔을 고르시오. ·················· ( )

① 노란색　　　② 초록색
③ 분홍색　　　④ 파란색

G: Jason, is this blue bag yours?

B: Yes, it is.

G: Your bag is nice. You have many ＿＿＿＿＿＿＿ things, right?

B: Yes, my favorite color is blue. What's your ＿＿＿＿＿＿＿ ＿＿＿＿＿＿＿?

G: My favorite color is ＿＿＿＿＿＿＿.

yours 너의 것 | nice 멋진 | pink 분홍색

4

다음 그림을 보고, 그림과 일치하는 대화를 고르시오. ························· ( )

① ② ③ ④

❶ W: How many classes do you have today?

B: I have four.

❷ W: What's wrong, Jake?
You are _____ _____.

B: Sorry, I _____ _____ late this morning.

❸ W: What time does your school start?

B: It starts at 9 o'clock.

❹ W: _____ _____!
We don't have enough time.

B: What time is it now?

class 수업 | again 또, 다시 | wake up 일어나다 | start 시작하다 | hurry up 서두르다 | enough 충분한

TIPS 남자 아이가 교실에 9시 지나서 도착하는 그림으로 가장 어울리는 대화를 골라 보세요.

5

다음 대화를 듣고, 여자 아이가 겨울을 좋아하는 이유를 고르시오. ··············· ( )

① 눈사람을 만들 수 있어서
② 겨울 운동을 할 수 있어서
③ 눈싸움을 할 수 있어서
④ 바람이 많이 불어서

B: I like spring. It is nice and warm in spring.

G: Yes. But it's too windy.

B: Well, _____ _____ you?

G: I like winter.

B: Winter? It's _____ _____.

G: Right. But we have snow, and we can
_____ _____ _____.

spring 봄 | warm 따뜻한 | too 너무 | snowman 눈사람

TIPS 여자 아이는 겨울에 눈이 오고, 눈사람을 만들 수 있어 겨울을 좋아한다고 했습니다.

6

다음 대화를 듣고, 여자 아이가 사려는 선물을 고르시오. ··············· ( )

①  ②

③ ④

M: May I help you?

G: I'm looking for a present for my brother.
He's six years old.

M: How about this toy train?

G: He _____ has one at home.
How much is _____ _____?

M: It's 15 dollars.

G: That's great. I'll _____ _____.

present 선물 | toy train 장난감 기차 | already 이미 | robot 로봇

7

다음을 듣고, 남자 아이가 가려고 하는 곳을 고르시오. ·········· (   )

① ② ③ ④

B: Hi, Sujin.
   Where is the _____ _____?
G: Sorry?
B: The science room.
G: Go straight and _____ _____
   at the library. It's _____ the music room
   and the computer room.
B: Thanks.

science room 과학실 | straight 곧장 | library 도서관 | between ~ 사이에

TIPS [between A and B] 는 'A와 B 사이에'라는 의미입니다.

8

다음 대화를 듣고, 음악회 날짜를 고르시오.
·········· (   )

① 2월 10일   ② 2월 20일
③ 3월 20일   ④ 3월 22일

M: Sara, I am going to a concert.
   Will you come with me?
W: When is _____ _____?
M: _____ 20.
W: Pardon?
M: March 20. _____ _____.

concert 음악회 | come with 함께 가다 | pardon 뭐라고

TIPS pardon은 '뭐라고요'라는 의미로 상대방의 말을 알아듣지 못했을 때 다시 말해 달라는 뜻으로 하는 말입니다. pardon 대신 sorry를 이용해서 '뭐라고요, 뭐라고 하셨나요'라고 표현할 수 있습니다.
Sorry? Could you repeat the question?
뭐라고요? 그 질문 한 번 더 해 주시겠어요?

9

다음 대화를 듣고, 대화가 이루어지는 장소를 고르시오. ·········· (   )

① 꽃 가게   ② 서점
③ 도서관   ④ 편의점

M: May I help you?
W: I want to buy _____ _____.
M: What color do you want?
W: Do you have _____ _____?
M: Yes, the white roses are over there. _____
   _____ roses do you want?
W: Ten, please.

rose 장미 | over there 저쪽에 | how many 얼마나 많이

TIPS white ones는 white roses를 의미합니다.

10

다음 대화를 듣고, 남자 아이 삼촌의 나이를 고르시오. ·············· (   )

① 18살   ② 21살
③ 28살   ④ 38살

G: Kevin, who is that man over there?

B: He's _____ _____.

G: Wow, your uncle is very tall and handsome. _____ _____ is he?

B: He's _____ years old.

G: Does he live with you?

B: No, he lives in Busan.

uncle 삼촌 | handsome 잘생긴 | how old 몇 살 | live in ~에 살다

11

다음 대화를 듣고, 여자 아이 아버지의 직업을 고르시오. ·············· (   )

① ② ③ ④

G: Who is this man in the picture?

B: He is my father. He is a teacher. _____ _____ your father do?

G: He is a firefighter.

B: That's awesome! I want to _____ _____ _____, too.

picture 사진 | firefighter 소방관 | awesome 굉장한, 멋진 | too 역시

12

다음 대화를 듣고, 대화가 자연스럽지 않은 것을 고르시오. ·············· (   )

① ② ③ ④

❶ M: Where is the hospital?

　W: It's _____ _____ the bakery.

❷ M: I'm thirsty. Can I have some water?

　W: Sure. _____ _____ _____.

❸ M: Is this your new hair pin?

　W: Yes, my mom bought it for me.

❹ M: What _____ _____ _____ this weekend?

　W: I _____ _____.

hospital 병원 | next to ~ 옆에 | bakery 빵집 | thirsty 목마른 | weekend 주말 | go camping 캠핑 가다

TIPS What will you do this weekend?의 질문에 대한 올바른 대답은 I will go to the beach. 등과 같이 조동사 will이나 [be going to + 동사원형]을 이용해서 대답해야 합니다.

13

다음 대화를 듣고, 남자 아이가 이번 주 토요일에 할 일을 고르시오. ··········· (   )

① 생일 파티 참석   ② 결혼식 참석
③ 병원 방문   ④ 친척 방문

G: Chris, can you come to my birthday party?
B: When is it?
G: It's _____ _____.
B: This Saturday? I'm sorry, but I can't.
G: _____ _____?
B: I have to _____ my uncle's _____.

birthday party 생일 파티 | **attend** 참석하다 | **wedding** 결혼
TIPS [have to + 동사원형]은 '~해야 한다'라는 의미입니다.

14

다음 대화를 듣고, 무엇에 관해 이야기하고 있는지 고르시오. ··················· (   )

① 좋아하는 TV 프로그램
② TV 드라마
③ 좋아하는 운동
④ 좋아하는 영화

W: Kevin, what are you doing?
M: I'm watching TV.
W: What kind of _____ _____ do you like to watch?
M: I like watching sports on TV. What about you?
W: I _____ _____.

kind 종류 | **program** 프로그램 | **sport** 스포츠 | **documentary** 다큐멘터리
TIPS [What kind/sort of + 명사]는 '어떤 종류의'라는 의미입니다.
What kind/sort of movie do you like? 어떤 종류의 영화를 좋아하니?

15

다음 대화를 듣고, 어떤 상황에서 이루어지는 대화인지 고르시오. ··············· (   )

① 축하하는 상황
② 도움을 요청하는 상황
③ 사과하는 상황
④ 제안을 거절하는 상황

W: Tony, are you doing anything?
B: Nothing. Why do you ask?
W: _____ _____ _____ me?
B: Sure. What can I do for you?
W: Can you _____ _____ _____?
B: Okay.

nothing 아무것도 아닌 | **why** 왜 | **wash the dishes** 설거지하다

16

다음 대화를 듣고, 내용과 <u>다른</u> 것을 고르시오. ··················· (   )

① 남자 아이는 봄을 좋아한다.
② 여자 아이는 겨울을 좋아한다.
③ 여자 아이는 스키 타는 것을 좋아한다.
④ 여자 아이는 겨울에 일주일에 2번 스키를 탄다.

G: What's your favorite season?
B: My favorite season is spring. How about you?
G: I like winter because I _____ _____.
B: Oh, really? _____ _____ do you go skiing?
G: I go skiing _____ _____
_____.

season 계절 | **because** 왜냐하면, 때문에 | **really** 정말 | **often** 자주 | **once** 한 번
TIPS 여자 아이는 일주일에 한 번 스키를 탄다.
twice a week 일주일에 두 번   three times a week 일주일에 세 번

17

다음을 듣고, 설명하는 운동을 고르시오.
.... (   )

① ② ③ ④

W: This is a sport. We play this sport on a large field. We _____ _____ _____ with a bat. We use a _____ _____ _____ a ball.

large 커다란 | field 경기장 | hit 치다 | bat 방망이 | glove 글러브 | catch 잡다

18

다음 대화를 듣고, 이어질 말로 알맞은 것을 고르시오. .... (   )

W _____

① I like listening to the radio.
② I can play the violin.
③ I listen to music every day.
④ I like K-pop.

M: What are you doing, Jessie?

W: I'm listening to music.

M: _____ _____ of _____ do you like?

W: _____

listen to music 음악을 듣다 | kind 종류 | radio 라디오 | violin 바이올린 | every day 매일

TIPS What kind of music ~?으로 질문했으므로 음악의 종류로 대답해야 합니다.

19

다음 대화를 듣고, 이어질 말로 알맞은 것을 고르시오. .... (   )

B _____

① I took the subway.
② I built a sandcastle on the beach.
③ It was very fun.
④ It was very sunny.

G: Paul, what did you do last Sunday?

B: I went to the _____.

G: Oh, did you?

_____ _____ _____ do there?

B: _____

last Sunday 지난 일요일 | beach 해변 | by subway 지하철로 | sandcastle 모래성

TIPS What did you do ~?로 질문했으므로 과거형 동사를 이용해서 답합니다. I took the subway.가 올바른 대답이 되려면 How did you go there?로 물어야 합니다.

20

다음 대화를 듣고, 이어질 말로 적절하지 않은 것을 고르시오. .... (   )

B _____

① I got up late.
② I missed the bus.
③ It snowed a lot this morning.
④ I usually walk to school.

G: How do you go to school, Mike?

B: I usually _____ a _____ to school, but I took the subway today.

G: _____ _____ _____ take the subway?

B: _____

usually 보통 | take a bus 버스를 타다 | subway 지하철 | why 왜

TIPS Why did you~ ?(왜 ~했니?)라고 질문하고 있으므로 과거형 동사를 이용해서 답합니다.

Word Check

● 다음 들려주는 단어의 의미를 쓰세요.

	단어	의미
01	exercise	운동하다
02	fasten	
03	enough	
04	snowman	
05	present	
06	pardon	
07	handsome	
08	firefighter	
09	weekend	
10	attend	
11	wedding	
12	documentary	
13	awesome	
14	sandcastle	
15	field	

● 앞에 모의고사에 나오는 문장들을 잘 듣고, 빈칸을 완성하세요.

01 Cindy, _____ fasten _____ your _____ seat _____ _____ belt _____.

02 I exercised _____ _____ last night.

03 I _____ _____ _____ this morning.

04 We don't have _____ _____.

05 We have snow, and we can _____ _____ _____.

06 It's _____ the music room _____ the computer room.

07 Your uncle is very _____ and _____.

08 I have to _____ my uncle's _____.

09 I like _____ _____ on TV.

10 Can you _____ _____ _____?

11 My _____ _____ is spring.

12 We use a glove to _____ _____ _____.

13 I _____ _____ to the radio.

14 It _____ _____ _____ this morning.

15 I _____ _____ a _____ to school.

영어 듣기 모의고사

보통 속도

빠른 속도

| 학습일 | 월 일 | 부모님 확인 | 점수 |

1

다음을 듣고, 그림과 일치하는 설명을 고르시오. ·····························( )

① ② ③ ④

2

다음 대화를 듣고, 언제 나누는 대화인지 고르시오. ···························( )

① 위로할 때   ② 칭찬할 때
③ 헤어질 때   ④ 사과할 때

3

다음 대화를 듣고, 무엇에 관해 이야기하고 있는지 고르시오. ·················( )

① 좋아하는 과목   ② 좋아하는 과일
③ 아침식사   ④ 좋아하는 색깔

4

다음 그림을 보고, 그림과 일치하는 대화를 고르시오. ·······················( )

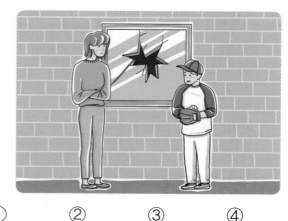

① ② ③ ④

5

다음 대화를 듣고, 대화가 자연스럽지 <u>않은</u> 것을 고르시오. ···················( )

① ② ③ ④

6

다음 대화를 듣고, 현재 날씨를 고르시오.
···································· (   )

①
② 
③ 
④

7

다음 대화를 듣고, 사진에서 여자 아이의 어머니를 고르시오. ···················· (   )

①   ②   ③   ④

8

다음 그림을 보고, 여자가 할 말로 알맞은 것을 고르시오. ···················· (   )

①   ②   ③   ④

9

다음 대화를 듣고, 남자가 슬퍼하는 이유를 고르시오. ························· (   )

① 물건을 잃어버려서
② 시합에 져서
③ 친구가 교통사고가 나서
④ 시험을 못 봐서

10

다음 대화를 듣고, 남자 아이의 장래 희망으로 알맞은 것을 고르시오. ·············· (   )

① 화가   ② 사진사
③ 의사   ④ 음악가

11

다음 대화를 듣고, 남자가 어젯밤에 한 일을 고르시오. ···················· (   )

① 영화 감상　　　② 숙제

③ 청소　　　　　④ 산책

12

다음 대화를 듣고, 두 사람이 만날 시각을 고르시오. ························· (   )

① 5시　　　　　② 5시 30분

③ 6시　　　　　④ 6시 30분

13

다음 대화를 듣고, 남자가 살 물건과 가격이 바르게 짝지어진 것을 고르시오. ······ (   )

① 10달러　　②  12달러

③  13달러　　④  20달러

14

다음 대화를 듣고, 대화가 이루어지는 장소를 고르시오. ······················ (   )

① 휴대전화기 판매점

② 분실물 보관소

③ 경찰서

④ 휴대전화기 수리점

15

다음을 듣고, 친구와 헤어질 때 할 수 있는 말을 고르시오. ···················· (   )

①　　　　②　　　　③　　　　④

16

다음 대화를 듣고, 두 사람이 어떤 관계인지 고르시오. ······················ (   )

① 의사 – 환자　　② 식당 종업원 – 손님

③ 학생 – 선생님　④ 호텔 직원 – 손님

17

다음 대화를 듣고, 두 사람이 만날 장소를 고르시오. ·············· (   )

① 지하철 역   ② 박물관 앞
③ 버스 정류장   ④ 집 앞

19

다음 대화를 듣고, 이어질 말로 알맞은 것을 고르시오. ·············· (   )

W _____

① Yes, I can walk fast.
② Good. See you then.
③ Where is the park?
④ The park is near my house.

18

다음 대화를 듣고, 이어질 말로 알맞은 것을 고르시오. ·············· (   )

M _____

① That's too bad.
② Sounds good.
③ I'm glad to meet you.
④ I have a good idea.

20

다음 대화를 듣고, 이어질 말로 적절하지 <u>않은</u> 것을 고르시오. ·············· (   )

B _____

① That's a good idea.
② That's too bad.
③ Okay. What time shall we meet?
④ Sorry. I can't swim.

| 학습일 | 월 일 | 부모님 확인 | 점수 |

● 잘 듣고, 빈칸에 알맞은 말을 쓰세요.

1

다음을 듣고, 그림과 일치하는 설명을 고르시오. ·························· (　　　)

① ② ③ ④

W: ❶ Please do not park here.

❷ Please _____ _____ _____ here.

❸ Please do not swim here.

❹ Please do not _____ here.

park 주차하다 | smoke 담배 피우다

2

다음 대화를 듣고, 언제 나누는 대화인지 고르시오. ·························· (　　　)

① 위로할 때 　　② 칭찬할 때
③ 헤어질 때 　　④ 사과할 때

W: Peter, what's wrong? You look sad.

M: Yes, I'm sad.

I _____ _____ _____.

W: Really? I'm _____ to hear that.

I hope you will find your dog _____.

M: Thank you.

look sad 슬퍼 보이다 | lost 잃어버리다(lose)의 과거형 | hope 바라다 | soon 곧

TIPS 남자가 개를 잃어버렸다고 하자 여자가 위로하는 대화입니다.

3

다음 대화를 듣고, 무엇에 관해 이야기하고 있는지 고르시오. ·························· (　　　)

① 좋아하는 과목 　　② 좋아하는 과일
③ 아침식사 　　④ 좋아하는 색깔

W: Tony, what do you eat for breakfast?

M: I have bananas for breakfast.

W: Do you _____ _____?

M: Yes, I do. How about you?

What's your _____ _____?

W: I like oranges.

breakfast 아침식사 | banana 바나나 | fruit 과일 | orange 오렌지

4

다음 그림을 보고, 그림과 일치하는 대화를 고르시오. ·················· (   )

①   ②   ③   ④

❶ W: Did you clean the window?

   B: No, I didn't.

❷ W: _____ is the girl _____ the window?

   B: She's my friend, Jessie.

❸ W: Would you close the _____?

   B: Okay.

❹ W: Did you _____ the _____?

   B: Yes, I did. I'm _____, Mom.

clean 청소하다 | window 창문 | break 깨다 | sorry 미안한

TIPS 남자 아이가 창문을 깬 상황에 가장 어울리는 대화를 고르세요.
by the window는 '창문 옆'이라는 의미로 by 대신 next to를 이용해서 next to the window라고 해도 됩니다.

5

다음 대화를 듣고, 대화가 자연스럽지 않은 것을 고르시오. ·················· (   )

①   ②   ③   ④

❶ G: When does your first class start?

   B: It _____ _____ 9 o'clock.

❷ G: Where are you going?

   B: I'm going to the station.

❸ G: Do you have any _____ or _____?

   B: No, they are _____ my brothers.

❹ G: What do you want for your birthday?

   B: I want a computer.

first 첫 번째 | class 수업 | station 역 | brothers or sisters 형제나 자매

TIPS Do you have brothers or sisters?에 대한 올바른 대답은 Yes, I have two older sisters.(응, 누나가 2명 있어.)나 No, I'm the only son.(아니, 외동아들이야.) 등입니다.

6

다음 대화를 듣고, 현재 날씨를 고르시오.
·················· (   )

①   ②

③    ④

W: Are you _____ _____?

B: Yes. How is the weather today?

W: It's _____. They said it's _____ _____ _____ in the afternoon.

go out 외출하다 | weather 날씨 | cloudy 흐린 | rain 비 오다 | in the afternoon 오후에

TIPS 현재는 흐리고 오후에 비가 온다고 했습니다.

7

다음 대화를 듣고, 사진에서 여자 아이의 어머니를 고르시오. ·········· (   )

①   ②   ③   ④

B: Is this your mother?

G: No, she's my aunt. My mom has long hair, and she is _____ _____ _____.

B: Is she wearing a _____ _____?

G: Yes, she's the one.

aunt 고모, 이모 | long hair 긴 머리 | thin 마른 | wear 입다

8

다음 그림을 보고, 여자가 할 말로 알맞은 것을 고르시오. ·········· (   )

①   ②   ③   ④

W: ① _____ _____ are these cookies?

② I'm baking cookies.

③ _____ _____ _____ these cookies.

④ What do you want to eat for lunch?

how much 얼마 | bake 굽다 | lunch 점심식사

TIPS 과자를 먹으라고 권하는 상황에 어울리는 말을 고르세요.
[Help yourself to + 음식]은 '음식을 마음껏 드세요'라는 의미입니다.

9

다음 대화를 듣고, 남자가 슬퍼하는 이유를 고르시오. ·········· (   )

① 물건을 잃어버려서
② 시합에 져서
③ 친구가 교통사고가 나서
④ 시험을 못 봐서

W: You look sad. What's the matter?

M: I studied hard, but I _____ the test.

W: _____ _____. I'm sure you will _____ _____ next time.

M: Thanks.

matter 일 | fail 실패하다 | test 시험 | cheer up 기운 내다 | sure 확실한 | better 더 나은 | next time 다음번에

TIPS fail the test는 시험에 불합격하다   pass the test 시험에 합격하다

10

다음 대화를 듣고, 남자 아이의 장래 희망으로 알맞은 것을 고르시오. ·········· (   )

① 화가   ② 사진사
③ 의사   ④ 음악가

G: Wow, this drawing is great. When did you draw this?

B: I _____ it last month.

G: I think you're really _____ _____ drawing.

B: Thank you. I want to be an artist in the future.

G: I think you will be a _____ _____.

draw 그리다 | be good at ~을 잘하다 | artist 화가, 예술가 | think 생각하다

11

다음 대화를 듣고, 남자가 어젯밤에 한 일을 고르시오. ·················· (   )

① 영화 감상   ② 숙제
③ 청소   ④ 산책

W: Mike, I _____ _____ last night, but your phone was off.

M: I _____ _____ _____ _____, so I turned it off.

W: I see. How was the movie?

M: It was really good.

call 전화하다 | last night 지난밤에 | movie 영화 | turn off 끄다

TIPS turn something off는 '(전기 · 가스 · 수도 등을) 끄다'라는 의미이고, turn something on은 '(전기 · 가스 · 수도 등을) 켜다'라는 의미입니다.

12

다음 대화를 듣고, 두 사람이 만날 시각을 고르시오. ·················· (   )

① 5시   ② 5시 30분
③ 6시   ④ 6시 30분

[Cellphone rings.]

B: Hello.

G: Hello, Jacob. This is Susan.
   Do you want to go to the K-pop concert with me tonight? The concert starts at 6:30.

B: Okay. What time shall we meet?

G: _____ _____ at 5.

B: That's _____ _____.
   How about _____?

G: Good.

concert 콘서트 | tonight 오늘 밤 | meet 만나다 | too early 너무 이른

13

다음 대화를 듣고, 남자가 살 물건과 가격이 바르게 짝지어진 것을 고르시오. ······ (   )

① 10달러   ② 12달러
③ 13달러   ④ 20달러

W: Good afternoon. May I help you?

M: I'm looking for a tie.

W: How about this one?

M: It looks good, but I want a _____ _____.

W: Then, how about this one?
   It's _____ _____.

M: It's nice. I'll _____ _____.

tie 넥타이 | take 사다

TIPS 넥타이는 necktie 또는 tie라고 말합니다.

14

다음 대화를 듣고, 대화가 이루어지는 장소를 고르시오. ················ (   )

① 휴대전화기 판매점
② 분실물 보관소
③ 경찰서
④ 휴대전화기 수리점

M: How can I help you?

W: My cellphone _____ _____.

M: Oh, I see. Let me take a look.

W: Can you _____ _____?

M: Yes. I think it will _____ _____ _____ to fix it.

cellphone 휴대폰 | **work** 작동하다 | **take a look** 보다 | **fix** 고치다

TIPS 동사 work은 '일하다'라는 의미 이외에 '(기계 장치 등이) 작동되다, 기능하다'라는 의미를 가지고 있습니다.

15

다음을 듣고, 친구와 헤어질 때 할 수 있는 말을 고르시오. ················ (   )

①   ②   ③   ④

W: ❶ How have you been?

   ❷ How are you doing?

   ❸ Bye! _____ _____.

   ❹ How is the _____ _____?

weather 날씨 | **today** 오늘

TIPS Take care.는 '몸 건강해, 조심해.'라는 의미로 헤어질 때 하는 인사말입니다.
A: How have you been? 어떻게 지냈니?
B: I've been good. 잘 지냈어.

16

다음 대화를 듣고, 두 사람이 어떤 관계인지 고르시오. ················ (   )

① 의사 – 환자   ② 식당 종업원 – 손님
③ 학생 – 선생님   ④ 호텔 직원 – 손님

M: Are you ready to _____?

W: Yes. I'll have the steak.

M: How would you like your steak?

W: _____, please.

M: What would you _____ _____ _____?

W: A Diet Coke, please.

order 주문하다 | **steak** 스테이크 | **medium** 중간 | **drink** 마시다

TIPS 고기 굽기 정도
rare: 가장 덜 익힌 상태   medium: 중간 정도 굽기
medium well: 중간보다 조금 더 구운 상태   well done: 바싹 구운 상태

17

다음 대화를 듣고, 두 사람이 만날 장소를 고르시오. ……………………… (   )

① 지하철 역   ② 박물관 앞
③ 버스 정류장   ④ 집 앞

[Cellphone rings.]

G: Hello.

B: Hello, Helen. _____ _____?

G: I'm going to the library tomorrow.

   Do you want to come with me?

B: Sure, _____ _____ shall we meet?

G: Let's meet at 3 o'clock at the _____

   _____.

B: Okay.

library 도서관 | tomorrow 내일 | meet 만나다 | bus stop 버스 정류장

TIPS What's up?은 '무슨 일이야?' 또는 '요즘 어때?', '잘 지냈어?(How are you doing?)' 등의 의미로 사용됩니다.

18

다음 대화를 듣고, 이어질 말로 알맞은 것을 고르시오. ……………………… (   )

M _____

① That's too bad.
② Sounds good.
③ I'm glad to meet you.
④ I have a good idea.

M: How are you today, Jessie?

W: Not good. I _____ _____ _____.

M: _____

have a cold 감기에 걸리다 | glad 기쁜 | idea 생각

TIPS 친구가 감기에 걸렸으므로, 위로하는 말이 오는 것이 어울립니다.
       That's too bad. 대신 I'm sorry to hear that.으로 대답해도 됩니다.

19

다음 대화를 듣고, 이어질 말로 알맞은 것을 고르시오. ……………………… (   )

W _____

① Yes, I can walk fast.
② Good. See you then.
③ Where is the park?
④ The park is near my house.

M: Sara, let's _____ _____

   _____ at the park tomorrow morning.

W: Sounds good.

M: _____ _____ _____ at 7

   in front of the park?

W: _____

take a walk 산책하다 | tomorrow morning 내일 아침 | in front of ~ 앞에 | then 그때 |
near 가까운

20

다음 대화를 듣고, 이어질 말로 적절하지 <u>않은</u> 것을 고르시오. ……………… (   )

B _____

① That's a good idea.
② That's too bad.
③ Okay. What time shall we meet?
④ Sorry. I can't swim.

G: Kevin, what are you going to do after school?

B: I'm going to read a book. _____?

G: It's hot today. Let's _____ _____.

B: _____

hot 더운 | go swimming 수영하러 가다

TIPS That's too bad.는 '그것 참 안됐다, (그렇다니) 유감이다.'라는 의미로
       [Let's + 동사원형~ .]('~하자')에 대한 대답으로 알맞지 않습니다.

● 다음 들려주는 단어의 의미를 쓰세요.

단어	의미
01 smoke	담배 피우다
02 hope	
03 soon	
04 fruit	
05 break	
06 bake	
07 matter	
08 fail	
09 sure	
10 artist	
11 tonight	
12 fix	
13 work	
14 glad	
15 then	

15 회 Sentence Check

● 앞에 모의고사에 나오는 문장들을 잘 듣고, 빈칸을 완성하세요.

01 Please _____do_____ _____not_____ _____smoke_____ here.

02 I hope you will _____ your dog _____.

03 Did you _____ _____ _____?

04 Do you have any _____ _____ _____?

05 They said it's _____ _____ _____ in the afternoon.

06 My mom has long hair, and she is _____ _____ _____.

07 _____ _____ to these cookies.

08 I studied hard, but I _____ _____ _____.

09 I'm sure you will _____ _____ next time.

10 I think you're really _____ _____ painting.

11 I called you last night, but your _____ _____ _____.

12 My cellphone _____ _____.

13 _____ _____ at 3 o'clock at the bus stop.

14 I'm _____ _____ _____ you.

15 Let's take a walk at the park _____ _____.

● 다음 단어들을 듣고, 뜻을 미리 알아보세요.

01	idea	생각
02	later	나중에
03	draw	그리다
04	flower	꽃
05	today	오늘
06	sandwich	샌드위치
07	weekend	주말
08	special	특별한
09	plan	계획
10	family	가족
11	happen	(일이) 일어나다
12	use	사용하다
13	mean	의미하다
14	fun	재미
15	stay	머무르다

16	job	직업
17	firefighter	소방관
18	remember	기억하다
19	gym	체육관
20	number	번호
21	rectangular	직사각형의
22	think	생각하다
23	competition	대회
24	here you are	여기 있다
25	live in	～에 살다
26	fried rice	볶음밥
27	go camping	캠핑 가다
28	a few minutes	몇 분
29	no problem	천만에
30	first prize	1등

● 다음 단어들을 듣고, 뜻을 미리 알아보세요.

01	kitchen	부엌	16	company	회사
02	ready	준비된	17	soon	곧
03	fly	날다	18	wrong	잘못된
04	beach	해변	19	wonderful	멋진
05	special	특별한	20	hurry	서두르다
06	usually	보통	21	plan	계획
07	library	도서관	22	grandparents	조부모
08	umbrella	우산	23	wash the dishes	설거지하다
09	phone	전화기	24	table tennis	탁구
10	cellphone	휴대폰	25	free time	여가 시간
11	sign	표지판	26	go out	외출하다
12	yesterday	어제	27	on Tuesdays	화요일마다
13	scientist	과학자	28	all day	하루 종일
14	nurse	간호사	29	wear glasses	안경을 쓰다
15	move	이사하다	30	so much	무척

● 다음 단어들을 듣고, 뜻을 미리 알아보세요.

01	chef	주방장	**16**	fever	열
02	sleepy	졸린	**17**	check	확인하다
03	flute	플루트	**18**	instead	대신에
04	guitar	기타	**19**	rest	휴식
05	right	맞는	**20**	people	사람들
06	turn	변하다, 바꾸다	**21**	great	훌륭한
07	borrow	빌리다	**22**	something	무언가
08	outside	밖에	**23**	flu	독감
09	pretty	꽤, 무척	**24**	wash a car	세차하다
10	season	계절	**25**	until late	늦게까지
11	autumn	가을	**26**	go to bed	자러 가다
12	present	선물	**27**	musical instrument	악기
13	show	보여주다	**28**	watch out	조심하다
14	whole	전체의	**29**	runny nose	콧물
15	center	중심지	**30**	fruit juice	과일 주스

4 회 **Voca**bulary

● 다음 단어들을 듣고, 뜻을 미리 알아보세요.

01	lend	빌려주다	**16**	kindness	친절
02	straight	곧장	**17**	prize	상
03	still	여전히	**18**	another	다른
04	dream	꿈	**19**	catch	잡다
05	lesson	수업	**20**	country	나라
06	classmate	반 친구	**21**	congratulations	축하해
07	cucumber	오이	**22**	pleasure	즐거움
08	each	각각	**23**	hospital	병원
09	magazine	잡지	**24**	turn right	오른쪽으로 돌다
10	return	돌려주다	**25**	be over	끝나다
11	light	가벼운	**26**	in the middle of	~의 가운데에
12	park	공원, 주차하다	**27**	this afternoon	오늘 오후
13	usually	보통	**28**	by bus	버스로
14	walk	산책시키다	**29**	go fishing	낚시하러 가다
15	cellphone	휴대폰	**30**	a little	조금

● 다음 단어들을 듣고, 뜻을 미리 알아보세요.

01	news	소식	16	question	질문
02	past	~을 지나서	17	exciting	흥미진진한
03	zoo	동물원	18	cereal	시리얼
04	order	주문하다	19	really	정말
05	during	~ 동안	20	first	처음의
06	table tennis	탁구	21	together	함께
07	subject	과목	22	Korean food	한국 음식
08	myself	나 자신	23	have a haircut	머리를 자르다
09	baker	제빵사	24	swimming pool	수영장
10	special	특별한	25	every Friday	금요일마다
11	paint	페인트칠하다	26	in the future	장래에
12	invite	초대하다	27	take pictures	사진을 찍다
13	sure	물론, 그럼	28	car accident	자동차 사고
14	headache	두통	29	cheer up	기운 내다
15	better	더 나은	30	every day	매일

6 ^회 Vocabulary

● 다음 단어들을 듣고, 뜻을 미리 알아보세요.

01	onion	양파	16	tent	텐트
02	thirsty	목마른	17	bring	가져다주다
03	practice	연습하다	18	idea	생각
04	park	공원, 주차하다	19	noodles	국수
05	hold	들다	20	Internet	인터넷
06	crayon	크레용	21	anything else	그밖에 다른 것
07	whose	누구의	22	stay up late	늦게까지 안 자다
08	guess	추측하다	23	take a walk	산책하다
09	essay	에세이	24	go to bed	자러 가다
10	contest	대회	25	art class	미술 수업
11	catch	잡다	26	over there	저쪽에
12	water	물을 주다	27	first prize	1등
13	twice	두 번	28	be proud of	～이 자랑스럽다
14	cousin	사촌	29	feel well	건강이 좋다
15	cellphone	휴대폰	30	take some medicine	약을 좀 먹다

● 다음 단어들을 듣고, 뜻을 미리 알아보세요.

01	together	함께	16	floor	바닥, 마루
02	tonight	오늘 밤, 오늘 저녁	17	pet	반려동물
03	camera	카메라	18	think	생각하다
04	weather	날씨	19	cheap	싼
05	beach	해변	20	popular	인기 있는
06	strawberry	딸기	21	teens	십대
07	already	이미, 벌써	22	veterinarian	수의사
08	different	다른	23	wake up	일어나다
09	trip	여행	24	for a minute	잠깐
10	fun	재미	25	in the future	장래에
11	concert	음악회	26	comedy	코미디
12	station	역	27	romance movie	로맨스 영화
13	subway	지하철	28	hurry up	서두르다
14	far	먼	29	take care of	~을 돌보다
15	anything	아무것	30	feel good	기분이 좋다

● 다음 단어들을 듣고, 뜻을 미리 알아보세요.

01	really	정말
02	put	놓다
03	call	전화하다
04	yesterday	어제
05	congratulations	축하해
06	picture	사진
07	glasses	안경
08	weekend	주말
09	sick	아픈
10	pear	배
11	favorite	좋아하는
12	hobby	취미
13	cafeteria	구내식당
14	snack	과자
15	check	확인하다

16	smartphone	스마트폰
17	baker	제빵사
18	plan	계획
19	floor	바닥
20	lie	눕다
21	salad	샐러드
22	medium-sized	중간 크기의
23	be good at	~을 잘하다
24	have a cold	감기 걸리다
25	how many	얼마나 많이
26	have lunch	점심을 먹다
27	swimming lesson	수영 수업
28	last night	지난밤
29	anything else	뭐 다른 것
30	birthday party	생일 파티

● 다음 단어들을 듣고, 뜻을 미리 알아보세요.

01	here	여기	16	know	알다
02	subject	과목	17	soon	곧
03	cheese	치즈	18	campfire	모닥불
04	where	어디	19	mountain	산
05	toothache	치통	20	happen	일어나다
06	dentist	치과의사	21	second	두 번째
07	again	또, 다시	22	grade	학년
08	lovely	사랑스러운	23	watch out	조심하다
09	same	같은	24	take a walk	산책하다
10	stage	무대	25	fried rice	볶음밥
11	sunglasses	선글라스	26	go to school	학교에 가다
12	minute	분	27	set up	세우다
13	near	가까운	28	younger brother	남동생
14	kick	차다	29	movie ticket	영화표
15	sign	표지판	30	be gone	사라지다

10회 Vocabulary

● 다음 단어들을 듣고, 뜻을 미리 알아보세요.

01	trash	쓰레기
02	beautiful	아름다운
03	ask	묻다
04	cool	멋진
05	season	계절
06	because	왜냐하면
07	under	~ 아래에
08	straight	곧장, 똑바로
09	parents	부모
10	show	(길 등을) 가리키다
11	way	길
12	corner	모퉁이
13	between	~ 사이에
14	practice	연습하다
15	feather	깃털

16	wing	날개
17	bookstore	서점
18	afternoon	오후
19	choice	선택
20	yet	아직
21	festival	축제
22	turn on	(불 등을) 켜다
23	pick up	줍다
24	last weekend	지난 주말
25	wash one's car	세차하다
26	colorful leaf	단풍
27	remote control	리모컨
28	until late	늦게까지
29	get off	내리다
30	summer vacation	여름 방학

● 다음 단어들을 듣고, 뜻을 미리 알아보세요.

01	worry	걱정하다	16	absent	결석한
02	everything	모든 것	17	practice	연습하다
03	notebook	공책	18	diligent	부지런한
04	park	주차하다	19	hobby	취미
05	sleepy	졸린	20	clean	청소하다
06	tomorrow	내일	21	cellphone	휴대전화
07	language	언어	22	over there	저쪽에
08	contest	대회	23	until midnight	자정까지
09	usually	보통	24	weather report	일기예보
10	near	가까운	25	take care of	～을 돌보다
11	start	시작하다	26	bus stop	버스 정류장
12	bowling	볼링	27	living room	거실
13	headache	두통	28	every weekend	주말마다
14	garage	차고	29	sick in bed	아파서 누워 있는
15	socks	양말	30	fairy tale	동화

● 다음 단어들을 듣고, 뜻을 미리 알아보세요.

01	pleasure	즐거움	16	package	소포
02	goodbye	잘 가	17	different	여러 가지의
03	delicious	맛있는	18	member	회원
04	sandwich	샌드위치	19	clock	시계
05	join	함께하다	20	club	동아리
06	because	왜냐하면	21	aquarium	수족관, 아쿠아리움
07	art	미술	22	on the wall	벽에
08	interesting	재미있는	23	get up	일어나다
09	become	~이 되다	24	make dinner	저녁을 만들다
10	arm	팔	25	I see	알다
11	stairs	계단	26	fall down	넘어지다
12	slip	미끄러지다	27	at night	밤에
13	ice	얼음	28	by airmail	항공우편으로
14	rectangular	직사각형의	29	next to	~ 옆에
15	furniture	가구	30	eat out	외식하다

● 다음 단어들을 듣고, 뜻을 미리 알아보세요.

01	light	빛, 불
02	speak	말하다
03	language	언어
04	market	시장
05	comedy	코미디
06	park	공원, 주차하다
07	bookstore	서점
08	pants	바지
09	check	확인하다
10	think	생각하다
11	writer	작가
12	sick	아픈
13	practice	연습하다
14	contest	대회
15	concert	콘서트

16	aquarium	수족관
17	straight	곧장
18	room	방
19	pass	건네다
20	first	먼저
21	month	달
22	a little	조금
23	wake up	일어나다
24	good night	잘 자
25	turn on	(불 등을) 켜다
26	watch movies	영화를 보다
27	runny nose	콧물
28	feel better	더 낫다
29	police officer	경찰
30	no problem	문제없다

14회  Vocabulary

● 다음 단어들을 듣고, 뜻을 미리 알아보세요.

01	exercise	운동하다	16	attend	참석하다
02	jog	조깅하다	17	wedding	결혼
03	again	또, 다시	18	program	프로그램
04	start	시작하다	19	documentary	다큐멘터리
05	enough	충분한	20	awesome	굉장한, 멋진
06	warm	따뜻한	21	season	계절
07	snowman	눈사람	22	often	자주
08	present	선물	23	field	경기장
09	between	~ 사이에	24	sandcastle	모래성
10	pardon	뭐라고	25	fasten one's seat belt	안전벨트를 매다
11	handsome	잘생긴	26	toy train	장난감 기차
12	firefighter	소방관	27	science room	과학실
13	too	역시	28	listen to music	음악을 듣다
14	thirsty	목마른	29	last Sunday	지난 일요일
15	weekend	주말	30	by subway	지하철로

15회 Vocabulary

● 다음 단어들을 듣고, 뜻을 미리 알아보세요.

01	smoke	담배 피우다	16	fix	고치다
02	hope	바라다	17	steak	스테이크
03	soon	곧	18	work	작동하다
04	fruit	과일	19	medium	중간
05	break	깨다	20	glad	기쁜
06	station	역	21	idea	생각
07	thin	마른	22	then	그때
08	bake	굽다	23	brothers or sisters	형제나 자매
09	matter	일, 문제	24	go out	외출하다
10	fail	실패하다	25	in the afternoon	오후에
11	sure	확실한	26	cheer up	기운 내다
12	artist	예술가, 화가	27	turn off	(불 등을) 끄다
13	tonight	오늘 밤, 오늘 저녁	28	take a walk	산책하다
14	tie	넥타이	29	in front of	～ 앞에
15	cellphone	휴대폰	30	go swimming	수영하러 가다

Listening mentor joy

Longman

LEVEL **4**

정답 및 해석

Pearson

Longman

Listening mentor joy

정답 및 해석

4
LEVEL

Pearson

1회 영어 듣기 모의고사

본책 p. 06

1 ④	**2** ③	**3** ③	**4** ②	**5** ④	**6** ②	**7** ②	**8** ②	**9** ①	**10** ②
11 ③	**12** ④	**13** ③	**14** ③	**15** ④	**16** ②	**17** ③	**18** ②	**19** ④	**20** ④

듣기 대본
본책 p. 10

1 W: Jim, where is your bag?
　 B: It's in front of the desk.

2 M: ① See you later.
　　　② That's a good idea.
　　　③ I'd love to, but I can't.
　　　④ Here you are.

3 B: Jina, what are you doing?
　 G: I'm drawing.
　 B: What are you drawing?
　 G: I'm drawing flowers.

4 M: I am small. I live in a pond.
　　　I can jump high with my legs.

5 G: What did you eat for lunch today?
　 B: I had fried rice. How about you?
　 G: I had a sandwich.
　 B: What kind of sandwich did you have?
　 G: I had a cheese sandwich.

6 G: Tony, what are you going to do this weekend?
　 B: I will visit my grandparents.
　 G: Where do they live?
　 B: They live in Suwon. Do you have any special plans?
　 G: I'll go camping with my family.

7 G: ① What day is it today?
　　　② What happened to your leg?
　　　③ Can I use your computer?
　　　④ What's your name?

8 W: Is your brother in this room?
　 M: Yes, he's over there.
　 W: Do you mean the boy with long hair?
　 M: No, he has short hair. He is playing with a ball.

해석

1 W: 짐, 네 가방 어디에 있니?
　 B: 책상 앞에 있어요.

2 M: ① 나중에 봐.
　　　② 좋은 생각이야.
　　　③ 나도 그러고 싶은데 할 수 없어.
　　　④ 여기 있어.

3 B: 지나야, 뭐하고 있어?
　 G: 나 그림 그리고 있어.
　 B: 무엇을 그리고 있니?
　 G: 나는 꽃을 그리고 있어.

4 M: 나는 작다. 나는 연못에서 산다.
　　　나는 내 다리로 높이 뛰어오를 수 있다.

5 G: 오늘 점심에 뭐 먹었어?
　 B: 나 볶음밥 먹었어. 너는 어때?
　 G: 나는 샌드위치 먹었어.
　 B: 무슨 샌드위치 먹었어?
　 G: 나는 치즈 샌드위치 먹었어.

6 G: 토니야, 이번 주말에 뭐할 거야?
　 B: 조부모님 댁에 방문할 거야.
　 G: 어디에 사시는데?
　 B: 수원에 사셔. 너는 특별한 계획 있어?
　 G: 나는 가족이랑 캠핑을 갈 거야.

7 G: ① 오늘 무슨 요일이야?
　　　② 너 다리에 무슨 일이야?
　　　③ 네 컴퓨터를 사용해도 되니?
　　　④ 네 이름이 뭐야?

8 W: 네 남동생이 이 방에 있니?
　 M: 응, 저기에 있어.
　 W: 긴 머리 소년을 말하는 거야?
　 M: 아니, 짧은 머리야. 공을 갖고 놀고 있어.

9 G: What did you do yesterday, Jim?
B: I went to the zoo.
G: Did you have fun?
B: Yes, very much. How was your weekend?
Did you go camping?
G: No, I stayed home and did my homework.

10 M: How's the weather today? Is it sunny?
W: No, it isn't. It's cloudy.
M: Is it cold?
W: No, it isn't, but it's windy.

11 G: What does your father do?
B: Do you mean my father's job?
G: Yes.
B: He's a firefighter. His job is to put out fires.

12 W: May I help you?
M: Yes, I'm looking for some potatoes.
W: They're over there. How many potatoes do
you need?
M: I need six.

13 M: What are you doing, Cindy?
G: I'm looking for my baseball cap. Did you see it?
M: Yes, I saw it on the desk over there a few
minutes ago.
G: Oh, thanks.
M: No problem.

14 B: Do you remember our plan for tomorrow?
G: Sure. The basketball game starts at 7 o'clock.
What time shall we meet?
B: How about 6 o'clock?
G: That's too early. Let's meet at 6:30 in front of
the gym.
B: Okay. See you then.

15 M: How can I help you?
W: I left my bag on the bus yesterday.
M: Do you remember the bus number?
W: I took bus number 30.
M: What does your bag look like?
W: It is red and rectangular.

9 G: 어제 뭐했어, 짐?
B: 나 동물원에 갔어.
G: 재미있었어?
B: 응, 아주 많이. 네 주말은 어땠어?
캠핑 갔니?
G: 아니, 집에 있으면서 숙제를 했어.

10 M: 오늘 날씨 어때? 맑니?
W: 아니, 흐려.
M: 추워?
W: 아니, 하지만 바람이 불어.

11 G: 너의 아버지는 뭐하시니?
B: 아버지 직업을 묻는 거야?
G: 응.
B: 소방관이셔. 그의 일은 불을 끄는 거야.

12 W: 도와드릴까요?
M: 예. 감자를 좀 찾고 있어요.
W: 저쪽에 있어요. 감자가 얼마나 필요하시죠?
M: 여섯 개 필요해요.

13 M: 신디, 뭐하고 있어?
G: 내 야구모자를 찾고 있어요. 보셨어요?
M: 응, 몇 분 전에 저기 책상 위에서 봤어.
G: 오, 감사해요.
M: 천만에.

14 B: 내일 우리 계획 기억하지?
G: 물론. 야구 경기가 7시에 시작하잖아.
우리 몇 시에 만날까?
B: 6시 어때?
G: 너무 일러. 체육관 앞에서 6시 30분에 만나자.
B: 좋아. 그때 보자.

15 M: 어떻게 도와드릴까요?
W: 어제 버스에 가방을 두고 내렸어요.
M: 버스 번호 기억하시나요?
W: 30번 버스를 탔어요.
M: 가방이 어떻게 생겼나요?
W: 빨간색이고 직사각형 모양이에요.

16 ① B: What did you do last Sunday?
G: I went shopping.
② B: <u>How was</u> your vacation?
G: I went there <u>by train</u>.
③ B: What do you think of my picture?
G: Wow, you're very good at painting.
④ B: What do you want to be in the future?
G: I want to be a <u>pianist</u>.

16 ① B: 지난 일요일에 뭐했어?
G: 쇼핑했어.
② B: 방학 어땠어?
G: 나는 기차를 타고 갔어.
③ B: 내 그림 어떻게 생각해?
G: 와우, 너 그림 무척 잘 그리네.
④ B: 장래에 뭐가 되고 싶어?
G: 나는 피아니스트가 되고 싶어.

17 W: ① Where is your computer?
② Can I play computer games?
③ Could you <u>stop playing</u> the computer game?
④ Whose computer is this?

17 W: ① 네 컴퓨터는 어디에 있니?
② 컴퓨터 게임을 해도 되나요?
③ 컴퓨터 게임을 그만할래?
④ 이것은 누구의 컴퓨터니?

18 B: You <u>look happy</u> today.
Do you have any good news?
G: Yes, I won <u>first prize</u> in the English language competition.
B: ① That's too bad.
② Wow! <u>Congratulations</u>!
③ See you later.
④ It's warm and windy.

18 B: 너 오늘 행복해 보여.
무슨 좋은 소식이 있니?
G: 응, 나 영어 경시 대회에서 1등을 했어.
B: ① 그거 안됐다.
② 와우! 축하해!
③ 나중에 보자.
④ 따뜻하고 바람이 불어.

19 M: Do you like dogs, Amy?
W: Yes, I love dogs. <u>What about</u> you?
M: I like dogs very much.
W: Do you like cats, too?
M: ① No, I don't have any pets.
② There are three cats over there.
③ Yes, I want a dog.
④ Yes, I love all animals.

19 M: 너 개를 좋아하니, 에이미?
W: 응, 나 개를 사랑해. 너는 어때?
M: 나는 개를 매우 좋아해.
W: 고양이도 좋아하니?
M: ① 아니, 나는 반려동물이 하나도 없어.
② 저기에 고양이 세 마리가 있어.
③ 응, 나는 개를 원해.
④ 응, 나는 모든 동물을 사랑해.

20 M: May I help you?
W: I'd like a sandwich, please.
M: <u>Anything to drink</u>?
W: ① Yes, I have some water.
② I don't drink coffee.
③ No, we don't have milk.
④ Orange juice, please.

20 M: 도와드릴까요?
W: 샌드위치 주세요.
M: 마실 것은요?
W: ① 예, 저는 물이 좀 있어요.
② 저는 커피를 마시지 않아요.
③ 아니요, 우리는 우유가 없어요.
④ 오렌지 주스 주세요.

Word Check
본책 p. 16

01 나중에	**04** 특별한	**07** 의미하다	**10** 기억하다	**13** 직사각형의
02 샌드위치	**05** 계획	**08** 머무르다	**11** 체육관	**14** 생각하다
03 주말	**06** 일어나다	**09** 소방관	**12** 번호	**15** 대회, 경쟁

Sentence Check

01 That's a good idea.
02 I can jump high with my legs.
03 I will visit my grandparents.
04 He is playing with a ball.
05 I stayed home and did my homework.
06 His job is to put out fires.
07 I'm looking for some potatoes.
08 I saw it on the desk over there a few minutes ago.
09 The basketball game starts at 7 o'clock.
10 Let's meet at 6:30 in front of the gym.
11 I left my bag on the bus yesterday.
12 You're very good at painting.
13 I won first prize in the English language competition.
14 That's too bad.
15 Anything to drink?

2회 영어 듣기 모의고사

1 ③	**2** ③	**3** ④	**4** ②	**5** ②	**6** ③	**7** ③	**8** ③	**9** ②	**10** ②
11 ③	**12** ③	**13** ④	**14** ③	**15** ②	**16** ②	**17** ②	**18** ①	**19** ②	**20** ①

듣기 대본

1 W: Where is Jim?
　　M: He's in the kitchen.
　　W: Is he cooking?
　　M: No, he's washing the dishes.

2 B: Jina, what's your favorite sport?
　　G: I like table tennis. How about you?
　　B: I like soccer. Do you like soccer?
　　G: No, I don't, but I like baseball.
　　B: I like baseball, too.

3 M: ① Are you ready to go?
　　　② Have some more pizza.
　　　③ Do you need any help?
　　　④ Happy birthday, Alice. This is for you.

4 M: I am a bird, but I can't fly.
　　　I'm good at swimming and I like to eat fish.

5 G: Mike, what are you going to do after school?
　　B: I don't have any special plans.
　　G: Then, can you help me do my math homework?
　　B: Sure. Let's meet at the library at 4.
　　G: Okay.

6 W: What do you do in your free time?
　　M: I play computer games. How about you?
　　W: I usually play the piano or read books.
　　M: That's good. I like reading, too.

해석

1 W: 짐 어디에 있어?
　　M: 부엌에 있어.
　　W: 요리하고 있니?
　　M: 아니, 설거지하고 있어.

2 B: 지나, 네가 좋아하는 운동이 뭐야?
　　G: 나는 탁구를 좋아해. 너는 어때?
　　B: 나는 축구를 좋아해. 너 축구 좋아하니?
　　G: 아니, 하지만 나는 야구는 좋아해.
　　B: 나도 야구 좋아해.

3 B: ① 갈 준비됐니?
　　　② 피자를 좀 더 먹어.
　　　③ 도움이 필요하니?
　　　④ 생일 축하해, 엘리스. 이거 너를 위한 거야.

4 M: 나는 새지만 날 수 없다. 나는 수영을 잘하고 물고기 먹는 것을 좋아한다.

5 G: 마이크, 방과 후에 뭐할 거야?
　　B: 특별한 일은 없어.
　　G: 그러면, 내 수학 숙제 도와줄 수 있니?
　　B: 물론. 도서관에서 4시에 만나자.
　　G: 좋아

6 W: 여가 시간에 뭐해?
　　M: 컴퓨터 게임을 해. 너는 어때?
　　W: 나는 보통 피아노를 치거나 책을 읽어.
　　M: 좋네. 나도 책 읽는 것을 좋아해.

7
W: Are you going out?
M: Yes, I'm going to the library now.
W: I think you should take an umbrella.
M: Is it raining now?
W: No, it's not, but it looks like it will rain soon.

7
W: 나갈 거야?
M: 응, 지금 도서관에 갈 거야.
W: 너 우산을 가져가야 할 거 같아.
M: 지금 비가 오고 있어?
W: 아니, 하지만 곧 비가 올 거 같아.

8
M: Julie, what are you doing?
W: I'm talking on the phone.
M: Look at that sign.
   You can't use your cellphone here.
W: Oh! I see. I didn't know that.

8
M: 줄리, 뭐하고 있어?
W: 나 휴대폰으로 통화하고 있어.
M: 저기 표지판을 봐.
   여기서는 휴대폰을 사용할 수 없어.
W: 오! 알았어. 그걸 몰랐어.

9
M: Stella, where are you going?
W: I'm going to the shopping mall.
M: What day is it today?
   Is it Tuesday or Wednesday?
W: It's Tuesday.
M: The shopping mall is closed on Tuesdays.

9
M: 스텔라, 어디 가고 있어?
W: 쇼핑몰에 가고 있어.
M: 오늘 무슨 요일이야?
   화요일 아니면 수요일?
W: 화요일이야.
M: 쇼핑몰은 화요일마다 문을 닫아.

10
G: Did you go camping yesterday?
B: No, I didn't.
G: Why? Were you busy?
B: No, I was sick, so I stayed home all day.
G: Oh, that's too bad.

10
G: 어제 캠핑 갔니?
B: 아니, 안 갔어.
G: 왜? 바빴어?
B: 아니, 아파서 집에서 하루 종일 있었어.
G: 오, 그거 안됐다.

11
B: What do you want to be in the future?
G: I'd like to be a scientist. How about you, Mike?
B: I want to be a nurse like my mother.
G: Your mom is a nurse?
B: Yes. She works at the hospital next to our school.

11
B: 너는 장래에 무엇이 되고 싶어?
G: 나는 과학자가 되고 싶어. 너는 어때, 마이크?
B: 나는 어머니처럼 간호사가 되고 싶어.
G: 네 엄마가 간호사셔?
B: 응. 우리 학교 옆에 있는 병원에서 일하고 계셔.

12
B: Hello, everyone. I'm John Brown. I'm from Canada. I moved to Seoul last year. My dad works at a computer company here in Korea. I like playing baseball. My favorite food is pizza. I'm happy to meet you.

12
B: 안녕, 여러분. 나는 존 브라운이야. 나는 캐나다에서 왔어. 나는 작년에 서울로 이사왔어. 나의 아빠는 여기 한국에 있는 컴퓨터 회사에 다니셔. 나는 야구하는 것을 좋아해. 내가 좋아하는 음식은 피자야. 여러분을 만나서 반가워.

13
B: What's for lunch today?
W: I'm making fried rice. Do you like it?
B: Yes, that's one of my favorite foods.
W: Good. Lunch will be ready soon. Wash your hands before lunch.
B: Okay.

13
B: 오늘 점심이 뭐예요?
W: 볶음밥을 만들고 있어. 너 좋아하니?
B: 예, 제가 좋아하는 음식 중 하나예요.
W: 잘됐다. 점심이 곧 준비될 거야.
   점심식사 전에 손을 씻어라.
B: 알겠어요.

14 ① M: What's wrong?

W: I have a headache.

② M: Cathy, what are you doing?

W: I'm cleaning my room.

③ M: Where shall we meet tomorrow?

W: Let's meet at 7 o'clock.

④ M: How was your summer vacation?

W: It was wonderful.

14 ① M: 무슨 일이야?

W: 나 두통이 있어.

② M: 캐시, 뭐하고 있어?

W: 나 내 방을 청소하고 있어.

③ M: 내일 어디에서 만날까?

W: 7시에 만나자.

④ M: 네 여름휴가가 어땠어?

W: 멋졌어.

15 G: Jim, where are you going?

B: I'm going to the shopping mall.

G: Why?

B: I'm going to buy a birthday present for my older brother. Tomorrow is his birthday.

G: He is turning sixteen years old, isn't he?

B: No, he's turning fourteen years old.

15 G: 짐, 어디 가고 있니?

B: 나 쇼핑몰에 가고 있어.

G: 왜?

B: 형의 생일 선물을 사려고 가고 있어. 내일이 형 생일이야.

G: 16살이 되지, 그렇지 않니?

B: 아니, 14살이 돼.

16 M: Where is your sister, Minji?

W: She's over there. She's wearing a skirt.

M: Do you mean the girl wearing glasses?

W: No, she's not wearing glasses. She has a book in her hand.

M: Oh, I found her.

16 M: 네 여동생 어디에 있어, 민지?

W: 저쪽에 있어. 치마를 입고 있어.

M: 안경 쓴 소녀 말하는 거야?

W: 아니, 안경을 쓰지 않아. 손에 책을 들고 있어.

M: 오, 찾았어.

17 G: Billy, what time does the swimming class start?

B: It starts at 5:30.

G: What time is it now?

B: It's ten past five.

G: Really? Let's hurry.

17 G: 빌리, 몇 시에 수영 수업이 시작하니?

B: 수영 수업은 5시 30분에 시작해.

G: 지금 몇 시야?

B: 5시 10분이야.

G: 정말? 서두르자.

18 G: Do you have any plans after school?

B: No, I don't.

G: Then, let's go swimming.

B: ① That's a good idea.

② You had a great time.

③ Yes, I need some water.

④ Thank you so much.

18 G: 방과 후에 계획 있니?

B: 아니, 없어.

G: 그러면, 수영하러 가자.

B: ① 좋은 생각이야.

② 즐거운 시간 보냈구나.

③ 응, 나 물이 좀 필요해.

④ 무척 고마워.

19 W: What are you going to do this weekend?

M: I'm going to visit my grandparents. How about you?

W: I am going to the beach with my cousins.

M: Have a good weekend, Cindy. See you on Monday.

W: ① I want to talk to you.

② You too! See you later.

③ Long time no see.

④ I don't feel good today.

19 W: 이번 주말에 뭐할 거야?

M: 조부모님 댁에 방문할 거야. 너는 어때?

W: 나는 사촌들과 해변에 갈 거야.

M: 즐거운 주말 보내, 신디. 월요일에 봐.

W: ① 너랑 말하고 싶어.

② 너도! 나중에 봐.

③ 오랜만이야.

④ 나 오늘 기분이 좋지 않아.

20 W: May I help you?
M: Yes, I'm <u>looking for</u> a T-shirt.
W: <u>How about</u> this red one?
M: ① No, I don't have money.
② It looks good, but I want a yellow shirt.
③ How much is it?
④ It's too small for me. Do you have one in a larger size?

20 W: 도와드릴까요?
M: 예, 티셔츠를 찾고 있어요.
W: 이 빨간 것은 어때요?
M: ① 아니요, 나는 돈이 없어요.
② 좋아 보여요, 하지만 저는 노란 티셔츠를 원해요.
③ 얼마예요?
④ 저한테 너무 작아요. 더 큰 사이즈 있나요?

Word Check
본책 p. 28

01 해변
02 부엌
03 보통
04 여가 시간
05 특별한
06 선물
07 휴대폰
08 표지판
09 간호사
10 회사
11 곧
12 잘못된
13 멋진
14 서두르다
15 조부모

Sentence Check
본책 p. 29

01 Have some **more pizza**.
02 I'm good at **swimming and I like to eat fish**.
03 I don't have any **special plans**.
04 I usually play **the piano or read books**.
05 I think **you should take an umbrella**.
06 It looks like it will **rain soon**.
07 You can't use your **cellphone here**.
08 The shopping mall is closed **on Tuesdays**.
09 I was sick, so I stayed home **all day**.
10 I want to be a nurse **like my mother**.
11 My dad works at a **computer company here in Korea**.
12 Lunch will **be ready soon**.
13 I'm going to buy a birthday present for my **older brother**.
14 She has a book **in her hand**.
15 Have a **good weekend**.

3회 영어 듣기 모의고사
본책 p. 30

| 1 ④ | 2 ④ | 3 ② | 4 ② | 5 ① | 6 ④ | 7 ③ | 8 ② | 9 ③ | 10 ② |
| 11 ③ | 12 ① | 13 ④ | 14 ③ | 15 ② | 16 ② | 17 ③ | 18 ④ | 19 ① | 20 ② |

본책 p. 34

1 ① W: Is he cooking?
M: No, he's <u>washing</u> the car.
② W: What does your mother do?
M: She's a <u>chef</u>.
③ W: Would you like something to drink?
M: Orange juice, please.
④ W: Would you like to <u>try this cake</u>?
M: Sure, thanks.

1 ① W: 그는 요리하고 있니?
M: 아니, 그는 세차하고 있어.
② W: 네 어머니 뭐하셔?
M: 주방장이셔.
③ W: 뭐 마실래요?
M: 오렌지주스 주세요.
④ W: 이 케이크 먹어볼래?
M: 물론, 고마워.

2 B: I'm so sleepy.
G: What did you do last night?
B: I did my homework <u>until</u> <u>late</u> at night.
G: What time did you go to bed?
B: I <u>went</u> <u>to</u> <u>bed</u> at 11:40 and got up at 5:30 today.

2 B: 나 무척 졸려.
G: 어젯밤에 뭐했니?
B: 밤에 늦게까지 숙제를 했거든.
G: 몇 시에 자러 갔는데?
B: 11시 40분에 자서 오늘 5시 30분에 일어났어.

3 B: Michelle, can you play the flute?
G: Yes, I can.
B: What other musical instruments can you play?
G: I can <u>play</u> the <u>piano</u> and the <u>violin</u>. How about you?
B: I can play the <u>guitar</u>.

3 B: 미쉘, 너 플루트 연주할 수 있니?
G: 응, 할 수 있어.
B: 다른 악기는 무엇을 연주할 수 있어?
G: 피아노랑 바이올린을 연주할 수 있어. 너는 어때?
B: 나는 기타를 칠 수 있어.

4 B: Is your mother in this picture?
G: Yes, my mom has <u>long</u> <u>hair</u> and is wearing a skirt.
B: Is this your mother?
G: No, she isn't. She's wearing a <u>blue</u> <u>skirt</u>.
B: Oh, this is your mom. Right?
G: <u>That's</u> <u>right</u>.

4 B: 이 사진에 네 어머니가 계시니?
G: 응, 나의 엄마는 긴 머리에 치마를 입고 계셔.
B: 이분이 네 어머니셔?
G: 아니야. 엄마는 파란 치마를 입고 계셔.
B: 오, 이분이 네 엄마구나. 맞지?
G: 맞아.

5 B: ① Let's <u>wait</u> <u>for</u> the red light to turn green.
② <u>Watch</u> <u>out</u>! There is a car coming.
③ Can I borrow your bike?
④ Let's play outside.

5 B: ① 빨간불이 초록불로 바뀔 때까지 기다려요.
② 조심하세요! 차가 오고 있어요.
③ 당신 자전거 빌릴 수 있나요?
④ 밖에서 놀아요.

6 M: I'm going to have a <u>birthday</u> <u>party</u>. Can you come?
W: Sure. When is the party?
M: It's <u>on</u> <u>July</u> 10.
W: Okay. See you then.

6 M: 생일 파티를 할 거야. 올 수 있니?
W: 물론이지. 파티가 언제야?
M: 7월 10일이야.
W: 알았어. 그때 보자.

7 B: Alice, do you like spring?
G: Yes, I do. How about you, Tony?
B: I like spring, too. But my <u>favorite</u> <u>season</u> is autumn.
G: <u>Why</u> do you like autumn most?
B: I like <u>cool</u> <u>weather</u>.

7 B: 앨리스, 봄 좋아하니?
G: 응, 그래. 너는 어때, 토니?
B: 나도 봄을 좋아해. 하지만 내가 가장 좋아하는 계절은 가을이야.
G: 왜 가을을 가장 좋아해?
B: 나는 시원한 날씨가 좋아.

8 W: May I help you?
B: Yes, I'm looking for a <u>present</u> for my sister.
W: How about this Barbie doll?
B: She has many Barbie dolls. Can you show me the <u>teddy</u> <u>bear</u> over there?
W: Do you mean this one?
B: Yes, <u>how</u> <u>much</u> is it?

8 W: 도와드릴까요?
B: 예, 여동생을 위한 선물을 찾고 있어요.
W: 이 바비인형은 어때요?
B: 바비인형이 많이 있어요. 저기에 있는 테디베어 보여주시겠어요?
W: 이거 말하는 거예요?
B: 예, 얼마예요?

9 G: How was your weekend, Minsu?
B: It was great. I visited my grandparents.
G: Where do they live?
B: They live in Incheon. How about you? Did you have a good weekend?
G: No, I didn't. I stayed home the whole weekend because I was sick.

9 G: 주말 어땠어, 민수야?
B: 좋았어. 조부모님 댁에 방문했어.
G: 어디 사시는데?
B: 인천에 사셔. 너는 어때? 즐거운 주말 보냈니?
G: 아니. 주말 내내 아파서 집에 있었어.

10 W: What did you do last Sunday?
M: I went to the museum.
W: Where is the museum?
M: It is in the center of Seoul.
W: Did you take a bus?
M: No. I took the subway.

10 W: 지난 일요일에 뭐했어?
M: 박물관에 갔어.
W: 박물관이 어디에 있어?
M: 서울 중심지에 있어.
W: 버스 탔니?
M: 아니, 지하철 탔어.

11 B: Mom, where is Alice?
W: She's in the front yard.
B: What is she doing there?
W: She's washing my car.
B: Really? I'll go and help her.

11 B: 엄마, 앨리스 어디 있어요?
W: 앞마당에 있어.
B: 거기서 뭐해요?
W: 내 차를 세차하고 있어.
B: 정말요? 가서 도와줄게요.

12 W: What time does our train leave?
M: It leaves here at 11:20.
W: What time is it now?
M: Oh, it's ten to eleven. I mean it's 10:50.
W: I see.

12 W: 우리 기차 몇 시에 출발해?
M: 11시 20분에 여기서 출발해.
W: 지금 몇 시야?
M: 오, 11시 10분 전이야. 10시 50분이라고.
W: 알았어.

13 M: May I help you?
W: I need some balloons for a birthday party.
M: How many balloons do you want?
W: I want five blue balloons and ten red balloons.

13 M: 도와드릴까요?
W: 생일 파티에 풍선이 좀 필요해요.
M: 풍선을 얼마나 많이 원하세요?
W: 파란 풍선 5개와 빨간 풍선 10개 주세요.

14 ① B: This present is for you.
G: Thank you very much.
② B: Whose book is this?
G: It's mine.
③ B: Where are you from?
G: I'm in the classroom.
④ B: Who is that girl?
G: She's my friend, Sally.

14 ① B: 이 선물 너를 위한 거야.
G: 무척 고마워.
② B: 이게 누구 책이야?
G: 내 거야.
③ B: 어디에서 왔니?
G: 나는 교실에 있어.
④ B: 저 소녀 누구야?
G: 그녀는 내 친구, 샐리야.

15 M: What's wrong?
W: I have a fever and a runny nose.
M: Let me check. I think you have a cold.
W: Do I have to take medicine?
M: No, you don't have to. Instead, drink lots of water and get some rest.

15 M: 무슨 일이죠?
W: 열이 나고 콧물이 흘러요.
M: 확인해 볼게요. 감기에 걸리신 거 같아요.
W: 약을 먹어야 하나요?
M: 아니요, 그럴 필요는 없어요. 대신에, 물을 많이 마시고 휴식을 취하세요.

16 W: ① There is a bird on the tree.
② Leaves are falling from the tree.
③ There are many flowers in the garden.
④ Some people are swimming in the river.

16 W: ① 나무에 새가 있다.
② 나무에서 나뭇잎들이 떨어지고 있다.
③ 정원에 많은 꽃들이 있다.
④ 몇몇 사람들이 강에서 수영하고 있다.

17 ① B: What are you doing?
G: I'm listening to music.
② B: What's wrong with him?
G: He has the flu.
③ B: Let's go to the library.
G: I'm sorry, but I can't.
④ B: How do you go to school?
G: I go to school by bus.

17 ① B: 뭐하고 있어?
G: 음악 듣고 있어.
② B: 그에게 무슨 일이야?
G: 독감에 걸렸어.
③ B: 도서관 가자.
G: 미안한데 갈 수 없어.
④ B: 학교에 어떻게 가?
G: 버스로 학교에 가.

18 W: Would you like something cold to drink?
M: Sure. What do you have?
W: We have three kinds of fruit juice and iced tea.
M: ① That's a good idea.
② No, thanks. I'm full.
③ How about this one?
④ I'll have iced tea.

18 W: 시원한 마실 것 드릴까요?
M: 예. 무엇이 있죠?
W: 세 종류의 과일 주스와 아이스티가 있어요.
M: ① 좋은 생각이에요.
② 아니, 감사해요. 배불러요.
③ 이것은 어때요?
④ 아이스티로 할게요.

19 W: Do you have any hobbies?
M: I enjoy playing soccer.
W: Sounds interesting! How often do you play soccer?
M: ① I play soccer three times a week.
② It's 20 dollars.
③ What a nice hobby!
④ I'd like to, but I can't.

19 W: 취미가 좀 있니?
M: 나 축구하는 거 즐겨.
W: 재미있겠다! 얼마나 자주 축구를 해?
M: ① 일주일에 세 번 축구해.
② 20달러야.
③ 정말 멋진 취미구나!
④ 그러고 싶은데 그럴 수 없어.

20 M: Jenny. Long time no see.
How have you been?
W: Pretty good. How was your vacation?
M: ① It was fun. I went camping.
② I will stay at a hotel.
③ It was great! I went to Hawaii with my cousin.
④ It was amazing.

20 M: 제니. 오랜만이야.
어떻게 지냈어?
W: 꽤 좋아. 너는 휴가 어땠어?
M: ① 재미있었어. 나는 캠핑을 갔어.
② 나는 호텔에서 머무를 거야.
③ 훌륭했어! 사촌이랑 하와이에 갔어.
④ 멋졌어.

Word Check

본책 p. 40

01 변하다, 바꾸다	**04** 꽤, 무척	**07** 전체의	**10** 확인하다	**13** 떨어지다
02 빌리다	**05** 계절	**08** 중심지	**11** 대신에	**14** 훌륭한
03 밖에	**06** 가을	**09** 열	**12** 휴식	**15** 무언가

Sentence Check

01 I did my homework until late at night.

02 She's wearing a blue skirt.

03 Let's wait for the red light to turn green.

04 I'm going to have a birthday party.

05 Can you show me the teddy bear over there?

06 I stayed home the whole weekend because I was sick.

07 It is in the center of Seoul.

08 She's washing my car.

09 It leaves here at 11:20.

10 I have a fever and a runny nose.

11 Leaves are falling from the tree.

12 I need some balloons for a birthday party.

13 Would you like something cold to drink?

14 Do you have any hobbies?

15 Long time no see.

4 영어 듣기 모의고사

| 1 ② | 2 ③ | 3 ② | 4 ② | 5 ④ | 6 ④ | 7 ② | 8 ② | 9 ③ | 10 ④ |
| 11 ① | 12 ① | 13 ② | 14 ① | 15 ④ | 16 ④ | 17 ② | 18 ④ | 19 ① | 20 ④ |

듣기 대본

1 B: ① Do you like reading books?
② Can I borrow your umbrella?
③ Can you lend me some money?
④ Can I use your phone?

2 ① W: That's too bad.
② W: What a nice car!
③ W: Help yourself.
④ W: Have a nice day.

3 M: Excuse me. Where is the library?
W: The library? Do you see the hospital?
M: That hospital?
W: Yes, go straight and turn right at the hospital. The library is next to the post office.
M: Thank you.

4 G: Mike, what are you doing?
B: I'm writing about my future job.
G: Do you still want to be a police officer?
B: No, I have a new dream now.
G: What is it?
B: I want to be a singer.

해석

1 B: ① 책 읽는 거 좋아하니?
② 네 우산 빌릴 수 있니?
③ 나한테 돈 좀 빌려줄래?
④ 네 전화기 써도 되니?

2 W: ① 안됐다.
② 정말 멋진 자동차구나!
③ 많이 먹어.
④ 즐거운 날 보내.

3 M: 실례합니다. 도서관이 어디에 있죠?
W: 도서관이요? 병원 보이시죠?
M: 저 병원이요?
W: 예, 곧장 가서 병원에서 오른쪽으로 도세요. 도서관은 우체국 옆에 있어요.
M: 감사합니다.

4 G: 마이크, 뭐하고 있어?
B: 미래 직업에 대해 적고 있어.
G: 여전히 경찰관이 되고 싶니?
B: 아니, 지금 새로운 꿈이 생겼어.
G: 뭔데?
B: 난 가수가 되고 싶어.

5 G: I get up at 7. I go to school at 8:30. School is over at 3. I do my homework after school. I have dinner at 6:30. I usually go for a walk after dinner.

6 G: Minsu, what time do you have lunch?
B: I have lunch at 12:30. After lunch, I usually play soccer with my classmates.
G: What time do you finish your class?
B: School is over at 3.
G: What do you do after school?
B: After school, I have a swimming lesson at 4.

7 M: May I help you?
W: I need some cucumbers. How much is this cucumber?
M: We are selling cucumbers for 200 won each.
W: Okay. Can I get five?

8 M: Jennie, what are you doing?
W: I'm reading a magazine.
M: Is it interesting?
W: Yes, it is.
M: Can I borrow your magazine?
W: Sorry, I can't lend it to you. I have to return it to the library today.

9 M: Hi, Alice. Long time no see.
W: Hi, Mike. Good to see you again. How are you?
M: I'm good. How was your vacation?
W: It was great.

10 M: This is a sport. We play this on a table. There is a net in the middle of the table. We need a racket and a small and light ball.

11 M: Where did you park your car?
W: My car is over there.
M: Do you mean the white car next to the tree?
W: No, the green one is mine.
M: What a nice car!

12 B: Do you like sports?
G: Yes, I do. I usually play tennis every Sunday. How about you?
B: I like sports, too.
G: What sport do you like most?
B: I like soccer most. I want to be a soccer player.

---

5 G: 나는 7시에 일어난다. 나는 8시 30분에 학교에 간다. 학교는 3시에 끝난다. 나는 방과 후에 숙제를 한다. 나는 6시 30분에 저녁을 먹는다. 나는 보통 저녁식사 후에 산책을 한다.

6 G: 민수야, 너는 몇 시에 점심을 먹어?
B: 나는 12시 30분에 점심을 먹어. 점심을 먹은 후, 보통 반 친구들과 축구를 해.
G: 수업은 몇 시에 끝나?
B: 수업은 3시에 끝나.
G: 방과 후에는 뭐해?
B: 방과 후에 4시에 수영 수업이 있어.

7 M: 도와드릴까요?
W: 오이가 좀 필요해요. 이 오이는 얼마예요?
M: 각각 200원에 오이를 팔고 있어요.
W: 좋아요. 다섯 개 주실 수 있나요?

8 M: 제니, 뭐하고 있어?
W: 잡지를 읽고 있어.
M: 재미있어?
W: 응, 그래.
M: 그 잡지 빌릴 수 있니?
W: 미안, 빌려줄 수 없어. 나는 오늘 도서관에 그것을 반납해야 해.

9 M: 안녕, 앨리스. 오랜만이야.
W: 안녕, 마이크. 다시 만나니 반갑다. 잘 지내?
M: 좋아. 네 휴가는 어땠어?
W: 좋았어.

10 M: 이것은 스포츠다. 우리는 이것을 테이블 위에서 한다. 테이블 가운데 네트가 있다. 우리는 라켓과 작고 가벼운 공이 필요하다.

11 M: 네 차 어디에 주차했어?
W: 내 차는 저쪽에 있어.
M: 나무 옆에 있는 하얀 차를 말하는 거야?
W: 아니, 초록색 차가 나의 차야.
M: 무척 멋진 차구나!

12 B: 운동 좋아하니?
G: 응, 그래. 나는 보통 일요일마다 테니스를 쳐. 너는 어때?
B: 나도 운동 좋아해.
G: 무슨 운동을 가장 좋아해?
B: 나는 축구를 가장 좋아해. 나는 축구 선수가 되고 싶어.

13 B: Minji, are you free this afternoon?
G: Yes, I am. Why?
B: I'll <u>walk</u> <u>my</u> <u>dog</u> at the park. Will you come with me?
G: Sure.
B: Then, <u>let's meet</u> at the park at 5.

13 B: 민지, 오늘 오후에 한가하니?
G: 응, 그래. 왜?
B: 나 공원에서 개를 산책시킬 거야. 같이 갈래?
G: 물론.
B: 그러면 공원에서 5시에 만나자.

14 ① B: Hi, Mary. <u>How</u> <u>are</u> <u>you</u> doing?
G: I'm doing my homework.
② B: What's your favorite season?
G: I like <u>autumn</u> <u>best</u>.
③ B: Let's play baseball after school.
G: Sounds great!
④ B: How do you go to school?
G: I usually go to school <u>by</u> <u>bus</u>.

14 ① B: 안녕, 메리. 어떻게 지내?
G: 나는 숙제하고 있어.
② B: 네가 좋아하는 계절은 뭐야?
G: 나는 가을을 가장 좋아해.
③ B: 방과 후에 야구하자.
G: 좋아!
④ B: 학교에 어떻게 가?
G: 나는 보통 버스로 학교에 가.

15 M: What's wrong?
W: I can't find <u>my</u> <u>cellphone</u>.
M: Your cellphone?
W: Yes. Did you see it?
M: It's on the chair <u>next</u> <u>to</u> the TV.

15 M: 무슨 일이야?
W: 내 휴대폰을 찾을 수 없어.
M: 네 휴대폰?
W: 응. 그거 봤니?
M: TV 옆 의자 위에 있어.

16 ① M: See you tomorrow.
W: Bye. See you.
② M: What's the problem?
W: I <u>have</u> <u>a</u> <u>cold</u>.
③ M: Thank you for your kindness.
W: It's my pleasure.
④ M: I won a <u>prize</u> in a writing contest.
W: That's great. <u>Congratulations</u>.

16 ① M: 내일 보자.
W: 안녕. 그럼 또 보자.
② M: 무슨 문제야?
W: 나 감기에 걸렸어.
③ M: 친절에 감사해요.
W: 제가 즐겁죠.
④ M: 나 글짓기 대회에서 상 받았어.
W: 멋지다. 축하해.

17 M: What can I do for you?
W: I'm looking for a skirt.
M: How about this <u>blue</u> <u>one</u>?
W: Hmm... Do you have <u>another</u> <u>one</u> in pink?
M: Yes, we have <u>pink</u> <u>skirts</u> over there.

17 M: 무엇을 도와드릴까요?
W: 치마를 찾고 있어요.
M: 이 파란 것은 어때요?
W: 음… 분홍색으로 다른 거 없나요?
M: 예, 저쪽에 분홍 치마들이 있어요.

18 W: How was your weekend?
M: It was fun. I <u>went</u> <u>camping</u> with my family.
What did you do last weekend?
W: I <u>went</u> <u>fishing</u> with my dad.
M: ① My dad is busy.
② I feel good.
③ That's a good idea.
④ Did you catch many fish?

18 W: 주말 어땠어?
M: 재미있었어. 가족과 캠핑을 갔어.
너는 지난 주말에 뭐했어?
W: 나는 아빠랑 낚시하러 갔어.
M: ① 아빠는 바쁘셔.
② 기분 좋아.
③ 좋은 생각이야.
④ 물고기 많이 잡았어?

19 W: May I help you?
M: I want <u>these</u> <u>shoes</u>. How much are they?
W: They are <u>30</u> <u>dollars</u>.
M: ① Okay. I'll take them.
② They are not my shoes.
③ Sorry. I don't have money.
④ I'd like to, but I can't.

19 W: 도와드릴까요?
M: 이 신발을 사려고요. 얼마예요?
W: 30달러예요.
M: ① 좋아요. 그걸로 살게요.
② 그것은 내 신발이 아니에요.
③ 죄송해요. 나는 돈이 없었어요.
④ 그러고 싶은데 그럴 수 없어요.

20 W: Jim, can you <u>speak</u> Chinese?
M: Yes, I can. <u>Can you</u>?
W: ① No, I can't.
② Yes, I can speak Chinese a little bit.
③ No, but I want to learn.
④ Yes, China is a big country.

20 W: 짐, 중국어로 말할 수 있니?
M: 응, 할 수 있어. 너는?
W: ① 아니, 못 해.
② 응, 중국어를 조금 할 수 있어.
③ 아니, 하지만 배우고 싶어.
④ 응, 중국은 큰 나라야.

Word Check 본책 p. 52

01 빌려주다   **04** 오이   **07** 돌려주다   **10** 친절   **13** 나라

02 곧장   **05** 각각   **08** 가벼운   **11** 다른   **14** 축하하다

03 여전히   **06** 잡지   **09** 산책시키다   **12** 잡다   **15** 즐거움

Sentence Check 본책 p. 53

01 Help yourself.
02 Go straight and turn right at the hospital.
03 I'm writing about my future job.
04 I have a new dream now.
05 I usually go for a walk after dinner.
06 We are selling cucumbers for 200 won each.
07 I have to return it to the library today.
08 Good to see you again.

09 There is a net in the middle of the table.
10 What a nice car!
11 I usually play tennis every Sunday.
12 I walk my dog at the park.
13 Thank you for your kindness.
14 I won a prize in a writing test.
15 I went camping with my family.

1 ④	**2** ④	**3** ③	**4** ③	**5** ②	**6** ①	**7** ②	**8** ②	**9** ①	**10** ④
11 ④	**12** ③	**13** ①	**14** ③	**15** ②	**16** ②	**17** ④	**18** ②	**19** ④	**20** ③

듣기 대본
본책 p. 58

1 B: ① How much is the chair?
② What size do you want?
③ Can I have some water?
④ I would like to have a haircut.

2 M: ① Here you are.
② That's good news.
③ How can I help you?
④ How are you doing today?

3 W: What time is it now?
M: It's ten past three.
W: You mean it's 3:10?
M: Yes, it is.

4 B: How was your weekend, Cathy?
G: It was pretty good.
B: What did you do?
G: I went to the zoo. How about you?
B: I stayed home and watched TV.

5 W: Are you ready to order?
M: Yes, please. I'd like the spaghetti.
W: Would you like something to drink with that?
M: I'd like a Coke, please.

6 G: Tom, can you play table tennis?
B: Yes, I can. Can you?
G: No, I can't, but I'm going to learn during summer vacation.
B: What sports can you play?
G: I can play tennis.

7 G: Minsu, what are you doing?
B: I'm doing my math homework.
G: Do you like math?
B: No, I don't.
G: What's your favorite subject?
B: I like science.
G: I like it, too.

해석

1 B: ① 그 의자 얼마예요?
② 무슨 사이즈를 원하나요?
③ 물 좀 먹을 수 있나요?
④ 머리를 자르고 싶어요.

2 M: ① 여기 있어요.
② 좋은 소식이야.
③ 어떻게 도와드릴까요?
④ 오늘 어때?

3 W: 지금 몇 시야?
M: 3시 10분이야.
W: 3시 10분을 말하는 거 맞지?
M: 응, 그래.

4 B: 주말 어땠어, 캐시?
G: 무척 좋았어.
B: 뭐했는데?
G: 나는 동물원에 갔어. 너는 어때?
B: 나는 집에 있으면서 TV를 봤어.

5 W: 주문하실래요?
M: 예. 스파게티 주세요.
W: 그것과 함께 마실 것도 드릴까요?
M: 콜라로 주세요.

6 G: 톰, 탁구 칠 수 있니?
B: 응, 할 수 있어. 너는?
G: 나는 못해. 하지만 여름 방학 동안 배울 예정이야.
B: 무슨 운동 할 수 있어?
G: 나는 테니스 칠 수 있어.

7 G: 민수, 뭐하고 있어?
B: 나 수학 숙제하고 있어.
G: 너 수학 좋아해?
B: 아니.
G: 네가 좋아하는 과목은 뭐야?
B: 나 과학 좋아해.
G: 나도 그거 좋아해.

8 B: Jennie, where are you going?
  G: I'm going to the swimming pool. I have a swimming lesson <u>every</u> <u>Friday</u>.
  B: Friday? It's Thursday today.
  G: Really?
  B: Yes, <u>today</u> <u>is</u> <u>Thursday</u>.

8 B: 제니, 어디 가니?
  G: 나 수영장 가고 있어. 금요일마다 수영 수업이 있어.
  B: 금요일? 오늘 목요일이야.
  G: 정말?
  B: 응, 오늘은 목요일이야.

9 B: Would you like some cookies?
  G: Yes, thanks. Where did you get them?
  B: I made <u>them</u> <u>myself</u>.
  G: Really?
  B: Yes, I want to <u>be</u> <u>a</u> <u>baker</u> in the future.

9 B: 쿠키 좀 먹을래?
  G: 응, 고마워. 어디서 얻었어?
  B: 내가 직접 만들었어.
  G: 정말?
  B: 응, 나는 장래에 제빵사가 되고 싶어.

10 M: Alice, do you have <u>any</u> <u>plans</u> tomorrow?
  W: I don't have anything special to do. Why?
  M: Can you <u>help</u> <u>me</u>? I'm going to paint my house.
  W: Okay.

10 M: 앨리스, 내일 계획이 있니?
  W: 특별한 거는 없어. 왜?
  M: 나 도와줄 수 있니? 집을 페인트칠할 거야.
  W: 좋아.

11 B: Amy, your birthday is <u>next</u> <u>Sunday</u>, isn't it?
  G: Yes, it is. I'm going to invite my friends on my birthday.
  B: What do you want for your birthday?
  G: I want a <u>new</u> <u>computer</u>.
  B: You don't have a computer?
  G: I have a computer, but it's <u>very</u> <u>old</u>.

11 B: 에이미, 네 생일이 다음 주 일요일이지, 그렇지 않니?
  G: 응, 그래. 나는 내 생일에 친구들을 초대할 예정이야.
  B: 생일에 무엇을 원해?
  G: 나는 새 컴퓨터를 원해.
  B: 너 컴퓨터 없어?
  G: 컴퓨터가 있는데 너무 오래됐어.

12 B: Susie, what are you doing?
  G: I'm <u>taking</u> <u>photos</u> of flowers.
  B: Can I see them?
  G: Sure.
  B: Wow. You are <u>good</u> <u>at</u> taking photos.
  G: Thanks.

12 B: 수지, 뭐하고 있어?
  G: 꽃 사진을 찍고 있어.
  B: 봐도 되니?
  G: 물론.
  B: 와우. 너 사진 잘 찍는구나.
  G: 고마워.

13 ① M: What's wrong?
    G: I <u>have</u> <u>a</u> <u>fever</u> and a headache.
  ② M: How was your vacation?
    G: It was great.
  ③ M: What do you want for lunch?
    G: I'd like to have fried chicken.
  ④ M: <u>What</u> <u>time</u> do you have dinner?
    G: I have dinner at 7.

13 ① M: 무슨 일이죠?
    G: 열이 나고 두통이 있어요.
  ② M: 휴가 어땠어?
    G: 좋았어요.
  ③ M: 점심으로 뭐 먹고 싶어?
    G: 나 프라이드치킨 먹고 싶어요.
  ④ M: 몇 시에 저녁을 먹어?
    G: 7시에 저녁을 먹어요.

14 M: I'm sorry I'm late.
  W: <u>Why</u> were you late today?
  M: I had a <u>car</u> <u>accident</u>.
  W: Really? Are you okay?
  M: Yes, I am.

14 M: 늦어서 미안해.
  W: 오늘 왜 늦었어?
  M: 교통사고가 있었어.
  W: 정말? 괜찮아?
  M: 응, 괜찮아.

15 M: What are you doing here, Cindy?
W: I'm looking for <u>my watch</u>.
M: Your watch? Is this your watch?
W: No, it isn't.
M: What does your watch look like?
W: It is <u>round</u> and its color is <u>black</u>.

15 M: 여기서 뭐해, 신디?
W: 손목시계를 찾고 있어.
M: 네 손목시계? 이게 네 손목시계야
W: 아니야.
M: 네 손목시계 어떻게 생겼어?
W: 둥글고 검은색이야.

16 ① W: Sam, <u>how was</u> the party?
M: It was great.
② M: I got a C on the math test.
W: <u>Cheer up</u>! You'll do better next time.
③ M: Can I ask you a question?
W: Sure. What is it?
④ M: Did you see the soccer game yesterday?
W: Yes, it was <u>very exciting</u>.

16 ① W: 샘, 파티 어땠어?
M: 좋았어.
② M: 나 수학 시험에서 C 받았어.
W: 기운 내! 다음번에는 더 잘할 거야.
③ M: 질문하나 해도 되나요?
W: 물론이죠. 뭔데요?
④ M: 어제 축구 경기 봤니?
W: 응, 정말 흥미진진했어.

17 W: Jim, do you <u>have breakfast</u> every day?
M: Yes, I do.
W: What do you have for breakfast?
M: I <u>usually eat</u> cereal. How about you?
W: I don't have breakfast.

17 W: 짐, 너는 매일 아침을 먹니?
M: 응, 그래.
W: 아침에 뭐 먹어?
M: 보통 시리얼을 먹어. 너는 어때?
W: 나는 아침을 안 먹어.

18 G: Hi, John. <u>What time</u> does your first class start?
B: It starts <u>at 9</u>.
G: Really? My first class starts at 8:40. Then, what time does your school finish?
B: ① It's not my book.
② I usually finish at 4.
③ It's Monday.
④ I go to bed at 10.

18 G: 안녕, 존. 네 첫 수업은 몇 시에 시작해?
B: 9시에 시작해.
G: 정말? 내 첫 수업은 8시 40분에 시작해. 그러면 학교는 몇 시에 끝나?
B: ① 그것은 내 책이 아니야.
② 보통 4시에 끝나.
③ 월요일이야
④ 나는 10시에 자러 가.

19 W: I'm hungry. <u>Let's order</u> some pizza.
M: Sorry. I don't like pizza.
W: Then, <u>what</u> do you want to <u>have</u>?
M: ① I ate pizza for lunch.
② I want a new computer.
③ I don't like Korean food.
④ I want fried chicken.

19 W: 나 배고파. 피자를 좀 주문하자.
M: 미안해. 나 피자를 좋아하지 않아.
W: 그러면 뭐 먹고 싶어?
M: ① 난 점심에 피자를 먹었어.
② 나는 새 컴퓨터를 원해.
③ 나는 한국 음식은 좋아하지 않아.
④ 나 프라이드치킨 먹고 싶어.

20 W: You <u>look sad</u>. What's wrong?
M: I <u>lost</u> my bike.
W: ① Oh, that's too bad.
② What does your bike look like?
③ Where is your bike?
④ Really? Let's find it together.

20 W: 너 슬퍼 보여. 뭐 잘못됐어?
M: 자전거를 잃어버렸어.
W: ① 오, 정말 안됐다.
② 네 자전거 어떻게 생겼어?
③ 네 자전거 어디에 있어?
④ 정말? 같이 찾아보자.

01 소식 　　　**04** ~ 동안 　　　**07** 특별한 　　　**10** 두통 　　　**13** 흥미진진한

02 ~을 지나서 　**05** 탁구 　　　**08** 초대하다 　　**11** 더 나은 　　**14** 정말

03 사고 　　　　**06** 나 자신 　　**09** 물론, 그럼, 좋아 　**12** 시리얼, 곡물 　**15** 함께

Sentence Check   본책 p. 65

01 I would like to have a haircut.

02 That's good news.

03 I stayed home and watched TV.

04 I'm going to learn during summer vacation.

05 I have a swimming lesson every Friday.

06 I made them myself.

07 I'm going to paint my house.

08 I have a computer, but it's very old.

09 I'm taking photos of flowers.

10 I have a fever and a headache.

11 I had a car accident.

12 I got a C on math test.

13 My first class starts at 8:40.

14 Let's order some pizza.

15 I lost my bike.

6 영어 듣기 모의고사
본책 p. 66

| **1** ④ | **2** ③ | **3** ③ | **4** ③ | **5** ① | **6** ④ | **7** ② | **8** ② | **9** ① | **10** ④ |
| **11** ④ | **12** ④ | **13** ① | **14** ② | **15** ① | **16** ④ | **17** ① | **18** ③ | **19** ③ | **20** ② |

듣기 대본   본책 p. 70

1 W: May I help you?
　 M: I need some cucumbers.
　 W: Sorry. We don't have any cucumbers now.
　 M: Then, do you have onions?
　 W: Yes, we do. How many onions do you want?
　 M: Five.

2 B: ① Excuse me. Where is the bank?
　　 ② I'm sorry to hear that.
　　 ③ I'm thirsty. Can I have some water?
　　 ④ No, thanks. I'm full.

3 G: How is the weather today?
　 B: It's sunny. Let's take a walk after lunch.
　 G: Sorry, I can't. I have to practice the piano.
　 B: Oh, I see.

해석

1 W: 도와드릴까요?
　 M: 오이가 좀 필요해요.
　 W: 죄송합니다. 지금 오이가 없어요.
　 M: 그러면, 양파는 있나요?
　 W: 예, 있어요. 양파를 얼마나 원하세요?
　 M: 다섯 개요.

2 B: ① 실례합니다. 은행이 어디죠?
　　 ② 그 소식을 들으니 유감이네요.
　　 ③ 목이 말라요. 물을 좀 먹을 수 있나요?
　　 ④ 아니요, 감사합니다. 배가 불러요.

3 G: 오늘 날씨 어때?
　 B: 맑아. 점심식사 후 산책하자.
　 G: 미안한데 할 수없어. 나 피아노 연습을 해야 해.
　 B: 오, 알았어.

4 B: Where is Bob?
G: He's at the park.
B: Is he <u>playing</u> <u>soccer</u> there?
G: No, he isn't.
B: What is he doing?
G: He's <u>playing</u> <u>baseball</u> with his friends.

4 B: 밥이 어디 있어?
G: 공원에 있어.
B: 거기서 축구하고 있니?
G: 아니.
B: 뭐하고 있는데?
G: 친구들과 야구하고 있어.

5 W: Who is your sister in this picture?
M: She's wearing a <u>yellow</u> <u>cap</u>.
W: Is she your sister?
M: No, she's isn't. She's <u>holding</u> a teddy <u>bear</u> in her hand.

5 W: 이 사진에서 누구 네 여동생이니?
M: 노란 야구모자를 쓰고 있어.
W: 얘가 네 여동생이야?
M: 아니야. 그녀는 손에 곰 인형을 들고 있어.

6 G: ① What time do you <u>go</u> to <u>bed</u>?
② May I take your order?
③ What do you want for your birthday?
④ What a <u>nice</u> <u>watch</u>! Where did you get it?

6 G: ① 몇 시에 자러 가니?
② 주문하시겠어요?
③ 네 생일에 무엇을 원해?
④ 멋진 손목시계구나! 어디서 났어?

7 G: Minsu, where are you going?
B: I'm going to the <u>shopping</u> <u>mall</u>.
G: Why?
B: I have art classes at school, so I need <u>some</u> <u>crayons</u>.
G: Can I come with you?
B: Sure.

7 G: 민수, 어디 가고 있어?
B: 나 쇼핑몰에 가고 있어.
G: 왜?
B: 학교에서 미술 수업이 있어서 크레용이 좀 필요해.
G: 같이 가도 되니?
B: 물론.

8 ① M: <u>What</u> <u>time</u> is it now?
W: It's Saturday.
② M: <u>Whose</u> <u>car</u> is this?
W: It's my mom's car.
③ M: Who is the man over there?
W: Nice to meet you.
④ M: I have a fever and a headache.
W: Have a good time.

8 ① M: 지금 몇 시야?
W: 토요일이야.
② M: 이거 누구의 차야?
W: 내 엄마의 차야.
③ M: 저쪽에 있는 남자 누구야?
W: 만나서 반가워.
④ M: 열이 있고 두통이 있어요.
W: 좋은 시간 보내.

9 W: James, what do you eat <u>for</u> <u>breakfast</u>?
M: I eat bread. How about you?
W: I <u>usually</u> <u>eat</u> cereal and eggs.
M: Eggs?
W: Yes. I like scrambled eggs.

9 W: 제임스, 아침식사로 뭐 먹어?
M: 나는 빵을 먹어. 너는 어때?
W: 나는 보통 시리얼과 달걀을 먹어.
M: 달걀?
W: 응. 나 스크램블 에그 좋아해.

10 B: Guess what, Mom?
W: What?
B: I won <u>first</u> <u>prize</u> in the essay contest.
W: Really?
B: Yes, I did.
W: <u>Good</u> <u>job</u>! I'm proud of you.

10 B: 맞춰 보세요, 엄마?
W: 뭘?
B: 제가 백일장에서 1등 했어요.
W: 정말?
B: 예, 그래요.
W: 잘했어! 네가 자랑스러워.

11 M: Are you okay, Amy?
　　W: No, I don't <u>feel well</u>. I have a headache.
　　M: Sorry to hear that. Did you <u>take some</u> <u>medicine</u>?
　　W: No, I didn't. I don't have medicine for a headache.
　　M: Really? I'll <u>get you</u> some medicine.

11 M: 괜찮아, 에이미?
　　W: 아니, 몸이 좋지 않아. 두통이 있어.
　　M: 안됐다. 약을 좀 먹었어?
　　W: 아니. 두통약이 없어.
　　M: 정말? 내가 약을 좀 가져다줄게.

---

12 M: ① A boy is catching a ball.
　　　　② A boy is <u>eating</u> fish.
　　　　③ A boy is swimming in the river.
　　　　④ A boy is <u>catching fish</u>.

12 ① M: 한 소년이 공을 잡고 있다.
　　　② M: 한 소년이 생선을 먹고 있다.
　　　③ M: 한 소년이 강에서 수영하고 있다.
　　　④ M: 한 소년이 물고기를 잡고 있다.

---

13 M: Jennifer, what are you doing?
　　W: I'm watering the flowers <u>in the garden</u>.
　　M: How often do you water the flowers?
　　W: <u>Twice a week</u>.

13 M: 제니퍼, 뭐하고 있어?
　　W: 정원에서 꽃에 물을 주고 있어.
　　M: 얼마나 자주 꽃들에 물을 주니?
　　W: 일주일에 두 번.

---

14 M: Amy, how are you doing today?
　　W: I'm not good.
　　M: Why?
　　W: I <u>stayed up late</u> last night.
　　M: Did you play computer games?
　　W: No, I <u>watched</u> a soccer game <u>on TV</u>.

14 M: 에이미, 오늘 기분이 어때?
　　W: 좋지 않아.
　　M: 왜?
　　W: 지난밤에 늦게까지 안 잤어.
　　M: 컴퓨터 게임 했니?
　　W: 아니, TV로 축구 경기를 봤어.

---

15 B: Who is the woman in the picture?
　　G: She's <u>my cousin</u>, Ann.
　　B: Do you have a cousin?
　　G: Yes, she <u>lives in</u> Canada.
　　B: She's very tall. How old is she?
　　G: She's 14 years old.

15 B: 사진에 있는 여자 누구야?
　　G: 내 사촌, 앤이야.
　　B: 너 사촌이 있어?
　　G: 응, 캐나다에서 살고 있어.
　　B: 키가 매우 크다. 몇 살이야?
　　G: 14살이야.

---

16 [Cellphone rings.]
　　W: Hello.
　　M: Hi, Amy. <u>This is</u> Tom.
　　W: Oh, hi, Tom. What's up?
　　M: I'm going camping tomorrow, but I don't have a tent. Will you lend me <u>your tent</u>?
　　W: Sure. I'll <u>bring</u> it to your house.

16 [휴대폰이 울린다]
　　W: 여보세요.
　　M: 안녕, 에이미. 톰이야.
　　W: 오, 안녕, 톰. 무슨 일이야?
　　M: 나 내일 캠핑을 가는데 텐트가 없어. 텐트를 빌려줄 수 있니?
　　W: 물론이지. 네 집으로 가져다줄게.

---

17 W: What <u>do you think</u> about my plan?
　　M: ① It sounds good.
　　　　② I don't have any plans.
　　　　③ Yes, I'm busy.
　　　　④ It's not my idea.

17 W: 내 계획을 어떻게 생각해?
　　M: ① 좋은 거 같아.
　　　② 나는 어떤 계획도 없어.
　　　③ 응, 나는 바빠.
　　　④ 그것은 내 생각이 아니야.

18 M: Where did you get that T-shirt? It's so cool.
  W: ① It's not my T-shirt.
  ② I like that blue T-shirt.
  ③ I bought it at an online shopping mall.
  ④ It's 10 dollars.

19 W: What would you like to have?
  M: I'll have fried rice and a Coke.
  W: Anything else?
  M: ① I don't like noodles.
  ② No, thanks. I'm full.
  ③ No, that's all.
  ④ I have something for you.

20 B: Hi, Jessie?
  G: Oh, Mike. What's up?
  B: I'm going to the shopping mall this afternoon.
    Do you want to go with me?
  B: ① Okay. What time shall we meet?
  ② Yes, I went shopping yesterday.
  ③ I'd like to, but I have to do my homework.
  ④ I'm sorry, but I can't.

18 M: 그 티셔츠 어디서 났어? 무척 멋지다.
  W: ① 그것은 내 티셔츠가 아니야.
  ② 나는 그 파란 티셔츠가 좋아.
  ③ 나는 그것을 인터넷에서 샀어.
  ④ 그거 10달러야.

19 W: 뭐 드시겠어요?
  M: 저는 볶음밥하고 콜라 주세요.
  W: 그밖에 다른 것은요?
  M: ① 나는 국수를 좋아하지 않아요.
  ② 아니요, 고마워요. 배불러요.
  ③ 아니요, 그게 다예요.
  ④ 당신에게 줄 뭔가가 있어요.

20 B: 안녕, 제시?
  G: 오, 마이크. 무슨 일이야?
  B: 오늘 오후에 쇼핑몰에 갈 거야.
    나랑 같이 갈래?
  G: ① 좋아. 몇 시에 만날까?
  ② 응, 나는 어제 쇼핑했어.
  ③ 그러고 싶은데 숙제를 해야 해.
  ④ 미안한데 그럴 수 없어.

Word Check
본책 p. 76

01 양파	**04** 깨어 있다	**07** 추측하다	**10** 잡다	**13** 가져다주다
02 목마른	**05** 들다	**08** 에세이	**11** 두 번	**14** 생각
03 연습하다	**06** 크레용	**09** 대회	**12** 사촌	**15** 국수

Sentence Check
본책 p. 77

01 I have to practice the piano.
02 She's holding a teddy bear in her hand.
03 What a nice watch!
04 I have art classes at school.
05 I have a fever and a headache.
06 I usually eat cereal and eggs.
07 I won first prize in the essay contest.
08 I don't have medicine for a headache.

09 A boy is catching fish.
10 I'm watering the flowers in the garden.
11 I'm not good today.
12 I'll bring it to your house.
13 I don't have any plans.
14 I bought it at an on the Internet.
15 I'm going to the shopping mall this afternoon.

1 ③	**2** ①	**3** ①	**4** ②	**5** ①	**6** ④	**7** ②	**8** ③	**9** ②	**10** ④
11 ①	**12** ①	**13** ④	**14** ①	**15** ③	**16** ②	**17** ②	**18** ①	**19** ④	**20** ②

듣기 대본
본책 p. 82

1 W: ① Let's have dinner together.
　　② Wait here, please.
　　③ It's time to wake up.
　　④ Do you want some more?

2 M: Alice, are you going to the swimming pool tonight?
W: Yes, I am. Why?
M: I want to take the swimming lesson with you. Is it okay?
W: Sure. The lesson starts at 7:30. Let's meet in front of the pool at 7:10.
M: Okay.

3 B: Amy, is this your camera?
G: No, it isn't. It's my mom's.
B: Oh, I see. Whose cellphone is this?
G: It's mine.
B: Can I use it for a minute?
G: Of course.

4 G: How is the weather today?
B: It's sunny. Let's go to the beach.
G: Sorry, I can't. I have to clean my room.
B: Oh, I see.

5 W: ① There are some books on the round table.
　　② There is a book on the floor.
　　③ There are some pencils on the round table.
　　④ There are some apples on the table.

6 W: Donovan, what do you eat for breakfast?
M: I usually have some fruit.
W: What kind of fruit do you eat?
M: I eat apples.
W: Do you like apples?
M: Yes, but I like strawberries the most.

7 G: Jessie, did you see John?
B: Yes, he is in the library.
G: Is he reading a book there?
B: No, he isn't.
G: What is he doing there?
B: He's borrowing some books.

해석

1 W: ① 함께 저녁 먹자.
　　② 여기서 기다려 주세요.
　　③ 일어날 시간이다.
　　④ 좀 더 먹을래?

2 M: 앨리스, 오늘 저녁에 수영장에 갈 거니?
W: 응, 그래. 왜?
M: 너랑 같이 수영 수업을 받고 싶어. 괜찮니?
W: 물론이지. 수영 수업은 7시 30분에 시작해. 수영장 앞에서 7시 10분에 만나자.
M: 좋아.

3 B: 에이미, 이게 네 카메라니?
G: 아니, 그렇지 않아. 나의 엄마 거야.
B: 오, 알았어. 이것은 누구의 휴대폰이니?
G: 그것은 내 거야.
B: 내가 잠깐 이거 써도 되니?
G: 물론.

4 G: 오늘 날씨 어때?
B: 맑아. 해변에 가자.
G: 미안한데 안 돼. 내 방 청소를 해야 해.
B: 오, 알았어.

5 W: ① 둥근 탁자 위에 책이 몇 권 있다.
　　② 마루 위에 책이 한 권 있다.
　　③ 둥근 탁자 위에 연필들이 몇 개 있다.
　　④ 탁자 위에 사과가 몇 개 있다.

6 W: 도노반, 아침식사에 무엇을 먹어?
M: 나는 보통 과일을 좀 먹어.
W: 무슨 종류의 과일을 먹어?
M: 사과를 먹어.
W: 사과 좋아하니?
M: 응, 하지만 가장 좋아하는 것은 딸기야.

7 G: 제시, 존 봤니?
B: 응, 도서관에 있어.
G: 거기서 책을 읽고 있니?
B: 아니, 그렇지 않아.
G: 거시서 뭐하고 있는데?
B: 책을 좀 빌리고 있어.

8 ① M: What are you doing?

W: I'm playing a computer game.

② M: May I help you?

W: I'm <u>looking for</u> a computer.

③ M: Can I help you?

W: I think there is <u>something</u> <u>wrong</u> with my computer.

④ M: Whose computer is this?

W: It's <u>my</u> <u>dad's</u>.

8 ① M : 뭐하고 있어?

W : 나는 컴퓨터 게임을 하고 있어.

② M : 도와드릴까요?

W : 컴퓨터를 찾고 있어요.

③ M : 도와드릴까요?

W : 제 생각에 제 컴퓨터에 문제가 있는 거 같아요.

④ M : 이것은 누구의 컴퓨터니?

W : 그것은 나의 아빠 거야.

9 M: May I help you?

G: Yes, I'm looking for a bag.

M: How about this red one?

G: It's nice, but I already have a red bag. Can you show me a <u>different</u> <u>color</u>?

M: Then, how about this <u>blue</u> <u>one</u>?

G: I like it. <u>How</u> <u>much</u> is it?

9 M : 도와드릴까요?

G : 예. 가방을 사려고요.

M : 이 빨간 거 어때요?

G : 좋은데 전 이미 빨간 가방이 있어요. 다른 색으로 보여주시겠어요?

M : 그러면, 이 파란 거는 어때요?

G : 좋아요. 얼마예요?

10 ① G: What do you want to be in the future?

B: I'd like to be <u>a</u> <u>singer</u>.

② G: Hi, Paul. How was your trip to Korea?

B: It was good.

③ G: How are you doing?

B: <u>Pretty</u> <u>good</u>.

④ G: Would you like some pizza?

B: <u>No</u>, <u>thanks</u>. I like it very much.

10 ① G : 너는 장래에 무엇이 되고 싶어?

B : 나는 가수가 되고 싶어.

② G : 안녕, 폴. 한국 여행 어땠어?

B : 좋았어.

③ G : 어떻게 지내?

B : 아주 잘 지내.

④ G : 피자를 좀 먹을요?

B : 아니, 고마워. 나는 그것을 아주 좋아해.

11 M: Mira, what do you think about this movie?

W: It's a lot of fun. Do you like <u>comedy</u> <u>movies</u>?

M: Yes, I love comedy. What about you?

W: I like comedy, too. But I love <u>romance</u> <u>movies</u> the most.

11 M : 미라야, 이 영화 어떻게 생각해?

W : 매우 재미있어. 너 코미디 영화 좋아하니?

M : 응, 코미디 아주 좋아해. 너는 어때?

W : 나도 코미디 좋아해. 하지만 난 로맨스 영화가 가장 좋아.

12 M: Hurry up. We are <u>late</u> <u>for</u> the concert.

W: All right. Should we take the subway?

M: No, the subway station is <u>too</u> <u>far</u> from here.

W: Well, how about <u>taking</u> <u>a</u> <u>taxi</u>?

M: Okay. Let's go!

12 M : 서둘러. 우리 음악회에 늦었어.

W : 알았어. 지하철을 타야 할까?

M : 아니, 여기서 지하철역은 너무 멀어.

W : 그럼, 택시를 타는 게 어때?

M : 좋아. 가자!

13 G: Hi, Mike. What did you do last weekend?

B: I just stayed home. I couldn't <u>do</u> <u>anything</u>.

G: Really? Why?

B: My dog was sick. I had to <u>take</u> <u>care</u> of him.

G: I'm <u>sorry</u> to hear that.

13 G : 안녕, 마이크. 지난 주말에 뭐했어?

B : 그냥 집에 있었어. 아무것도 할 수 없었어.

G : 정말? 왜?

B : 내 개가 아팠어. 나는 개를 돌봐야만 했어.

G : 그 얘기 들으니 유감이다.

14 *[Cellphone rings.]*
　M: Hello.
　W: Hi, Ted. Where are you?
　M: I'm at home. What's up?
　W: I'm going to play basketball with Jane and Tony today. Will you join us?
　M: I'd like to, but I can't. I have to visit my uncle.

15 B: Susan, do you have a pet?
　G: Oh, yes, I have two cats and three dogs.
　B: Wow. I think you really like animals.
　G: Yes, I do. I want to be a veterinarian in the future. Do you have any pets?
　B: Yes, I have a cat.

16 W: May I help you?
　M: Yes, I'm looking for a pair of blue jeans. How much are these?
　W: They are $40.
　M: Do you have any cheaper ones?
　W: Those ones are $28.
　M: Oh, that's good, I'll take them.

17 M: Good evening. May I help you?
　G: Yes, I'm looking for a skirt.
　M: How about this one? It's very popular among teens.
　G: Can I try it on?
　M: Sure, the fitting room is right over there.

18 G: John, let's go to the park after school.
　B: Okay. What time shall we meet?
　　My class finishes at 3 today.
　G: ① Then, how about 4:30?
　　② It sounds good.
　　③ That's too bad.
　　④ I feel good today.

19 B: What's your favorite sport?
　G: I like baseball. How about you?
　B: I like tennis.
　G: Are you good at tennis?
　B: ① I play tennis after school.
　　② No, thanks.
　　③ Yes, I like it.
　　④ No, I'm not.

14 *[휴대폰이 울린다.]*
　B: 여보세요.
　G: 안녕, 테드. 어디 있어?
　B: 집이야. 무슨 일이야?
　G: 제인이랑 토니랑 오늘 농구할 거야. 같이 할래?
　B: 그러고 싶은데 못 해. 삼촌 댁에 방문해야 해.

15 B: 수잔, 너 반려동물 있니?
　G: 오, 응. 나는 고양이 두 마리와 개 세 마리 있어.
　B: 와우. 너 정말 동물을 좋아하는 거 같다.
　G: 응, 그래. 나는 장래에 수의사가 되고 싶어. 너는 반려동물 키우니?
　B: 응, 나는 고양이가 한 마리 있어.

16 W: 도와드릴까요?
　M: 예, 청바지를 찾고 있어요. 이거 얼마예요?
　W: 40달러예요.
　M: 더 싼 거 있나요?
　W: 저것들은 28달러예요.
　M: 오, 저거 좋네요. 저걸로 살게요.

17 M: 안녕하세요. 도와드릴까요?
　G: 예, 치마를 사려고요.
　M: 이것 어때요? 십대 사이에서 매우 인기 있어요.
　G: 입어 봐도 되나요?
　M: 물론이죠. 탈의실은 바로 저쪽에 있어요.

18 G: 존, 방과 후에 공원에 가자.
　B: 좋아. 몇 시에 만날까?
　　내 수업은 오늘 3시에 끝나.
　G: ① 그럼, 4시 30분 어때?
　　② 좋은 거 같아.
　　③ 너무 안됐다.
　　④ 오늘 기분이 좋아.

19 B: 네가 좋아하는 운동이 뭐야?
　G: 나는 야구 좋아해. 너는 어때?
　B: 나는 테니스 좋아해.
　G: 테니스 잘 치니?
　B: ① 나는 방과 후에 테니스를 쳐.
　　② 아니, 고마워.
　　③ 응, 그거 좋아해.
　　④ 아니, 잘 못 쳐.

20 B: Hi, Jessie. <u>Where</u> are you going?
G: I'm going to the shopping center. I'll <u>buy</u> <u>a</u> <u>gift</u> for my dad's birthday.
B: <u>When</u> is your dad's birthday?
G: ① It's tomorrow.
② It's not my dad's.
③ It's next Monday.
④ It's July 10.

20 B: 안녕, 제시. 어디 가고 있어?
G: 쇼핑센터에 가고 있어. 아빠 생신 선물을 살 거야.
B: 네 아빠 생신이 언제야?
G: ① 내일이야.
② 그것은 나의 아빠 것이 아니야.
③ 다음 주 월요일이야.
④ 7월 10일이야.

Word Check
본책 p. 88

01 함께	**04** 다른	**07** 역	**10** 아무것	**13** 싼
02 딸기	**05** 여행	**08** 지하철	**11** 둥근	**14** 인기 있는
03 이미, 벌써	**06** 음악회	**09** 먼	**12** 반려동물	**15** 십대

Sentence Check
본책 p. 89

01 It's time to <u>wake up</u>.
02 I want to <u>take</u> the swimming <u>lesson</u> with you.
03 Can I use it <u>for a minute</u>?
04 <u>Let's go</u> to the beach.
05 I usually have <u>some fruit</u>.
06 He's <u>borrowing some books</u>.
07 I think there is <u>something wrong</u> with my computer.
08 I love <u>romance movies</u> the most.
09 The subway station is too <u>far from here</u>.
10 I had to <u>take care of him</u>.
11 I'd <u>like to</u>, but I can't.
12 I want to be a veterinarian <u>in the future</u>.
13 It's very popular <u>among teens</u>.
14 The <u>fitting room</u> is right over there.
15 My class <u>finishes</u> at 3 today.

8회 영어 듣기 모의고사
본책 p. 90

1 ②	2 ④	3 ②	4 ①	5 ③	6 ④	7 ③	8 ①	9 ②	10 ②
11 ①	12 ③	13 ③	14 ③	15 ①	16 ③	17 ④	18 ①	19 ③	20 ①

본책 p. 94

1 B: Are you okay? You don't look happy.
G: I <u>lost</u> <u>my</u> <u>watch</u>.
B: Really?
G: Yes, I put my watch on the desk, but I can't find it.
B: Don't be <u>sad</u>. Let's find it together.

1 B: 괜찮아? 너 행복해 보이지 않아.
G: 나 시계를 잃어버렸어.
B: 정말?
G: 응, 시계를 책상 위에 놓았는데 찾을 수가 없어.
B: 슬퍼하지 마. 같이 찾아보자.

2 M: ① How many <u>books</u> do you have?
② Wow, what a nice <u>cap</u> you have!
③ Who is the man in the room?
④ Wow, you're very <u>good</u> at <u>painting</u>.

2 M: ① 너는 얼마나 많은 책이 있니?
② 와우, 너 무척 멋진 야구모자가 있구나!
③ 방에 그 남자 누구야?
④ 와우, 너 그림 매우 잘 그리는구나.

3 ① W: James, what's wrong?
    M: I have a cold.
② W: I'm <u>sorry for</u> not calling you yesterday.
    M: It's okay.
③ W: I won first prize in the singing contest.
    M: Wow! <u>Congratulations</u>!
④ W: Can I borrow your pencil?
    M: Sure. <u>Here you are</u>.

4 G: James, who is your cousin in this picture?
    B: She's wearing a <u>red skirt</u>.
    G: Is she wearing glasses?
    B: No, she's <u>holding some flowers</u>.
    G: Oh, I see.

5 B: Susan, how was your weekend?
    G: It was great. I went to the zoo with my family.
    What did you do <u>last weekend</u>?
    B: I went to the hospital.
    G: Were you sick?
    B: No, I <u>visited</u> my grandmother. She is <u>in the hospital</u>.

6 M: May I help you?
    W: Yes, I want some oranges.
    M: Sorry. We don't have any oranges now. How about <u>these pears</u>?
    W: Okay.
    M: <u>How many</u> pears do you want?
    W: <u>Six</u>.

7 B: What's your <u>favorite subject</u>?
    G: I like science. How about you?
    B: I like P.E.
    G: Why do you <u>like P.E.</u>?
    B: I like playing sports.

8 ① M: How can I <u>help you</u>?
    W: I want <u>some flowers</u> for my mom.
② M: Do you have any hobbies?
    W: I like drawing flowers.
③ M: What <u>kind</u> of flowers do you like?
    W: I like <u>roses</u>.
④ M: Are you ready to order?
    W: Yes, I'd like the chicken salad.

3 ① W : 제임스, 뭐 잘못됐니?
    M : 나 감기 걸렸어.
② W : 어제 전화 안 해서 미안해.
    M : 괜찮아.
③ W : 나 노래 대회에서 1등 했어.
    M : 와우! 축하해!
④ W : 네 연필 빌릴 수 있니?
    M : 물론, 여기 있어.

4 G : 제임스, 이 사진에서 네 사촌이 누구야?
    B : 빨간 치마를 입고 있어.
    G : 안경을 쓰고 있니?
    B : 아니, 인형을 들고 있어.
    G : 오, 알았어.

5 B : 수잔, 주말 어땠어?
    G : 좋았어. 가족이랑 동물원에 갔어.
    너는 지난 주말에 뭐했어?
    B : 나는 병원에 갔어.
    G : 너 아팠어?
    B : 아니, 할머니한테 갔어. 병원에 계시거든.

6 M : 도와드릴까요?
    W : 예, 오렌지를 좀 사려고요.
    M : 죄송합니다. 오렌지가 지금 없어요. 이 배는 어떠세요?
    W : 좋아요.
    M : 배를 얼마나 드릴까요?
    W : 6개요.

7 B : 네가 좋아하는 과목이 뭐야?
    G : 나는 과학 좋아해. 너는 어때?
    B : 나는 체육 좋아해.
    G : 왜 체육을 좋아해?
    B : 나는 운동하는 거 좋아해.

8 ① M : 도와드릴까요?
    W : 엄마를 위해 꽃을 좀 사려고요.
② M : 취미가 있나요?
    W : 꽃 그리는 거 좋아해요.
③ M : 무슨 종류의 꽃을 좋아하나요?
    W : 장미를 좋아해요.
④ M : 주문하시겠어요?
    W : 예, 치킨 샐러드 주세요.

9 B: Alice, did you see Jane?
　　G: Yes, she is <u>at the</u> <u>cafeteria</u> now.
　　B: Really?
　　G: Yes, she is <u>having</u> <u>lunch</u> there.
　　B: Oh, I see. Thanks.

9 B: 앨리스, 제인 봤니?
　　G: 응, 지금 구내식당에 있어.
　　B: 정말?
　　G: 응, 거기서 점심 먹고 있어.
　　B: 오, 알았어. 고마워.

10 B: Mary, what are you doing?
　　G: I'm eating some snacks.
　　B: What time does your <u>swimming</u> <u>lesson</u> start?
　　G: It starts at 6 o'clock.
　　B: Hurry up! It's <u>fifteen</u> to <u>six</u>.
　　G: Really? I'm going to be late!

10 B: 메리, 뭐하고 있어?
　　G: 나 과자 먹고 있어.
　　B: 네 수영 수업 몇 시에 시작해?
　　G: 6시에 시작해.
　　B: 서둘러! 6시 15분 전이야.
　　G: 정말? 나 늦겠다!

11 B: It's hot today. How about swimming in the river?
　　G: I don't like swimming.
　　B: Then, how about <u>going</u> to <u>the</u> <u>movies</u>?
　　G: Sounds good! Let me check what movies are <u>on</u> <u>today</u>.

11 B: 오늘 덥다. 강에서 수영하는 거 어때?
　　G: 난 수영하는 걸 좋아하지 않아.
　　B: 그러면 영화 보러 가는 거 어때?
　　G: 좋아! 내가 오늘 무슨 영화하는지 확인해 볼게.

12 G: How was your Christmas?
　　B: It was great.
　　G: <u>What</u> <u>gifts</u> did you get?
　　B: I got a <u>backpack</u>. What about you?
　　G: I got a <u>smartphone</u> from my uncle.
　　B: Really? That's cool.

12 G: 크리스마스 어땠어?
　　B: 좋았어.
　　G: 무슨 선물 받았어?
　　B: 배낭 받았어. 너는 어때?
　　G: 난 삼촌한테 스마트폰 받았어.
　　B: 정말? 멋지다.

13 B: Wow, Susan. This cake is really good.
　　G: Thanks, my mom <u>made</u> <u>it</u> for me yesterday.
　　B: Really? Is your mom a baker?
　　G: No, she's a <u>teacher</u>. Will you have some more cake?
　　B: No, thanks. I'm <u>very</u> <u>full</u>.

13 B: 와우, 수잔. 이 케이크 정말 맛있다.
　　G: 고마워. 엄마가 어제 나에게 만들어주셨어.
　　B: 정말? 엄마가 제빵사야?
　　G: 아니, 선생님이야. 케이크 좀 더 먹을래?
　　B: 아니, 고마워. 정말 배불러.

14 ① W: Tony, do you have <u>any</u> <u>plans</u> this weekend?
　　　M: No, I don't have any special plans.
　　② W: Bob, how was the party?
　　　M: It was great.
　　③ W: Chris, what <u>are</u> you <u>going</u> <u>to</u> do today?
　　　M: I went to the park <u>last</u> <u>night</u>.
　　④ W: Hi, Mike. How are you doing?
　　　M: I'm doing very well. Thanks.

14 ① W: 토니, 이번 주말에 계획 있니?
　　　M: 아니, 나는 특별한 계획은 없어.
　　② W: 밥, 파티 어땠어?
　　　M: 멋졌어.
　　③ W: 크리스, 오늘 뭐할 거야?
　　　M: 지난밤에 공원에 갔어.
　　④ W: 안녕, 마이크. 어떻게 지내?
　　　M: 아주 잘 지내. 고마워.

15 *[Telephone rings.]*
W: Hello, Star Pizza. May I help you?
B: I'd like to make an order.
W: What would you like?
B: I want a medium–sized potato pizza.
W: Anything else?
B: No, that's all.

16 W: ① A man is talking on the phone.
② A man is lying on the floor.
③ A man is sleeping on the sofa.
④ A man is sitting on the sofa.

17 W: Sam, can you help me?
B: Sure. What can I do for you?
W: Can you wash the dishes after dinner?
B: Sure, Mom. Anything else?
W: That's all. Thank you.

18 W: What are you going to have for lunch?
M: I'll have a tuna sandwich. How about you?
W: ① I'll have a chicken salad.
② I don't like sandwiches.
③ That's not my sandwich.
④ I'll go to the park after lunch.

19 W: What did you do yesterday?
M: I went to the park and took many photos of flowers.
W: Wow, that's cool. Can you show me the photos you took?
M: ① It's not my camera.
② I'm sorry to hear that.
③ Okay. Here they are.
④ What kind of flowers do you like?

20 G: Happy birthday, Mike.
B: Thank you for coming to my birthday party.
G: Here is your present.
B: Oh, thanks. Can I open it now?
G: ① No, I can't.
② Of course. Open it!
③ Sure.
④ Yes, I hope you like it.

---

15 *[전화가 울린다.]*
W: 안녕하세요. 스타 피자입니다. 도와드릴까요?
B: 주문하고 싶어요.
W: 무엇을 원하세요?
B: 중간 크기의 포테이토 피자요.
W: 다른 것은요?
B: 아니요. 그게 다예요.

16 W: ① 한 남자가 전화 통화를 하고 있다.
② 한 남자가 바닥에 누워 있다.
③ 한 남자가 소파에서 자고 있다.
④ 한 남자가 소파에 앉아 있다.

17 W: 샘, 나 도와줄래?
B: 물론이죠. 뭐 도와드릴까요?
W: 저녁식사 후에 설거지 좀 해줄래?
B: 예, 엄마. 뭐 다른 거는요?
W: 그게 다야. 고마워.

18 W: 점심으로 뭐 먹을 거야?
M: 참치 샌드위치 먹을 거야. 너는 어때?
W: ① 나는 치킨 샐러드 먹을 거야.
② 나는 샌드위치 좋아하지 않아.
③ 저것은 내 샌드위치가 아니야.
④ 나는 점심 먹고 공원에 갈 거야.

19 W: 어제 뭐했어?
M: 공원에 가서 많은 꽃 사진을 찍었어.
W: 와우, 멋지다. 네가 찍은 사진들을 보여줄 수 있니?
M: ① 그것은 내 카메라가 아니야.
② 그것을 들으니 유감이다.
③ 좋아. 여기 있어.
④ 무슨 종류의 꽃을 좋아하니?

20 G: 생일 축하해, 마이크.
B: 내 생일 파티에 와줘서 고마워.
G: 여기 네 선물이야.
B: 오, 고마워. 지금 열어봐도 되니?
G: ① 아니, 난 할 수 없어.
② 물론이지. 열어봐!
③ 물론.
④ 응. 네가 좋아했으면 좋겠다.

Word Check

01 정말	04 축하해	07 좋아하는	10 확인하다	13 중간 크기의
02 전화하다	05 배낭	08 구내식당	11 주문, 주문하다	14 바닥
03 참치	06 주말	09 과자	12 사진	15 넓다

Sentence Check

01 You don't look happy.
02 You're very good at painting.
03 I'm sorry for not calling you yesterday.
04 She's holding some flowers.
05 She is in the hospital.
06 I want some flowers for my mom.
07 Let me check what movies are on today.
08 I got a smartphone from my uncle.

09 I don't have any special plans.
10 I'm doing very well.
11 A man is talking on the phone.
12 A man is sleeping on the sofa.
13 What are you going to have for lunch?
14 I took many photos of flowers.
15 Thank you for coming to my birthday party.

9 영어 듣기 모의고사

1 ④	2 ②	3 ②	4 ④	5 ②	6 ②	7 ①	8 ①	9 ①	10 ③
11 ①	12 ③	13 ②	14 ②	15 ③	16 ①	17 ②	18 ③	19 ①	20 ④

듣기 대본

1 G: ① How much is it?
   ② It's sunny today.
   ③ Let's take a walk.
   ④ Watch your step!

2 M: ① Can I help you?
   ② Would you like some cookies?
   ③ Can I have some cake?
   ④ How much is this cheese?

3 ① B: May I help you?
   G: Yes, I want some cookies.
   ② B: Where are you from?
   G: I'm from China.
   ③ B: What are you doing here?
   G: I'm doing my homework.
   ④ B: What is your favorite subject?
   G: I like music.

해석

1 G: ① 그거 얼마예요?
   ② 오늘은 맑다.
   ③ 산책하자.
   ④ 발 조심해!

2 M: ① 도와드릴까요?
   ② 쿠키 좀 더 먹을래요?
   ③ 케이크 좀 먹어도 되나요?
   ④ 이 치즈는 얼마예요?

3 ① B: 도와드릴까요?
   G: 예, 쿠키를 좀 주세요.
   ② B: 어디서 왔니?
   G: 중국에서 왔어.
   ③ B: 여기서 뭐하고 있어?
   G: 나는 숙제하고 있어.
   ④ B: 네가 좋아하는 과목이 뭐야?
   G: 난 음악을 좋아해.

4
G: What's wrong, Mike?
B: I have a toothache.
G: Did you go to the dentist?
B: Yes, I did.
G: I think you should stop eating candy.

5
M: Susan, what do you want to have for lunch?
W: I want to eat pizza.
M: Again? We had pizza yesterday. How about chicken fried rice?
W: That sounds good. It's my favorite.

6
B: Who is that girl over there?
G: She's my younger sister, Amy.
B: She's very lovely. How old is she?
G: She's ten years old.
B: Does she go to the same school as you?
G: Yes, we walk to school together.

7
G: James, did you see the soccer game on TV yesterday?
B: No, I didn't.
G: Then, what did you do yesterday?
B: I went fishing with my dad.
G: Really? Did you catch lots of fish?
B: Yes, we did.

8
B: Look! There is my uncle on the stage.
G: Really? What musical instrument is he playing?
B: He's playing the guitar.
G: Is he wearing a baseball cap?
B: No, he's wearing sunglasses.

9
B: Mary, how do you go to school?
G: I usually ride my bike to school.
B: How long does it take from your house to your school?
G: It takes about ten minutes. What about you?
B: My school is near my house, so I walk to school.

10
M: This is a very popular sport. Players cannot use their hands. Players have to use their feet and heads. Players kick a round ball.

11
M: Susan, are you taking photos?
W: Yes. Do you want to see the photos?
M: Look at that sign. You can't take photos here.
W: Oh! I see. I didn't know that.

4
G: 뭐, 잘못됐어, 마이크?
B: 치통이 있어.
G: 치과에는 갔니?
B: 응, 갔어.
G: 너 사탕 먹는 것을 그만두는 게 좋을 것 같아.

5
M: 수잔, 점심으로 뭐 먹고 싶어?
W: 피자 먹고 싶어.
M: 또? 우리 어제 피자 먹었잖아. 치킨 볶음밥 먹는 거 어때?
W: 좋을 것 같아. 그거 내가 좋아하는 거야.

6
B: 저쪽에 있는 소녀 누구야?
G: 내 여동생, 에이미야.
B: 무척 사랑스럽네. 몇 살이야?
G: 10살이야.
B: 너랑 같은 학교에 다니니?
G: 응, 우리는 함께 학교에 걸어가.

7
G: 제임스, 어제 TV로 축구 경기 봤니?
B: 아니, 못 봤어.
G: 그러면 어제 뭐했는데?
B: 아빠랑 낚시하러 갔어.
G: 정말? 물고기 많이 잡았니?
B: 응, 그랬어.

8
B: 봐! 무대 위에 내 삼촌이 있어.
G: 정말? 그가 연주하는 악기가 뭐야?
B: 기타를 연주하고 있어.
G: 야구모자를 쓰고 있니?
B: 아니, 선글라스를 쓰고 있어.

9
B: 메리, 학교에 어떻게 가니?
G: 보통 자전거를 타고 학교에 가.
B: 네 집에서 학교까지 얼마나 걸려?
G: 대략 10분 정도 걸려. 너는 어때?
B: 학교가 집에서 가까워서 학교에 걸어가.

10
M: 이것은 매우 인기 있는 스포츠이다. 선수들은 손을 사용할 수 없다. 선수들은 그들의 발이나 머리를 사용해야 한다. 선수들은 둥근 공을 찬다.

11
M: 수잔, 사진 찍고 있는 거야?
W: 응. 사진 보고 싶어?
M: 저 표지판을 봐. 여기서는 사진을 찍을 수 없어.
W: 오! 알았어. 그것을 몰랐어.

12 W: David, what are you doing?
   B: I'm reading a book.
   W: Can you <u>help me</u>? I'm cleaning the living room.
   B: Sorry, Mom. I'm going to <u>have online classes</u> soon.

12 W : 데이비드, 뭐하고 있니?
   B : 책 읽고 있어요.
   W : 나를 도와줄래? 거실을 청소하고 있어.
   B : 죄송해요, 엄마. 저 곧 온라인으로 수업을 들을 거예요.

13 M: Jane, <u>look up</u> at the sky.
   W: Wow, there are so many stars.
   M: Yeah. Let's <u>set up</u> the tent over there.
   W: Okay. Can we make a <u>campfire</u> here?
   M: No, we can't make a campfire <u>in the mountains</u>.
   W: Oh, I see.

13 M : 제인, 하늘을 봐라.
   W : 와우, 별들이 무척 많아.
   M : 그래. 저쪽에 텐트를 세우자.
   W : 좋아. 여기에 모닥불을 피울 수 있니?
   M : 아니, 우리는 산에서 모닥불을 피울 수 없어.
   W : 오, 알았어.

14 ① M: Where did you buy the bag?
     W: I bought it at the mall.
  ② M: How was your <u>vacation</u>?
     W: It will <u>be sunny</u> tomorrow.
  ③ M: What happened to your leg?
     W: I broke it last week.
  ④ M: Do you like movies?
     W: Yes, I <u>love watching</u> movies.

14 ① M : 그 가방 어디서 샀어?
     W : 쇼핑몰에서 샀어.
  ② M : 네 휴가 어땠어?
     W : 내일 맑을 거야.
  ③ M : 네 다리 무슨 일이야?
     W : 지난주에 부러졌어.
  ④ M : 영화 좋아하니?
     W : 응, 나 영화 보는 거 무척 좋아해.

15 G: Mike, do you have any brothers?
   B: Yes, I have a younger brother.
   G: How old is he?
   B: He's <u>nine years old</u>.
   G: Is he in the second grade?
   B: No, he's in the <u>third grade</u>.

15 G : 마이크, 너 형제 있니?
   B : 응, 남동생이 있어.
   G : 몇 살이야?
   B : 9살이야.
   G : 2학년이야?
   B : 아니, 3학년이야.

16 [Cellphone rings.]
   G: Hello.
   B: Hello, Alice. Where are you?
   G: I'm at home. Why?
   B: I have movie tickets. Do you want to <u>go to the movies</u> with me tonight?
   G: I'm sorry, but I can't. I have to take care of my <u>younger brother</u>.

16 [휴대폰이 울린다.]
   G : 여보세요.
   B : 안녕, 앨리스. 너 어디 있어?
   G : 나 집이야. 왜?
   B : 나 영화표가 있어. 오늘 저녁에 나와 같이 영화 보러 갈래?
   G : 미안한데 못 가. 나 남동생을 돌봐야 해.

17 G: Sam, what's wrong?
   B: I lost my pencil case.
   G: Really?
   B: Yes, I left it on my desk, but it's gone. <u>Can I borrow</u> your pencil?
   G: Sure. <u>Here you are</u>.

17 G : 샘, 뭐 잘못됐어?
   B : 나 필통을 잃어버렸어.
   G : 정말?
   B : 응, 책상 위에 뒀는데 사라졌어. 네 연필 빌릴 수 있니?
   G : 물론. 여기 있어.

18 G: What did you do last night?
B: I watched a <u>basketball</u> <u>game</u> at the gym.
G: <u>How</u> <u>was</u> the game?
B: ① I don't like baseball.
② It was windy last night.
③ It was exciting.
④ We will do it again.

18 G: 지난밤에 뭐했어?
B: 나 체육관에서 농구 경기를 봤어.
G: 경기 어땠어?
B: ① 나는 야구를 좋아하지 않아.
② 지난밤에 바람이 불었어.
③ 흥미진진했어.
④ 우리는 그걸 또 할 거야.

19 W: May I help you?
M: Can I get three potatoes?
W: Sure. Here you are. <u>Anything</u> <u>else</u>?
M: I need four carrots, too.
W: Okay. <u>Is that</u> <u>all</u>?
M: ① Yes, that's all. Thank you.
② Are you all right?
③ I'm tired today.
④ Yes, I love it.

19 W: 도와드릴까요?
M: 감자 세 개 주실 수 있나요?
W: 물론이요. 여기 있어요. 또 다른 것은요?
M: 당근 네 개도 주세요.
W: 알겠어요. 그게 다인가요?
M: ① 예, 다예요. 감사해요.
② 괜찮아요?
③ 나 오늘 피곤해.
④ 예, 그거 무척 좋아해요.

20 M: Excuse me. How can I <u>get</u> <u>to</u> <u>the</u> <u>museum</u> from here?
W: ① You can get there by subway.
② Go straight one block and turn right.
③ Sorry, I'm new here, too.
④ It opens on Sundays.

20 M: 실례합니다. 여기서 박물관에 어떻게 가죠?
W: ① 지하철로 갈 수 있어요.
② 한 블록 곧장 가서 오른쪽으로 도세요.
③ 죄송한데, 저도 여기 처음이에요.
④ 그것은 일요일마다 열어요.

Word Check
본책 p. 112

01 과목	**04** 사랑스러운	**07** 선글라스	**10** 차다	**13** 일어나다
02 치통	**05** 같은	**08** 당근	**11** 곧	**14** 두 번째
03 또, 다시	**06** 무대	**09** 가까운, 가까이	**12** 모닥불	**15** 학년

Sentence Check
본책 p. 113

01 Watch your step!
02 I think you should stop eating candy.
03 I have a toothache.
04 It's my favorite.
05 We walk to school together.
06 I went fishing with my dad.
07 He's wearing sunglasses.
08 I usually ride my bike to school.

09 It takes about ten minutes.
10 Players cannot use their hands.
11 You can't take photos here.
12 I'm going to have online classes soon.
13 We can't make a campfire in the mountains.
14 He's in the third grade.
15 I have to take care of my younger brother.

1 ④	**2** ②	**3** ②	**4** ③	**5** ②	**6** ①	**7** ②	**8** ③	**9** ②	**10** ③
11 ①	**12** ④	**13** ②	**14** ②	**15** ③	**16** ②	**17** ②	**18** ④	**19** ①	**20** ④

듣기 대본
본책 p. 118

1 G: ① Nice to meet you.
② Wash your hands.
③ Please turn on the light.
④ Let's pick up the trash.

2 M: ① How is the weather?
② How beautiful she is!
③ How old are you?
④ How much is this?

3 ① M: Who is that man?
　 W: He's my dad.
② M: Nice to meet you.
　 W: Nice to meet you, too.
③ M: May I help you?
　 W: Yes, I'm looking for a cake.
④ M: Can I ask you something?
　 W: Sure. What is it?

4 B: What did you do last weekend, Cindy?
G: I went camping with my family.
B: Oh, that's cool. Was it fun?
G: Yes, it was. What did you do?
B: I washed my dad's car.

5 M: Susan, what's your favorite season?
W: I like summer because I can swim in the sea.
　 What about you?
M: I like fall.
W: Why do you like it?
M: I love the colorful leaves in fall.

6 M: Susie, what are you doing?
W: I'm looking for the remote control.
　 Did you see it?
M: No, I didn't. Did you look under the sofa?
W: No, I'll check there now.

7 G: Sam, your birthday is coming soon.
B: Yeah. Can you come to my birthday party?
G: Of course. What do you want from your
　 parents? Do you want a smartphone?
B: No, I don't. I want a puppy.

해석

1 G: ① 만나서 반가워.
② 손을 씻어라.
③ 불을 켜 주세요.
④ 쓰레기를 줍자.

2 M: ① 날씨가 어때?
② 그녀는 무척 아름답구나!
③ 너는 몇 살이니?
④ 이것은 얼마니?

3 ① M: 저 남자는 누구니?
　 W: 그는 나의 아빠야.
② M: 만나서 반갑습니다.
　 W: 저도 만나서 반갑습니다.
③ M: 도와드릴까요?
　 W: 예, 케이크를 찾고 있어요.
④ M: 뭐 물어봐도 되니?
　 W: 물론이지. 뭔데?

4 B: 지난 주말에 뭐했어, 신디?
G: 가족이랑 캠핑을 갔어.
B: 오, 멋지다. 재미있었어?
G: 응, 그래. 너는 뭐했어?
B: 나는 아빠 차를 세차했어.

5 M: 수잔, 네가 좋아하는 계절은 뭐야?
W: 나는 바다에서 수영할 수 있어서 여름을 좋아해.
　 너는 언제?
M: 나는 가을을 좋아해.
W: 왜 좋아해?
M: 나는 가을에 단풍을 아주 좋아해.

6 M: 수지야, 뭐하고 있어?
W: 리모컨을 찾고 있어.
　 봤니?
M: 아니, 소파 아래 찾아봤어?
W: 아니, 지금 확인해 볼게.

7 G: 샘, 네 생일이 곧 오네.
B: 응. 내 생일 파티에 올 수 있니?
G: 물론. 부모님께 무엇을 받고 싶어?
　 스마트폰을 원하니?
B: 아니, 나는 강아지를 원해.

8 B: Do you have any hobbies?
  G: I play tennis every weekend. Do you play tennis?
  B: No, but I play table tennis after school.
    Can you play table tennis?
  G: Yes, I can, but I'm not good at it.

8 B: 너는 취미가 있니?
  G: 나는 주말마다 테니스를 쳐. 너 테니스 치니?
  B: 아니, 하지만 방과 후에 탁구를 쳐.
    너 탁구 칠 수 있니?
  G: 어, 할 수 있는데 잘하지는 못해.

9 W: Excuse me. Would you show me the way to
    the museum?
  M: Yes. Go straight and turn right at the corner.
  W: Go straight and turn right?
  M: Yes. It's between the church and the post office.
  W: Thank you so much.

9 W: 실례합니다. 저에게 박물관 가는 길 좀 알려주시겠어요?
  M: 예. 곧장 가서 모퉁이에서 오른쪽으로 도세요.
  W: 곧장 가서 오른쪽으로 돌아요?
  M: 예. 교회와 우체국 사이에 있어요.
  W: 정말 감사합니다.

10 M: I am an animal. I have feathers and wings.
    I can fly.

10 M: 나는 동물이다. 나는 깃털과 날개가 있다.
    나는 날 수 있다.

11 W: John, you look tired. What's wrong?
  M: I didn't sleep well last night.
  W: Did you play computer games again?
  M: No, my dog was sick, so I took care of him
    until late at night.
  W: I'm sorry to hear that.

11 W: 존, 피곤해 보여. 뭐 잘못됐어?
  M: 지난밤에 잠을 잘 못 잤어.
  W: 또 컴퓨터 게임을 했니?
  M: 아니, 내 개가 아파서 밤에 늦게까지 돌봐야 했어.
  W: 그 소리 들으니 유감이다.

12 G: Jason, long time no see.
  B: Hi, Cindy, How are you?
  G: I'm good. Where are you going?
  B: I'm going to the bookstore. How about you?
  G: I'm going to the museum.
    Oh, I have to get off this stop. See you.

12 G: 제이슨, 오랜만이야.
  B: 안녕, 신디. 잘 지냈니?
  G: 난 좋아. 어디 가고 있어?
  B: 나 서점에 가고 있어. 너는 어때?
  G: 나는 박물관에 가고 있어.
    오, 나 이번 정류장에서 내려야 해. 잘 가.

13 ① W: Where are you from?
    M: I'm from India.
  ② W: What do you want to have for dinner?
    M: I had sandwiches this morning.
  ③ W: Peter, I have something to ask you.
    M: What is that?
  ④ W: When is your birthday?
    M: It's November 10.

13 ① W: 어디서 왔니?
    M: 나 인도에서 왔어.
  ② W: 저녁으로 뭐 먹고 싶어?
    M: 나는 오늘 아침에 샌드위치 먹었어.
  ③ W: 피터, 너한테 묻고 싶은 게 있어.
    M: 그게 뭔데?
  ④ W: 네 생일이 언제야?
    M: 11월 10일이야.

14 W: Mike, what did you do yesterday?
  M: I made dinner for my sister. Yesterday was her
    birthday.
  W: Really? Can you cook?
  M: Yes, I took a cooking class last year.
  W: What kind of food did you make?
  M: I made some tomato pasta.
  W: Wow, that's cool.

14 W: 마이크, 어제 뭐했어?
  M: 여동생에 줄 저녁을 만들었어. 어제가 생일이었어.
  W: 정말? 너 요리할 수 있어?
  M: 응, 작년에 요리 수업을 들었어.
  W: 무슨 종류의 음식을 만들었어?
  M: 토마토 파스타 만들었어.
  W: 와우, 멋지다.

15 [Cellphone rings.]
G: Hello.
B: Hello, Alice. Where are you?
G: I'm <u>at home</u>.
B: How about <u>going</u> <u>swimming</u> this afternoon?
G: Sorry, but I can't.
B: Do you have to do your homework?
G: No, I have to <u>clean</u> my <u>room</u>.

15 [휴대폰이 울린다.]
G: 여보세요.
B: 안녕, 앨리스. 어디야?
G: 나 집이야.
B: 오후에 수영하러 가는 거 어때?
G: 미안한데, 못 가.
B: 숙제해야 하니?
G: 아니, 방 청소를 해야 해.

16 W: What are you going to do during <u>summer</u> <u>vacation</u>?
M: I'm going to Busan.
W: I love it there. That's a great choice.
M: <u>How</u> <u>about</u> you?
W: I don't have any <u>special</u> <u>plans</u> yet.

16 W: 여름 휴가 동안 뭐할 거야?
M: 부산에 갈 거야.
W: 나 거기 너무 좋아. 훌륭한 선택이야.
M: 너는 어때?
W: 나는 무슨 특별한 계획이 아직 없어.

17 G: Jason, where are you going?
B: I'm going to my piano lesson.
G: Do you have a <u>piano</u> <u>lesson</u> today?
B: Yes, I have piano lessons on Tuesdays and Fridays.
G: I thought today was Wednesday.
B: No, <u>today</u> is <u>Tuesday</u>.

17 G: 제이슨, 어디 가고 있어?
B: 나 피아노 수업 가고 있어.
G: 너 오늘 피아노 수업이 있어?
B: 응, 화요일과 금요일에 피아노 수업이 있어.
G: 오늘 화요일이야? 나는 오늘이 수요일이라고 생각했어.
B: 아니, 오늘은 화요일이야.

18 G: Peter, you <u>look</u> <u>tired</u>. What did you do last night?
B: I practiced dancing for the festival.
G: <u>When</u> <u>is</u> the festival?
B: ① I like dancing.
　② It's at the corner.
　③ It is very fun.
　④ It's this Saturday.

18 G: 피터, 피곤해 보여. 지난밤에 뭐했어?
B: 축제를 위해서 춤 연습을 했어.
G: 축제가 언제야?
B: ① 나는 춤추는 것을 좋아해.
　② 그것은 모퉁이에 있어.
　③ 그것은 무척 즐거워.
　④ 이번 주 토요일이야.

19 W: Brian, what are you doing?
M: Why? Do you need something?
W: Yes. Can you <u>help</u> <u>me</u> move this box? It's <u>too</u> <u>heavy</u> for me.
M: ① Okay. No problem.
　② No, it's not my book.
　③ I'm sorry to hear that.
　④ What a nice book!

19 W: 브라이언, 뭐하고 있어?
M: 왜? 뭐 필요하니?
W: 응. 이 상자 옮기는 거 도와줄래? 나에게는 너무 무거워.
M: ① 좋아. 문제 없어.
　② 아니, 그것은 내 책이 아니야.
　③ 그거 들으니 유감이다.
　④ 무척 멋진 책이구나!

20 B: Amy, is this <u>your</u> <u>camera</u>?
G: Yes, it is.
B: It's very nice. Where did you <u>get</u> <u>it</u>?
G: ① I bought it last week.
　② My dad bought it for me.
　③ I borrowed it from my friend.
　④ It's on the table.

20 B: 에이미, 이거 네 카메라니?
G: 응, 그래.
B: 무척 멋지다. 어디서 났어?
G: ① 지난주에 샀어.
　② 아빠가 나에게 사주셨어.
　③ 내 친구한테 빌렸어.
　④ 그것은 식탁 위에 있어.

01 동물	04 곧장, 똑바로	07 리모컨	10 깃털	13 선택
02 계절	05 연습하다	08 모퉁이	11 날개	14 아직
03 형형색색의	06 (길 등을) 가리키다	09 쓰레기	12 무거운	15 축제

Sentence Check 본책 p. 125

01 Let's pick up the trash.
02 How beautiful she is!
03 Can I ask you something?
04 I washed my dad's car.
05 I like summer because I can swim in the sea.
06 I love the colorful leaves in fall.
07 I'm looking for the remote control.
08 I play tennis every weekend.
09 Go straight and turn right at the corner.
10 I have feathers and wings.
11 I took care of him until late at night.
12 I have to get off this stop.
13 I have something to ask you.
14 I don't have any special plans yet.
15 I practiced dancing for the festival.

11 영어 듣기 모의고사
본책 p. 126

| 1 ③ | 2 ④ | 3 ③ | 4 ② | 5 ① | 6 ② | 7 ④ | 8 ③ | 9 ② | 10 ④ |
| 11 ③ | 12 ① | 13 ① | 14 ③ | 15 ④ | 16 ① | 17 ② | 18 ④ | 19 ① | 20 ③ |

듣기 대본 본책 p. 130

1 W: ① I'm sorry, but I can't help you.
② Thank you for helping me.
③ Don't worry. Everything will be okay.
④ Let's have dinner together.

2 B: ① Where is your notebook?
② How much is this book?
③ I don't play computer games.
④ Can I use your phone?

3 M: Alice, what did you have for lunch?
W: I had pasta.
M: Again?
W: Yes, it's my favorite.
What's your favorite food?
M: I like gimbap.

4 B: ① Do not jump here.
② Do not swim here.
③ Do not run here.
④ Do not park here.

해석

1 W: ① 미안한데 너를 도울 수가 없어.
② 나를 도와줘서 고마워.
③ 걱정하지 마. 모든 것이 잘 될 거야.
④ 함께 저녁을 먹자.

2 B: ① 네 공책 어디에 있어?
② 이 책 얼마야?
③ 나는 컴퓨터 게임을 하지 않아.
④ 네 전화기 써도 되니?

3 M: 앨리스, 점심으로 뭐 먹었어?
W: 파스타 먹었어.
M: 또?
W: 응, 그게 내가 좋아하는 거야.
네가 좋아하는 음식은 뭐야?
M: 나는 김밥 좋아해.

4 B: ① 여기서 뛰지 마라.
② 여기서 수영하지 마라.
③ 여기서 달리지 마라.
④ 여기에 주차하지 마라.

5 B: How are you, Susie?

G: I'm fine. Thanks. How are you?

B: I don't feel good today. I'm <u>tired</u> and <u>sleepy</u>.

G: Why?

B: I did my homework <u>until</u> <u>midnight</u>.

5 B: 잘 지내니, 수지?

G: 좋아. 고마워. 너는 어때?

B: 나는 오늘 기분이 좋지 않아. 피곤하고 졸려.

G: 왜?

B: 자정까지 숙제를 했거든.

6 M: Cathy, what are you going to do tomorrow?

W: I'm going to the beach with my friends.

M: Did you check the <u>weather report</u>?

W: No, I didn't.

M: It said it would <u>be rainy</u> tomorrow.

W: Oh, no.

6 W: 캐시, 내일 뭐할 거야?

M: 친구들하고 해변에 갈 거야.

W: 일기예보 확인했니?

M: 아니, 안 했는데.

W: 내일 비가 올 거라고 했어.

M: 오, 안돼.

7 G: James do you like pizza?

B: Yes, I do. It's my <u>favorite</u>.

G: I'm going to the pizza store with Jane after school. Do you want to <u>come with us</u>?

B: Sorry, I can't. I have to take an <u>English</u> language <u>program</u> after school.

7 G: 제임스, 피자 좋아하니?

B: 응, 그래. 내가 무척 좋아하는 거야.

G: 나 방과 후에 제인이랑 피자 가게 갈 거야. 우리랑 같이 갈래?

B: 미안해, 갈 수 없어. 방과 후 영어 프로그램에 참석해야 해.

8 W: Good afternoon. May I help you?

M: Good afternoon. I want to buy <u>some apples</u> and strawberries.

W: Sorry, we don't have any apples today.

M: Then, I'll just <u>buy strawberries</u>.

W: How many boxes of strawberries do you want?

M: <u>Three</u>.

8 W: 안녕하세요. 도와드릴까요?

M: 안녕하세요. 사과랑 딸기를 좀 사려고요.

W: 죄송해요, 오늘 사과가 없어요.

M: 그러면 딸기만 사야겠네요.

W: 딸기 몇 상자 원하세요?

M: 세 개요.

9 ① B: How much is this toy car?

G: It's 20 dollars.

② B: I won <u>first prize</u> in the contest.

G: Wow, <u>congratulations</u>.

③ B: Where did you get that?

G: I <u>bought it</u> last week.

④ B: What are you doing?

G: I'm looking for my bag.

9 ① B: 이 장난감 자동차 얼마예요?

G: 20달러예요.

② B: 나 대회에서 1등 했어.

G: 와우, 축하해.

③ B: 그거 어디에서 났어?

G: 지난주에 샀어.

④ B: 뭐하고 있어?

G: 내 가방을 찾고 있어.

10 G: John, what time do you get up?

B: I <u>usually</u> get up at 7.

G: Do you have breakfast <u>every day</u>?

B: Yes, I have scrambled eggs and milk for breakfast.

G: How do you go to school?

B: My school is near my house, so I <u>walk to school</u>.

G: What time does your school start?

B: It starts at 9:30.

10 G: 존, 몇 시에 일어나?

B: 나는 보통 7시에 일어나.

G: 매일 아침식사를 하니?

B: 응, 스크램블 에그와 우유를 아침으로 먹어.

G: 학교에는 어떻게 가?

B: 학교가 집에서 가까워서 걸어서 가.

G: 학교는 몇 시에 시작해?

B: 9시 30분에 시작해.

11 M: Hi, Cindy, did you go shopping yesterday?
W: No, I didn't.
M: Then, what did you do?
W: I cooked dinner for my family.
M: Oh, that's great.

11 M: 안녕, 신디. 어제 쇼핑하러 갔니?
W: 아니, 안 갔어.
M: 그러면, 뭐했어?
W: 가족을 위해 저녁을 만들었어.
M: 오, 훌륭하다.

12 M: Jennifer, are you busy tomorrow?
W: No, I'm not.
M: How about going to the museum?
W: Sounds good.
M: Then, let's meet at the bus stop at 2 o'clock.
W: Okay. See you tomorrow.

12 M: 제니퍼, 내일 바쁘니?
W: 아니, 안 바빠.
M: 박물관 가는 거 어때?
W: 좋아.
M: 그러면, 버스 정류장에서 2시에 만나자.
W: 좋아. 내일 봐.

13 M: Jane, do you like tennis?
W: No, I don't.
M: What's your favorite sport?
W: I like bowling.
M: Me too. I go bowling every weekend.
Let's go bowling together tomorrow.
W: Okay.

13 M: 제인, 테니스 좋아하니?
W: 아니, 안 좋아해.
M: 좋아하는 운동이 뭐야?
W: 나 볼링 좋아해.
M: 나도 그래. 난 주말마다 볼링하러 가.
내일 함께 볼링 치러 가자.
W: 좋아.

14 ① G: What's your favorite color?
B: My favorite color is blue.
② G: Did you make this cake?
B: Yes, I did.
③ G: What does your father do?
B: He is in the living room.
④ G: Is this your pencil?
B: No, it's not mine.

14 ① G: 네가 좋아하는 색이 뭐야?
B: 내가 좋아하는 색은 파란색이야.
② G: 이 케이크 네가 만들었니?
B: 응, 그래.
③ G: 네 아버지는 뭐하시니?
B: 거실에 계셔.
④ G: 이거 네 연필이니?
B: 아니, 내 것이 아니야.

15 [Cellphone rings.]
G: Hello.
B: Hello, Alice. Where are you?
G: I'm at home. What's up?
B: I can't meet you today.
G: Why?
B: I have a fever and a headache.
G: Oh, that's too bad. Take care of yourself.

15 [휴대폰이 울린다.]
G: 여보세요.
B: 안녕, 앨리스. 어디 있니?
G: 집이야. 무슨 일이야?
B: 오늘 널 못 만나.
G: 왜?
B: 열이 나고 두통이 있어.
G: 오, 안됐다. 몸조리 잘해.

16 B: Mom, where is Dad?
W: He's in the garage.
B: Is he washing the car there?
W: No, he's cleaning the garage.
B: Okay. I will go and help him.

16 B: 엄마, 아빠 어디 계세요?
W: 차고에 계셔.
B: 거기서 세차하고 계세요?
W: 아니, 차고 청소하고 있어.
B: 알겠어요. 가서 도와드릴게요.

17 G: Tomorrow is Jina's birthday. What are you going to buy for her?
B: I'm going to buy her a baseball cap.
G: Well... She doesn't like wearing baseball caps.
B: Then, how about socks?
G: Good. She told me she needed some socks.

17 G: 내일 지나의 생일이야. 그녀를 위해 뭘 살 거야?
B: 야구모자를 살 거야.
G: 음… 그녀는 야구모자 쓰는 것을 좋아하지 않아.
B: 그러면, 양말은 어때?
G: 좋아. 나한테 양말이 좀 필요하다고 말했어.

18 M: Look at those cats over there. Do you like cats, Julie?
W: Yes, I love cats. What about you?
M: ① They are not my cats.
② I don't have cats.
③ Yes, I want the cat.
④ I like cats very much.

18 M: 저쪽에 고양이들을 봐. 너 고양이 좋아하니, 줄리?
W: 응, 무척 좋아해. 너는 어때?
M: ① 그들은 내 고양이가 아니야.
② 나는 고양이가 없어.
③ 응, 나는 그 고양이를 원해.
④ 나 고양이 무척 좋아해.

19 B: Hi, Sara. Did you see Mike today?
G: No, he didn't come to school.
B: Do you know why he was absent?
G: ① He is sick in bed.
② He likes science.
③ I'll visit him after school.
④ He's my best friend.

19 B: 안녕, 사라. 오늘 마이크 봤니?
G: 아니, 오늘 학교에 오지 않았어.
B: 왜 결석했는지 아니?
G: ① 아파서 누워 있어.
② 과학을 좋아해.
③ 방과 후에 그를 방문할 거야.
④ 내 제일 친한 친구야.

20 B: Amy, what do you do after school?
G: I read books and practice the piano.
B: Wow, you are very diligent.
G: Thanks. Do you like reading books?
B: ① Yes, reading is my hobby.
② Yes, I like reading fairy tales.
③ No, I don't go to the library.
④ No, I don't like reading books.

20 B: 에이미, 방과 후에 뭐하니?
G: 나는 책을 읽고 피아노 연습을 해.
B: 와우, 무척 부지런하구나.
G: 고마워. 너 책 읽는 거 좋아하니?
B: ① 응, 독서는 내 취미야.
② 응, 나 동화책 읽는 거 좋아해.
③ 아니, 나는 도서관에 가지 않아.
④ 아니, 독서를 좋아하지 않아.

Word Check
본책 p. 136

01 걱정하다 **04** 내일 **07** 자정, 한밤중 **10** 두통 **13** 열
02 모든 것 **05** 대회 **08** 시작하다 **11** 차고 **14** 부지런한
03 주차하다, 공원 **06** 보통 **09** 볼링 **12** 결석한 **15** 취미

Sentence Check
본책 p. 137

01 Everything will be okay.
02 Do not park here.
03 I did my homework until midnight.
04 It said it would be rainy tomorrow.
05 I have to take an English language program after school.
06 I won first prize in the contest.
07 My school is near my house, so I walk to school.
08 Let's meet at the bus stop at 2 o'clock.
09 Let's go bowling together tomorrow.
10 I have a fever and a headache.
11 Take care of yourself.
12 I will go and help him.
13 She told me she needed some socks.
14 Look at those cats over there.
15 I read books and practice the piano.

| 1 ③ | 2 ④ | 3 ① | 4 ③ | 5 ④ | 6 ③ | 7 ② | 8 ④ | 9 ② | 10 ① |
| 11 ④ | 12 ② | 13 ④ | 14 ③ | 15 ③ | 16 ① | 17 ③ | 18 ③ | 19 ① | 20 ④ |

듣기 대본 본책 p. 142

1 ① M: What's your favorite color?
W: I like green.
② M: Alice, where do you live?
W: I live in Seoul.
③ M: Would you like to come to my house?
W: Okay. I'd love to.
④ M: Thank you for your help.
W: My pleasure.

2 W: ① Get up now. It's 8 o'clock.
② Hurry up. You're late.
③ Come in, this is my room.
④ Goodbye. See you tomorrow.

3 ① B: Do you want some more?
G: Yes, it's delicious.
② B: What are you doing?
G: I'm making dinner.
③ B: What did you do after lunch?
G: I played soccer.
④ B: Let's have sandwiches for lunch.
W: That's a great idea.

4 B: Hi, Susan. What are you going to do tomorrow?
G: I'll go skating with Sara.
B: Oh, that sounds fun.
G: Do you want to join us?
B: Sorry, I can't. I have a piano lesson.

5 B: Susie, did you find your bag?
G: No, I didn't.
B: Is your bag yellow?
G: No, it's green, and there is a bear on it.
B: Oh, I see.

6 G: What's your favorite subject?
B: I like art because I like drawing.
How about you?
G: I like science.
B: Why do you like it?
G: It's interesting, and I want to become a
scientist in the future.
B: I think you will be a great scientist.

해석

1 ① M : 네가 좋아하는 색이 뭐야?
W : 나는 초록색을 좋아해.
② M : 앨리스, 어디에서 살아?
W : 서울에 살아.
③ M : 나의 집에 올래?
W : 좋아. 그러고 싶어.
④ M : 도와줘서 고마워.
W : 천만에.

2 W : ① 지금 일어나. 8시야.
② 서둘러. 늦었어.
③ 들어와, 이게 네 방이야.
④ 잘 가. 내일 보자.

3 ① B : 더 먹을래?
G : 응, 맛있어.
② B : 뭐하고 있어?
G : 저녁을 만들고 있어.
③ B : 점심 먹고 뭐했어?
G : 축구를 했어.
④ B : 점심으로 샌드위치 먹자.
G : 좋은 생각이야.

4 B : 안녕, 수잔. 내일 뭐할 거야?
G : 사라와 스케이트 타러 갈 거야.
B : 오, 재미있을 것 같다.
G : 우리랑 같이 갈래?
B : 미안해, 갈 수 없어. 피아노 수업이 있거든.

5 B : 수지, 네 가방 찾았니?
G : 아니, 못 찾았어.
B : 네 가방이 노란색이니?
G : 아니, 초록색이고 위에 곰이 그려 있어.
B : 오, 알았어.

6 G : 네가 좋아하는 과목이 뭐야?
B : 나는 그리기를 좋아하기 때문에 미술을 좋아해.
너는 어때?
G : 나는 과학을 좋아해.
B : 왜 좋아하니?
G : 재미있고 장래에 과학자가 되고 싶거든.
B : 네가 훌륭한 과학자가 될 거라고 생각해.

7 G: What happened to your arm?
  B: ① I got into a car accident.
    ② I fell down the stairs.
    ③ I slipped on ice.
    ④ I fell down from a tree.

7 G: 네 팔 무슨 일이야?
  B: ① 자동차 사고를 당했어.
    ② 계단에서 넘어졌어.
    ③ 얼음에서 미끄러졌어.
    ④ 나무에서 떨어졌어.

8 W: This is a large, rectangular piece of furniture. You use this when you sleep at night. You can see this in your room.

8 W: 이것은 크고, 직사각형의 가구이다. 여러분은 이것을 밤에 잘 때 이용한다. 여러분 방에서 이것을 볼 수 있다.

9 W: Paul, what are you doing?
  B: I'm playing a computer game.
  W: It's time for bed.
    Turn off the computer.
  B: What time is it, Mom?
  W: It's 10:30.
  B: Okay. Good night.

9 W: 폴, 뭐하고 있니?
  B: 컴퓨터 게임을 하고 있어요.
  W: 잘 시간이야.
    컴퓨터를 꺼라.
  B: 몇 시예요, 엄마?
  W: 10시 30분이야.
  B: 알겠어요. 안녕히 주무세요.

10 W: Happy birthday, Mike. This is for you.
  B: Thank you. Can I open it now?
  W: Sure.
  B: Wow, what a nice watch!
  W: Do you like it?
  B: Yes, I love it. Thank you.

10 W: 생일 축하해, 마이크. 이거 널 위한 거야.
  B: 감사해요. 지금 열어봐도 되나요?
  W: 물론이지.
  B: 와우, 정말 멋진 시계예요!
  W: 마음에 드니?
  B: 예, 무척 좋아요. 감사해요.

11 W: May I help you?
  M: Yes, I'd like to send this package to Seoul.
  W: How do you want to send it?
  M: By airmail. How much is it?
  W: It's 20 dollars.

11 W: 도와드릴까요?
  M: 예, 이 소포를 서울로 보내고 싶어요.
  W: 어떻게 보내고 싶으세요?
  M: 항공우편으로요. 얼마예요?
  W: 20달러예요.

12 M: Hi, Jennifer. What did you do during this vacation?
  W: I went to Hawaii with my family. It was so fun. What about you?
  M: I took a cooking class.
  W: Really?
  M: Yes, I learned to make many different kinds of food.

12 M: 안녕, 제니퍼. 이번 휴가 동안 뭐했어?
  W: 가족이랑 하와이에 갔어.
    무척 재미있었어. 너는 어때?
  M: 난 요리 수업을 들었어.
  W: 정말?
  M: 응. 많은 여러 가지 음식 만드는 것을 배웠어.

13 M: Jane, what sport do you like?
  W: I like volleyball. I'm a member of the volleyball team.
  M: That's cool.
  W: What sport do you like?
  M: I like basketball. I play basketball in my free time.

13 M: 제인, 무슨 스포츠를 좋아해?
  W: 나는 배구를 좋아해. 나는 배구팀 회원이야.
  M: 멋지다.
  W: 너는 무슨 스포츠 좋아해?
  M: 나는 농구를 좋아해. 여가 시간에 농구를 해.

14 ① M: May I have some water?
W: Sure. <u>Here you are</u>.
② M: Would you like some more chicken?
W: No, thanks. I'm full.
③ M: What do you do in your <u>free time</u>?
W: I want to be <u>a teacher</u>.
④ M: Good morning, everyone.
W: Good morning, Mr. Brown.

14 ① M: 물 좀 먹을 수 있나요?
W: 물론이죠. 여기 있어요.
② M: 치킨 좀 더 먹을래요?
W: 아니요, 감사해요. 배불러요.
③ M: 여가 시간에 뭐해?
W: 나는 선생님이 되고 싶어.
④ M: 안녕하세요, 여러분.
W: 안녕하세요, 브라운 선생님.

15 W: ① A boy is <u>eating food</u>.
② There is some water in the cup.
③ A boy is <u>holding a cup</u>.
④ There is a clock on the wall.

15 W: ① 소년이 음식을 먹고 있다.
② 컵에 물이 좀 있다.
③ 소년이 컵을 들고 있다.
④ 벽에 시계가 있다.

16 B: Jina, which after-school clubs do you want to join?
G: I want to join the <u>swimming club</u>. How about you?
B: I don't know yet.
G: How about joining the <u>reading club</u>? You like reading books.
B: Oh, that's a <u>good idea</u>.

16 B: 지나, 무슨 방과 후 동아리 가입하고 싶어?
G: 수영 동아리에 가입하고 싶어. 너는 어때?
B: 아직 모르겠어.
G: 독서 동아리 가입하는 거 어때? 너 책 읽는 거 좋아하잖아.
B: 오, 좋은 생각이야.

17 M: Alice, when are you going to the aquarium?
W: Tomorrow.
M: Oh, <u>what day</u> is it today? Is it Thursday?
W: No, <u>it's Friday</u>.
M: Then, are you going there on Saturday?
W: Yes, I am.

17 M: 앨리스, 너 언제 아쿠아리움 갈 거니?
W: 내일.
M: 오, 오늘 무슨 요일이야? 목요일?
W: 아니, 금요일이야.
M: 그럼, 너 토요일에 거기 가는 거야?
W: 응, 그래.

18 G: What did you do <u>last weekend</u>?
B: I visited my uncle.
G: Where does <u>he live</u>?
B: ① He's a farmer.
② He's tall and handsome.
③ He lives in Incheon.
④ He's 21 years old.

18 G: 너 지난 주말에 뭐했어?
B: 나 삼촌댁을 방문했어.
G: 어디 사시는데?
B: ① 그는 농부야.
② 그는 키가 크고 잘생기셨어.
③ 그는 인천에 사셔.
④ 그는 21살이야.

19 G: Kevin, what does your mother do?
B: Do you mean <u>her job</u>?
G: Yes.
B: ① She works at a bank.
② She's busy every day.
③ My mom doesn't have a car.
④ She is in the living room now.

19 G: 케빈, 너의 어머니는 무슨 일을 하셔?
B: 엄마 직업을 말하는 거야?
G: 응.
B: ① 그녀는 은행에서 일하셔.
② 그녀는 매일 바쁘셔.
③ 나의 엄마는 자동차가 없으셔.
④ 그녀는 지금 거실에 있어.

20
W: Did you <u>eat</u> <u>out</u> last night?
M: Yes, I went to the new restaurant next to the bank.
W: Do you mean the Chinese <u>restaurant</u>?
M: Yes.
W: <u>How</u> <u>was</u> the food?
M: ① Really good.
② The fried rice was amazing.
③ Very tasty.
④ It was very boring.

20
W: 지난밤에 외식했니?
M: 응, 은행 옆에 있는 새로운 식당에 갔어.
W: 중국 식당 말하는 거야?
M: 응.
W: 음식 어땠어?
M: ① 정말 맛있었어.
② 볶음밥이 끝내줬어.
③ 아주 맛있었어.
④ 그거 무척 지루했어.

Word Check
본책 p. 148

01 즐거움	**04** 재미있는	**07** 미끄러지다	**10** 소포	**13** 시계
02 맛있는	**05** ~이 되다	**08** 직사각형의	**11** 여러 가지의	**14** 동아리
03 미술	**06** 계단	**09** 가구	**12** 회원	**15** 수족관, 아쿠아리움

Sentence Check
본책 p. 149

01 Thank you for your help.
02 That's a great idea.
03 I have a piano lesson.
04 I like art because I like drawing.
05 I think you will be a great scientist.
06 I fell down the stairs.
07 You use this when you sleep at night.
08 It's time for bed.

09 I'd like to send this package to Seoul.
10 I learned to make many different kinds of food.
11 I'm a member of the volleyball team.
12 I play basketball in my free time.
13 A boy is holding a cup.
14 What does your mother do?
15 I went to the new restaurant next to the bank.

13 ^하 영어 듣기 모의고사
본책 p. 150

1 ③	**2** ①	**3** ④	**4** ③	**5** ②	**6** ①	**7** ④	**8** ④	**9** ②	**10** ①
11 ④	**12** ④	**13** ①	**14** ②	**15** ②	**16** ①	**17** ④	**18** ④	**19** ①	**20** ④

1
M: ① It's time to <u>wake</u> <u>up</u>.
② Let's have dinner together.
③ Have a <u>good</u> <u>night</u>, Sally.
④ Turn on the light, please.

1
W: ① 일어날 시간이야.
② 함께 저녁 먹자.
③ 잘 자, 샐리.
④ 불을 켜 주세요.

2
M: Susan, can you speak any foreign languages?
W: Yes, I can <u>speak</u> Korean. How about you?
M: I can <u>speak</u> <u>Chinese</u> and Spanish.
W: Wow, that's cool.

2
M: 수잔, 너는 외국어를 말할 수 있니?
W: 응, 한국말을 할 수 있어. 너는 어때?
M: 나는 중국어와 스페인어를 말할 수 있어.
W: 와우, 멋지다.

3 ① M: Are there any strawberries in the box?
　　W: No, there aren't.
② M: Where are you going?
　　W: I'm going to the market.
③ M: What's your favorite fruit?
　　W: I like apples.
④ M: May I help you?
　　W: Yes, I want some strawberries.

3 ① M: 상자 안에 딸기가 좀 있니?
　　W: 아니, 없어.
② M: 어디 가고 있어?
　　W: 시장에 가고 있어.
③ M: 네가 좋아하는 과일이 뭐야?
　　W: 난 사과 좋아해.
④ M: 도와드릴까요?
　　W: 예, 딸기를 좀 주세요.

---

4 M: Sara, what do you do in your free time?
W: I watch movies.
M: What kind of movie do you like?
W: I like comedy.
M: I like comedy, too. They make me feel good.

4 M: 사라, 여가 시간에 뭐해?
W: 난 영화를 봐.
M: 무슨 종류의 영화를 좋아해?
W: 코미디 좋아해.
M: 나도 코미디 좋아해. 그것들은 기분을 좋게 만들어.

---

5 M: ① Do not run.
② Do not eat and drink here.
③ Do not park here.
④ Do not sit here.

5 M: ① 뛰지 마라.
② 여기서 먹거나 마시지 마라.
③ 여기에 주차하지 마라.
④ 여기에 앉지 마라.

---

6 W: Sam, how was the party last night?
M: It was very fun. Why didn't you come to the party?
W: I was busy last night.
M: Why?
W: My mom was sick, so I made dinner and took care of my younger brother.

6 W: 샘, 지난밤 파티 어땠어?
M: 매우 즐거웠어. 너는 왜 파티에 오지 않았어?
W: 지난밤에 바빴어.
M: 왜?
W: 엄마가 아프셔서 내가 저녁을 만들고 남동생을 돌봤어.

---

7 G: David, is your brother in the bookstore?
B: Yes, he's standing over there.
G: Is he wearing glasses?
B: No, he isn't. He's wearing a white T-shirt and blue pants.

7 G: 데이비드, 네 형이 서점 안에 있니?
B: 응, 저쪽에 서 있어.
G: 안경을 쓰고 있니?
B: 아니. 흰 티셔츠에 파란 바지를 입고 있어.

---

8 M: What's wrong?
G: I have a fever and a runny nose.
M: Let me check.
G: I have a headache, too.
M: You have a cold, so stay home and get some rest.

8 M: 어디가 아픈가요?
G: 열이 나고 콧물이 흘러요.
M: 확인해 볼게요.
G: 두통도 있어요.
M: 감기에 걸렸으니, 집에서 머물면서 휴식을 취하세요.

---

9 G: What do you want to be in the future?
B: I want to be a police officer. What about you?
G: I really want to be a writer like my dad.
B: I think you will be a great writer.
G: Thanks.

9 G: 너는 장래에 무엇이 되고 싶어?
B: 나는 경찰관이 되고 싶어. 너는 어때?
G: 나는 정말로 아빠처럼 작가가 되고 싶어.
B: 너는 훌륭한 작가가 될 수 있을 거라 생각해.
G: 고마워.

10 G: Hi, Paul. How was your weekend?
B: It was not good.
G: Why?
B: I was <u>sick</u> <u>in</u> <u>bed</u>.
G: Oh, I'm sorry to hear that. Are you okay now?
B: Yes, I <u>feel</u> <u>better</u>.

10 G: 안녕, 폴. 주말 어땠어?
B: 좋지 않았어.
G: 왜?
B: 아파서 누워 있었어.
G: 오, 그 말 들으니 안됐다. 지금은 괜찮아?
B: 응, 나아졌어.

11 G: Sam, what are you going to do after school?
B: I have a <u>tennis</u> <u>lesson</u> today. How about you?
G: I'm going to <u>practice</u> <u>the</u> <u>piano</u>.
B: Do you practice the piano every day?
G: Yes, the <u>piano</u> <u>contest</u> is next Saturday.
B: Oh, I see.

11 G: 샘, 방과 후에 뭐할 거야?
B: 나 테니스 수업이 오늘 있어. 너는 어때?
G: 나는 피아노 연습을 할 거야.
B: 너는 매일 피아노 연습을 하니?
G: 응, 피아노 대회가 다음 주 토요일이야.
B: 오, 알았어.

12 [Cellphone rings.]
B: Hello.
G: Hi, Mike. This is Alice. What are you doing now?
B: I'm watching TV at home. Why?
G: I'm going to <u>a concert</u> today. Will you come with me?
B: Sure. What time shall we meet?
G: <u>Let's</u> <u>meet</u> at the bus stop at 5.

12 [휴대폰이 울린다.]
B: 여보세요.
G: 안녕, 마이크. 나 앨리스야. 지금 뭐하고 있어?
B: 나 집에서 TV 보고 있어. 왜?
G: 나 오늘 음악회 보러 갈 거야. 나랑 같이 갈래?
B: 물론이지. 몇 시에 만날까?
G: 버스 정류장에서 5시에 만나자.

13 M: Excuse me. How can I get to the aquarium?
W: Let me see. <u>Go</u> <u>straight</u> one block and <u>turn</u> <u>left</u>.
M: Go straight one block and turn left?
W: Yes, it'll be on your right <u>next</u> <u>to</u> the hospital.
M: Oh, I see. Thank you very much.

13 M: 실례합니다. 수족관에 어떻게 가야 하나요?
W: 어디 봐요. 한 블록 곧장 가서 왼쪽으로 도세요.
M: 한 블록 곧장 가서 왼쪽으로 돌아요?
W: 예, 병원 옆에 당신 오른쪽에 있어요.
M: 오, 알겠어요. 무척 감사합니다.

14 W: ① He's dancing in the room
② He's <u>catching</u> <u>a</u> <u>ball</u>.
③ He's passing a ball.
④ He's <u>sitting</u> on the bench.

14 W: ① 그는 방에서 춤을 추고 있다.
② 그는 공을 잡고 있다.
③ 그는 공을 건네고 있다.
④ 그는 벤치에 앉아 있다.

15 B: Mom, <u>I'm</u> <u>home</u>.
W: How was your day at school?
B: It was a lot of fun today. I'm <u>a little</u> hungry. Can I have a snack?
W: Sure. But <u>wash</u> <u>your</u> <u>hands</u> first.
B: Okay, Mom.

15 B: 엄마, 집에 왔어요.
W: 학교에서 어땠어?
B: 오늘 많이 즐거웠어요. 조금 배고파요. 과자를 좀 먹어도 되나요?
W: 물론, 하지만 손 먼저 씻어라.
B: 알겠어요. 엄마.

16 B: Jessie, what's your <u>favorite</u> <u>month</u>?
G: I like <u>April</u>. I can see a lot of beautiful flowers in April. What's your favorite month?
B: I <u>like</u> <u>October</u>.
G: Why?
B: My birthday is in October.

16 B: 제시, 네가 좋아하는 달이 뭐야?
G: 나는 4월을 좋아해. 4월에는 아름다운 많은 꽃들을 볼 수 있어. 네가 좋아하는 달은 뭐야?
B: 나는 10월을 좋아해.
G: 왜?
B: 내 생일이 10월이거든.

17 G: Hello, everyone. My name is Alice Brown.
I live in Singapore. I'm 12 years old.
My favorite color is blue. I like swimming.
I'm good at playing the violin.

17 G: 안녕, 모두들. 내 이름은 앨리스 브라운이야. 나는 싱가포르에 살고 있어. 나는 12살이야. 내가 좋아하는 색은 파란색이야. 나는 수영을 좋아해. 나는 바이올린을 잘 연주해.

18 W: How was your summer vacation?
M: It was fun. I went to Busan.
W: What did you do there?
M: ① I went there by train.
② I stayed there for 4 days.
③ I stayed at a hotel.
④ I went swimming at the beach.

18 W: 네 여름휴가가 어땠어?
M: 재미있었어. 나 부산에 갔어.
W: 거기서 뭐했는데?
M: ① 거기에 기차 타고 갔어.
② 나는 4일 동안 거기 있었어.
③ 나는 호텔에서 머물렀어.
④ 해변에 수영하러 갔어.

19 G: Kevin, will you go to the library today?
B: Yes, I will. Why?
G: Can I go with you? I want to borrow some books.
B: ① Sure, no problem.
② No, I don't like reading books.
③ I'm glad you like it.
④ It's at seven in the evening.

19 G: 케빈, 오늘 도서관 갈 거니?
B: 응, 그래. 왜?
G: 나도 같이 가도 되니? 나 책을 좀 빌리고 싶어.
B: ① 물론이지, 문제없어.
② 아니, 나는 책 읽는 것을 좋아하지 않아.
③ 네가 좋아하니 내가 기뻐.
④ 저녁 7시야.

20 B: Is your school near your house?
G: No, it isn't.
B: Then, how do you go to school?
G: ① I ride my bike to school.
② My mom gives me a ride.
③ I go to school by bus.
④ I am often late for school.

20 B: 학교가 집에서 가깝니?
G: 아니, 그렇지 않아.
B: 그러면, 학교에 어떻게 가?
G: ① 나 자전거 타고 학교에 가.
② 엄마가 태워 주셔.
③ 버스로 학교에 가.
④ 나는 종종 학교에 늦어.

Word Check   본책 p. 160

01 말하다   **04** 코미디   **07** 보내다, 건네다   **10** 대회   **13** 곧장

02 언어   **05** 서점   **08** 경찰관   **11** 음악회   **14** 잡다

03 시장   **06** 콧물   **09** 미래, 장래   **12** 수족관   **15** 빌리다

Sentence Check   본책 p. 161

01 Have a good night.

02 I can speak Chinese and Spanish.

03 I'm going to the market.

04 They make me feel good.

05 I made dinner and took care of my younger brother.

06 He's standing over there.

07 I have a fever and a runny nose.

08 You have a cold, so stay home and get some rest.

09 I want to be a police officer.

10 I was sick in bed.

11 It'll be on your right next to the hospital.

12 I'm good at playing the violin.

13 I can see a lot of beautiful flowers in April.

14 I want to borrow some books.

15 I often late for school.

| 1 ④ | 2 ① | 3 ③ | 4 ② | 5 ① | 6 ② | 7 ① | 8 ③ | 9 ① | 10 ③ |
| 11 ③ | 12 ④ | 13 ② | 14 ① | 15 ② | 16 ④ | 17 ① | 18 ④ | 19 ② | 20 ④ |

듣기 대본
본책 p. 166

1 M: ① Do you have a car?
② We will be late for the concert.
③ How do you go to the market?
④ Cindy, fasten your seat belt.

2 G: Minsu, what's wrong? You look tired.
B: Do I? I exercised too much last night.
G: What did you do?
B: I went jogging at the park.

3 G: Jason, is this blue bag yours?
B: Yes, it is.
G: Your bag is nice. You have many blue things, right?
B: Yes, my favorite color is blue. What's your favorite color?
G: My favorite color is pink.

4 ① W: How many classes do you have today?
B: I have four.
② W: What's wrong, Jake? You are late again.
B: Sorry, I woke up late this morning.
③ W: What time does your school start?
B: It starts at 9 o'clock.
④ W: Hurry up! We don't have enough time.
B: What time is it now?

5 B: I like spring. It is nice and warm in spring.
G: Yes. But it's too windy.
B: Well, how about you?
G: I like winter.
B: Winter? It's too cold.
G: Right. But we have snow, and we can make a snowman.

6 M: May I help you?
G: I'm looking for a present for my brother. He's six years old.
M: How about this toy train?
G: He already has one at home. How much is this robot?
M: It's 15 dollars.
G: That's great. I'll take it.

해석

1 M: ① 너는 자동차가 있니?
② 우리는 음악회에 늦을 것이다.
③ 너는 시장에 어떻게 가니?
④ 신디, 안전벨트를 매.

2 G: 민수야, 무슨 일이야? 피곤해 보여.
B: 내가? 지난밤에 너무 많이 운동했어.
G: 뭐했는데?
B: 공원에서 조깅을 했어.

3 G: 제이슨, 이 파란 가방 너의 것이니?
B: 응, 그래.
G: 네 가방 멋있다. 너는 파란색들이 많은 거 같아, 맞지?
B: 응, 내가 좋아하는 색이 파란색이야. 네가 좋아하는 색은 뭐야?
G: 내가 좋아하는 색은 분홍색이야.

4 ① W: 너는 오늘 얼마나 많은 수업이 있어?
B: 네 개 있어요.
② W: 무슨 일이야, 제이크? 너 또 지각했어.
B: 죄송해요, 아침에 늦게 일어났어요.
③ W: 네 학교는 몇 시에 시작하니?
B: 9시에 시작해요.
④ W: 서둘러! 우리 충분한 시간이 없어.
B: 지금 몇 시예요?

5 B: 나는 봄을 좋아해. 봄은 날씨가 좋고 따뜻해.
G: 응. 하지만 너무 바람이 불어.
B: 음, 너는 어때?
G: 나는 겨울을 좋아해.
B: 겨울? 너무 춥잖아.
G: 맞아. 하지만 눈이 있고, 눈사람을 만들 수 있잖아.

6 M: 도와드릴까요?
G: 남동생을 위한 선물을 찾고 있어요. 6살이에요.
M: 이 장난감 기차 어때요?
G: 집에 이미 하나 있어요. 이 로봇은 얼마예요?
M: 15달러예요.
G: 좋네요. 이걸로 살게요.

7 B: Hi, Sujin. Where is the <u>science room</u>?
 G: Sorry?
 B: The science room.
 G: Go straight and <u>turn left</u> at the library. It's <u>between</u> the music room and the computer room.
 B: Thanks.

8 M: Sara, I am going to a concert. Will you come with me?
 W: When is <u>the concert</u>?
 M: <u>March</u> 20.
 W: Pardon?
 M: March 20. <u>This Friday</u>.

9 M: May I help you?
 W: I want to buy <u>some roses</u>.
 M: What color do you want?
 W: Do you have <u>white ones</u>?
 M: Yes, the white roses are over there. <u>How many</u> roses do you want?
 W: Ten, please.

10 G: Kevin, who is that man over there?
 B: He's <u>my uncle</u>.
 G: Wow, your uncle is very tall and handsome. <u>How old</u> is he?
 B: He's <u>28</u> years old.
 G: Does he live with you?
 B: No, he lives in Busan.

11 G: Who is this man in the picture?
 B: He is my father. He is a teacher. <u>What does</u> your father do?
 G: He is a firefighter.
 B: That's awesome! I want to <u>be a firefighter</u>, too.

12 ① M: Where is the hospital?
  W: It's <u>next to</u> the bakery.
 ② M: I'm thirsty. Can I have some water?
  W: Sure. <u>Here you are</u>.
 ③ M: Is this your new hair pin?
  W: Yes, my mom bought it for me.
 ④ M: What <u>will you do</u> this weekend?
  W: I <u>went camping</u>.

7 B: 안녕, 수진. 과학실이 어디야?
 G: 뭐라고?
 B: 과학실.
 G: 곧장 가서 도서관에서 왼쪽으로 가. 음악실이랑 컴퓨터실 사이에 있어.
 B: 고마워.

8 M: 사라, 나 콘서트에 갈 거야. 나랑 같이 갈래?
 W: 콘서트가 언제인데?
 M: 3월 20일.
 W: 뭐라고?
 M: 3월 20일. 이번 주 금요일이야.

9 M: 도와드릴까요?
 W: 장미를 좀 사려고 왔어요.
 M: 무슨 색을 원하세요?
 W: 하얀 게 있나요?
 M: 예, 하얀 장미는 저쪽에 있어요. 얼마나 많이 원하세요?
 W: 10송이 주세요.

10 G: 케빈, 저쪽에 남자 누구야?
 B: 내 삼촌이야.
 G: 와우, 네 삼촌 매우 키가 크고 잘생겼다. 몇 살이야?
 B: 28살이야.
 G: 너랑 같이 사니?
 B: 아니, 부산에 살아.

11 G: 사진 속 이 남자 누구야?
 B: 나의 아버지야. 선생님이셔. 네 아버지는 무슨 일을 하셔?
 G: 소방관이셔.
 B: 멋지다! 나도 소방관이 되고 싶어.

12 ① M: 병원이 어디 있어요?
  W: 빵집 옆에 있어요.
 ② M: 목말라요. 물을 좀 먹을 수 있나요?
  W: 물론이죠. 여기 있어요.
 ③ M: 이거 네 새 머리핀이니?
  W: 응, 엄마가 나에게 사주셨어.
 ④ M: 이번 주말에 뭐할 거야?
  W: 나 캠핑 갔었어.

13 G: Chris, can you come to my birthday party?
B: When is it?
G: It's this Saturday.
B: This Saturday? I'm sorry, but I can't.
G: Why not?
B: I have to attend my uncle's wedding.

13 G: 크리스, 내 생일 파티에 올 수 있니?
B: 언제야?
G: 이번 주 토요일이야.
B: 이번 주 토요일? 미안한데 갈 수 없어.
G: 왜?
B: 삼촌 결혼식에 참석해야 해.

14 W: Kevin, what are you doing?
M: I'm watching TV.
W: What kind of TV programs do you like to watch?
M: I like watching sports on TV. What about you?
W: I like documentaries.

14 W: 케빈, 뭐하고 있어?
M: 나 TV 보고 있어.
W: 무슨 종류의 TV 프로그램을 보는 거 좋아해?
M: 나는 TV로 스포츠 보는 거 좋아해. 너는 어때?
W: 나는 다큐멘터리를 좋아해.

15 W: Tony, are you doing anything?
B: Nothing. Why do you ask?
W: Can you help me?
B: Sure. What can I do for you?
W: Can you wash the dishes?
B: Okay.

15 W: 토니, 뭐하고 있니?
B: 아무 것도 안 해요. 왜 물으세요?
W: 나 좀 도와줄래?
B: 물론이죠. 무엇을 도와드릴까요?
W: 설거지 해줄래?
B: 알았어요.

16 G: What's your favorite season?
B: My favorite season is spring. How about you?
G: I like winter because I like skiing.
B: Oh, really? How often do you go skiing?
G: I go skiing once a week.

16 G: 네가 좋아하는 계절은 뭐야?
B: 내가 좋아하는 계절은 봄이야. 너는 어때?
G: 나는 스키를 좋아하기 때문에 겨울을 좋아해.
B: 오, 정말? 스키를 얼마나 자주 타?
G: 일주일에 한 번 스키 타러 가.

17 W: This is a sport. We play this sport on a large field. We hit a ball with a bat. We use a glove to catch a ball.

17 W: 이것은 스포츠다. 우리는 이 스포츠를 커다란 운동장에서 한다. 우리는 방망이로 공을 친다. 우리는 글러브를 이용해서 공을 잡는다.

18 M: What are you doing, Jessie?
W: I'm listening to music.
M: What kind of music do you like?
W: ① I like listening to the radio.
② I can play the violin.
③ I listen to music every day.
④ I like K-pop music.

18 M: 뭐하고 있어, 제시?
W: 나 음악 듣고 있어.
M: 무슨 종류의 음악을 좋아해?
W: ① 나는 라디오 듣는 거를 좋아해.
② 나는 바이올린을 켤 수 있어.
③ 나는 매일 음악을 들어.
④ 나는 케이팝 음악을 좋아해.

19 G: Paul, what did you do last Sunday?
B: I went to the beach.
G: Oh, did you? What did you do there?
B: ① I took the subway.
② I built a sandcastle on the beach.
③ It was very fun.
④ It was very sunny.

19 G: 폴, 지난 일요일에 뭐했어?
B: 나 해변에 갔어.
G: 오, 그랬어? 거기서 뭐했는데?
B: ① 나는 지하철을 탔어.
② 해변에서 모래성을 만들었어.
③ 무척 즐거웠어.
④ 매우 맑았어.

20 G: How do you go to school, Mike?
   B: I usually <u>take</u> a <u>bus</u> to school, but I took the subway today.
   G: <u>Why</u> <u>did</u> <u>you</u> take the subway?
   B: ① I got up late.
      ② I missed the bus.
      ③ It snowed a lot this morning.
      ④ I usually walk to school.

20 G: 학교에 어떻게 가, 마이크?
   B: 보통 버스 타고 학교에 가, 하지만 오늘은 지하철을 탔어.
   G: 왜 지하철을 탔는데?
   B: ① 늦게 일어났어.
      ② 버스를 놓쳤어.
      ③ 오늘 아침에 눈이 많이 왔어.
      ④ 나는 보통 걸어서 학교에 가.

Word Check
본책 p. 172

01 운동하다	**04** 눈사람	**07** 잘생긴	**10** 참석하다	**13** 굉장한, 멋진
02 매다, 채우다	**05** 선물	**08** 소방관	**11** 결혼	**14** 모래성
03 충분한	**06** 뭐라고	**09** 주말	**12** 다큐멘터리	**15** 경기장

Sentence Check
본책 p. 173

01 Cindy, fasten your seat belt.
02 I exercised too much last night.
03 I woke up late this morning.
04 We don't have enough time.
05 We have snow, and we can make a snowman.
06 It's between the music room and the computer room.
07 Your uncle is very tall and handsome.
08 I have to attend my uncle's wedding.
09 I like watching sports on TV.
10 Can you wash the dishes.
11 My favorite season is spring.
12 We use a glove to catch a ball.
13 I like listening to the radio.
14 It snowed a lot this morning.
15 I usually take a bus to school

15회 영어 듣기 모의고사
본책 p. 174

1 ②	**2** ①	**3** ②	**4** ④	**5** ③	**6** ③	**7** ④	**8** ③	**9** ④	**10** ①
11 ①	**12** ②	**13** ②	**14** ④	**15** ③	**16** ②	**17** ③	**18** ①	**19** ②	**20** ②

1 W: ① Please do not park here.
      ② Please <u>do</u> <u>not</u> <u>smoke</u> here.
      ③ Please do not swim here.
      ④ Please do not <u>sit</u> here.

2 W: Peter, what's wrong? You look sad.
   M: Yes, I'm sad. I <u>lost</u> <u>my</u> <u>dog</u>.
   W: Really? I'm <u>sorry</u> to hear that.
      I hope you will find your dog <u>soon</u>.
   M: Thank you.

1 W: ① 여기에 주차하지 마세요.
      ② 여기서 담배 피우지 마세요.
      ③ 여기서 수영하지 마세요.
      ④ 여기에 앉지 마세요.

2 W: 피터, 무슨 일이야? 너 슬퍼 보여.
   M: 응, 나 슬퍼. 내 개를 잃어버렸어.
   W: 정말? 그 말을 들으니 너무 안됐다.
      네 개를 곧 찾기를 바라.
   M: 고마워.

3 W: Tony, what do you eat for breakfast?
M: I have bananas for breakfast.
W: Do you like bananas?
M: Yes, I do. How about you? What's your favorite fruit?
W: I like oranges.

3 W: 토니, 아침식사로 무엇을 먹어?
M: 나는 아침으로 바나나를 먹어.
W: 너 바나나 좋아해?
M: 응, 그래. 너는 어때? 네가 좋아하는 과일은 뭐야?
W: 나는 오렌지 좋아해.

4 ① W: Did you clean the window?
B: No, I didn't.
② W: Who is the girl by the window?
B: She's my friend, Jessie.
③ W: Would you close the window?
B: Okay.
④ W: Did you break the window?
B: Yes, I did. I'm sorry, Mom.

4 ① W: 네가 창문을 청소했니?
B: 아니요.
② W: 창문 옆에 소녀는 누구니?
B: 그녀는 내 친구, 제시예요.
③ W: 창문 좀 닫아줄래?
B: 좋아요.
④ W: 네가 창문을 깼니?
B: 예, 죄송해요, 엄마.

5 ① G: When does your first class start?
B: It starts at 9 o'clock.
② G: Where are you going?
B: I'm going to the station.
③ G: Do you have any brothers or sisters?
B: No, they are not my brothers.
④ G: What do you want for your birthday?
B: I want a computer.

5 ① G: 네 첫 수업이 언제 시작해?
B: 9시에 시작해.
② G: 어디 가고 있어?
B: 역에 가고 있어.
③ G: 너는 형제자매가 있니?
B: 아니, 그들은 나의 형들이 아니야.
④ G: 생일 선물로 무엇을 원해?
B: 컴퓨터를 원해.

6 W: Are you going out?
B: Yes. How is the weather today?
W: It's cloudy. They said it's going to rain in the afternoon.

6 W: 너 외출하니?
B: 예. 오늘 날씨가 어때요?
W: 흐려. 오후에는 비가 올 거라고 했어.

7 B: Is this your mother?
G: No, she's my aunt. My mom has long hair, and she is tall and thin.
B: Is she wearing a red skirt?
G: Yes, she's the one.

7 B: 이분이 네 어머니야?
G: 아니, 내 고모야. 나의 엄마는 머리가 길고, 키가 크고 마르셨어.
B: 빨간 스커트를 입으셨니?
G: 응, 그녀야.

8 W: ① How much are these cookies?
② I'm baking cookies.
③ Help yourself to these cookies.
④ What do you want to eat for lunch?

8 W: ① 이 쿠키들은 얼마예요?
② 나는 쿠키를 굽고 있어.
③ 이 쿠키들 마음껏 먹어.
④ 너는 점심으로 무엇을 먹고 싶어?

9 W: You look sad. What's the matter?
M: I studied hard, but I failed the test.
W: Cheer up. I'm sure you will do better next time.
M: Thanks.

9 W: 너 슬퍼 보여. 무슨 일이야?
M: 열심히 공부했는데 시험에 불합격했어.
W: 기운 내. 다음번에는 더 잘할 거라고 확신해.
M: 고마워.

10 G: Wow, this drawing is great. When did you draw this?
   B: I <u>drew</u> it last month.
   G: I think you're really <u>good</u> <u>at</u> drawing.
   B: Thank you. I want to be an artist in the future.
   G: I think you will be a <u>great</u> <u>artist</u>.

10 G: 와우, 이 그림 훌륭하다. 이거 언제 그렸어?
   B: 지난달에 그렸어.
   G: 난 네가 정말 그림을 잘 그린다고 생각해.
   B: 고마워. 나는 장래에 화가가 되고 싶어.
   G: 너는 훌륭한 화가가 될 거라고 생각해.

11 W: Mike, I <u>called</u> <u>you</u> last night, but your phone was off.
   M: I <u>went</u> <u>to</u> <u>the</u> <u>movies</u>, so I turned it off.
   W: I see. How was the movie?
   M: It was really good.

11 W: 마이크, 내가 지난밤에 전화했는데 네 전화기가 꺼져 있었어.
   M: 나 영화 보러 갔어, 그래서 꺼놨어.
   W: 알았어. 영화는 어땠어?
   M: 정말 좋았어.

12 [Cellphone rings.]
   B: Hello.
   G: Hello, Jacob. This is Susan. Do you want to go to the K-pop concert with me tonight? The concert starts at 6:30.
   B: Okay. What time shall we meet?
   G: <u>Let's</u> <u>meet</u> at 5.
   B: That's <u>too</u> <u>early</u>. How about <u>5:30</u>?
   G: Good.

12 [휴대폰이 울린다.]
   B: 여보세요.
   G: 안녕, 제이콥. 나 수잔이야. 오늘 밤에 나랑 케이팝 콘서트 가고 싶니? 콘서트는 6시 30분에 시작해.
   B: 좋아. 몇 시에 만날까?
   G: 5시에 만나자.
   B: 너무 일러. 5시 30분 어때?
   G: 좋아.

13 W: Good afternoon. May I help you?
   M: I'm looking for a tie.
   W: How about this one?
   M: It looks good, but I want a <u>blue</u> <u>tie</u>.
   W: Then, how about this one? It's <u>12</u> <u>dollars</u>.
   M: It's nice. I'll <u>take</u> <u>it</u>.

13 W: 안녕하세요. 도와드릴까요?
   M: 넥타이를 찾고 있어요.
   W: 이것은 어때요?
   M: 좋아 보이지만, 파란색 넥타이를 원해요.
   W: 그러면, 이것은 어때요? 12달러예요.
   M: 좋네요. 그걸로 살게요.

14 M: How can I help you?
   W: My cellphone <u>doesn't</u> <u>work</u>.
   M: Oh, I see. Let me take a look.
   W: Can you <u>fix</u> <u>it</u>?
   M: Yes. I think it will <u>take</u> <u>two</u> <u>days</u> to fix it.

14 M: 어떻게 도와드릴까요?
   W: 제 핸드폰이 작동하지 않아요.
   M: 오, 알겠어요. 확인해 볼게요.
   W: 고칠 수 있나요?
   M: 예. 고치는 데 이틀 소요될 거 같아요.

15 W: ① How have you been?
   ② How are you doing?
   ③ Bye! <u>Take</u> <u>care</u>.
   ④ How is the <u>weather</u> <u>today</u>?

15 W: ① 어떻게 지냈니?
   ② 어떻게 지내?
   ③ 안녕! 몸 건강해.
   ④ 오늘 날씨가 어때?

16 M: Are you ready to <u>order</u>?
   W: Yes. I'll have the steak.
   M: How would you like your steak?
   W: <u>Medium</u>, please.
   M: What would you <u>like</u> <u>to</u> <u>drink</u>?
   W: A Diet Coke, please.

16 M: 주문하시겠어요?
   W: 예. 스테이크로 주세요.
   M: 스테이크는 어떻게 해드릴까요?
   W: 중간 굽기로 해주세요.
   M: 무엇을 마시겠어요?
   W: 다이어트 콜라 주세요.

17 *[Cellphone rings.]*
   G: Hello.
   B: Hello, Helen. <u>What's up</u>?
   G: I'm going to the library tomorrow. Do you want to come with me?
   B: Sure, <u>what time</u> shall we meet?
   G: Let's meet at 3 o'clock at the <u>bus stop</u>.
   B: Okay.

18 M: How are you today, Jessie?
   W: Not good. I <u>have a cold</u>.
   M: ① That's too bad.
      ② Sounds good.
      ③ I'm glad to meet you.
      ④ I have a good idea.

19 M: Sara, let's <u>take a walk</u> at the park tomorrow morning.
   W: Sounds good.
   M: <u>Can we meet</u> at 7 in front of the park?
   W: ① Yes, I can walk fast.
      ② Good. See you then.
      ③ Where is the park?
      ④ The park is near my house.

20 G: Kevin, what are you going to do after school?
   B: I'm going to read a book. <u>Why</u>?
   G: It's hot today. Let's <u>go swimming</u>.
   B: ① That's a good idea.
      ② That's too bad.
      ③ Okay. What time shall we meet?
      ④ Sorry. I can't swim.

17 *[휴대폰이 울린다.]*
   G: 여보세요.
   B: 안녕, 헬렌. 무슨 일이야?
   G: 나 내일 도서관 갈 거야. 나랑 같이 갈래?
   B: 물론이지, 몇 시에 만날까?
   G: 3시에 버스 정류장에서 만나자.
   B: 좋아.

18 M: 오늘 어때, 제시?
   W: 좋지 않아. 나 감기 걸렸어.
   M: ① 안됐다.
      ② 좋은 거 같아.
      ③ 만나서 반가워.
      ④ 나 좋은 생각이 있어.

19 M: 사라, 내일 아침에 공원에서 산책하자.
   W: 좋아.
   M: 공원 앞에서 7시에 만날 수 있니?
   W: ① 응, 난 빨리 걸을 수 있어.
      ② 좋아. 그때 보자.
      ③ 공원이 어디야?
      ④ 공원은 집이랑 가까워.

20 G: 케빈, 방과 후에 뭐할 거야?
   B: 책을 읽을 거야. 왜?
   G: 오늘 더워. 수영하러 가자.
   B: ① 그거 좋은 생각이야.
      ② 그거 안됐다.
      ③ 좋아. 몇 시에 만날까?
      ④ 미안해. 나 수영 못해.

Word Check
본책 p. 184

01 담배 피우다	**04** 과일	**07** 일, 문제	**10** 예술가, 화가	**13** 작동하다
02 바라다	**05** 깨다	**08** 실패하다	**11** 오늘 밤	**14** 기쁜
03 곧	**06** 굽다	**09** 확실한	**12** 고치다	**15** 그때

Sentence Check
본책 p. 185

01 Please do not smoke here.
02 I hope you will find your dog soon.
03 Did you break the window?
04 Do you have any brothers or sisters?
05 They said it's going to rain in the afternoon.
06 My mom has long hair, and she is tall and thin.
07 Help yourself to these cookies.
08 I studied hard, but I failed the test.
09 I'm sure you will do better next time.
10 I think you're really good at painting.
11 I called you last night, but your phone was off.
12 My cellphone doesn't work.
13 Let's meet at 3 o'clock at the bus stop.
14 I'm glad to meet you.
15 Let's take a walk at the park tomorrow morning.

memo

memo

Longman
Listening
mentor joy Series